Mental Health and Academic Learning in Schools

Mental Health and Academic Learning in Schools: Approaches for Facilitating the Wellbeing of Children and Young People investigates the many areas impacting on young people's learning and mental health in a unified manner. Offering a new model for teaching, learning and connecting with young people, it provides compelling evidence about the intertwined nature of students' academic performance, mental health and behaviour.

The book presents integrated models and strategies that serve to enhance student learning and promote wellbeing. Chapters explore issues relating to classroom management, school culture and leadership, staff wellbeing, pedagogy, inclusion and the curriculum. Placing students at the centre of decision making, the book showcases innovative models and strategies that schools might use for preventing problems, engaging students and identifying and addressing learning or mental health problems that some students might experience.

This book will appeal to academics, researchers and post-graduate students in the fields of mental health and education, and will also be of interest to school counsellors, educational psychologists and those working with young people in schools.

Andrea Reupert is Director of Psychology Programs in the Faculty of Education, Monash University, Australia.

The Mental Health and Well-being of Children and Adolescents
Series Editor: Garry Hornby
University of Plymouth

Mental health disorders in children and young people are increasing, with one in four under-16s experiencing mental health difficulties which will disrupt relationships, education and work. In addition to this, one in ten under-16s suffers from a diagnosed disorder. Access to up-to-date research and appropriate interventions minimises the mental health challenges these children and adolescents face and reduces their potentially lifelong impact.

It has been internationally recognised that the scale of mental health research is low in relation to the burden of the disorder. This research-focused series will consist of titles that consider key issues affecting young people's mental health and well-being, exploring preventative measures, promoting positive behaviour, and sharing research to develop effective and efficient treatment.

Aimed primarily at researchers and postgraduate students, this series will also be of interest to practitioners in the mental health field, such as psychologists, and some in the field of education, such as counsellors, who would like to implement research-based findings in their clinical practice.

Books in the series include:

School Bullying and Mental Health
Risks, Intervention and Prevention
Helen Cowie and Carrie-Anne Myers

Mental Health and Academic Learning in Schools
Approaches for Facilitating the Wellbeing of Children and Young People
Andrea Reupert

For more information about this series, please visit: www.routledge.com/The-Mental-Health-and-Well-being-of-Children-and-Adolescents/book-series/MHWCA

Mental Health and Academic Learning in Schools

Approaches for Facilitating the Wellbeing of Children and Young People

Andrea Reupert

LONDON AND NEW YORK

First published 2020
by Routledge
2 Park Square, Milton Park, Abingdon, Oxon, OX14 4RN

and by Routledge
52 Vanderbilt Avenue, New York, NY 10017

Routledge is an imprint of the Taylor & Francis Group, an informa business

© 2020 Andrea Reupert

The right of Andrea Reupert to be identified as the author of this work has been asserted by her in accordance with sections 77 and 78 of the Copyright, Designs and Patents Act 1988.

All rights reserved. No part of this book may be reprinted or reproduced or utilised in any form or by any electronic, mechanical, or other means, now known or hereafter invented, including photocopying and recording, or in any information storage or retrieval system, without permission in writing from the publishers.

Trademark notice: Product or corporate names may be trademarks or registered trademarks, and are used only for identification and explanation without intent to infringe.

British Library Cataloguing-in-Publication Data
A catalogue record for this book is available from the British Library

Library of Congress Cataloging-in-Publication Data
A catalog record for this book has been requested

ISBN: 9781138232976 (hbk)
ISBN: 9781315310930 (ebk)

Typeset in Bembo
by Apex CoVantage, LLC

This book is dedicated to students such as Alice, who have been through the wars of school and survived. May their voices be heard and from their experiences, changes made.

Contents

List of figures   x
List of tables   xi
Acknowledgements   xii
Series editor's foreword   xiii
GARRY HORNBY

1 **Alice's story**   1

2 **The role of schools in promoting children's mental health**   6
  Introduction 6
  The role of schools 6
  A question of priorities 8
  Key terms and concepts 9
  Why should schools be involved in promoting children's mental health? 11
  Finally . . . 21

3 **The relationship between mental illness, wellbeing and academic achievement**   26
  What is academic success and failure? 26
  Why do some children fail at school? 27
  A sequence of experiences 28
  Socio-economic factors, academic performance and mental illness 32
  Children's social and emotional competence and academic achievement 33
  Influence of schools on mental health and academic achievement 35
  What does this mean for schools? 37

4 **Towards a school-wide model for supporting students' mental health and academic learning**   42
  Programs to support students' mental health and academic learning 42

The evidence base 45
The rationale for developing a whole school, integrated approach for supporting children's academic learning and mental health needs 47
Tiered approaches 48
Examples of whole school, integrated approaches 50
A tiered system of common evidence-based practices 52
Problems and future opportunities for whole school approaches for supporting children's academic learning and mental health 56

5 School culture and climate — 60
School size 61
Screening 62
A help-seeking school 64
Leadership 65
School connectedness 69
Cultural competence and sensitivity 70
Safe schools 70
Relationships 71

6 Reconceptualising student behaviour — 80
The relationship between learning, mental health and behaviour 80
What is challenging behaviour? 81
Models of classroom management: what's our end goal? 83
"Teach more, manage less" (Richmond, 2007) 85
Promoting behaviour conducive to learning 86
"Consequences have consequences" (Lewis, 2015) 88
Motivating students 89
An approach based on mutual respect 91

7 Teaching and learning — 95
How excellent teachers teach 95
Feedback and assessment 100
Mental health topics 102
Teaching social and emotional skills 103
Teachers as role models 109

8 Partnerships — 113
Professional collaborations 114
Models of collaboration 116

Family partnerships 119
Children and youth 122

9 Inclusivity: celebrating diversity — 128
Why is inclusion important? 128
Inclusive education benefits all students 131
Basic principles of an inclusive education 134
How to be inclusive 134

10 Staff wellbeing — 144
Teacher social and emotional competence 144
Teacher and principal stress and wellbeing 146
Teachers' (potentially stressful) role in promoting young people's mental health and wellbeing 148
Promoting the wellbeing of school staff 150

11 Trauma-informed schools — 155
Trauma and its impact on young people 155
Schools and trauma 157
School-based formal programs 157
Managing specific traumatic events 161
Crisis plans 162
Synthesizing a trauma informed approach into school settings 163

12 Making a difference: are we there yet? — 167
What should schools be doing? Evidence-based programs and practice-based evidence 167
The place of monitoring and evaluation 169
The action research cycle 170
Reflective practice 173
Just do it 174
Take home messages 177
Students' voices 178

Index 183

Figures

2.1	Possible causes for student inattentiveness	16
3.1	The holistic, developmental needs of children across time	36
3.2	The interrelationships between mental health, illness, school performance and behaviour	37
4.1	A three-tiered approach for supporting children's mental health and academic learning needs	49
5.1	The different meanings of "at risk"	64
6.1	Continuum of control: behaviour and curriculum	84
8.1	Children at the centre of school partnerships	115
8.2	A continuum of collaboration between schools and external agencies and entities	117
8.3	A continuum of collaboration between students/caregivers and school staff	121
9.1	Framework of inclusive education	135
10.1	The relationships between individual and organisational factors, teacher wellbeing, stress and student outcomes	147
11.1	A school-based, tiered approach for supporting students exposed to trauma	164
12.1	The action research cycle for schools	171
12.2	A three-phase plan for implementing change in schools	175

Tables

3.1	Students' family income and SAT scores	32
5.1	Extending Hallinger's (2003) instructional leadership functions to wellbeing and mental health	66
6.1	The relative time provided in dominant learning versus dominant managing behaviour conversations	85
7.1	Implications of expert teachers' actions on student wellbeing and social and emotional development	97
12.1	Common barriers for implementing change and possible responses	176

Acknowledgements

There are several people to thank and acknowledge for their support in writing this book. First, my partner in life and work, Professor Darryl Maybery, for his never-ending support, positivity and openness to me taking on additional tasks and roles. To my children, Charlotte and Kellie, who are my inspiration and source of relief and delight. I also need to thank Jenny Rossiter, a friend and colleague, who read some early chapter drafts and provided wise and constructive feedback. Over the years, many university and school staff and students have challenged my thinking in many ways (even if, or perhaps especially if we do not always agree) in particular Professor Dennis Moore, Dr Stella Laletas, Dr Marie Hammer and Associate Professor Nicky Jacobs. One informative period was working as a school psychologist on the Atherton Tablelands in Far North Queensland under the supervision and guidance of Nello Raciti, working alongside many colleagues but in particular John Daly, Robbie Rourke, Anthony Porta, Annie Esdaile and John Harding. Our many shared experiences and discussions formed the backbone of this book and have helped shape my thinking ever since. Thank you.

Series editor's foreword

This book addresses the important issue of the role of schools in facilitating the mental health and wellbeing of children and young people, and considers this within the context of optimising academic learning. The book is the second in a series addressing the mental health and wellbeing of children and young people. The first book was specifically focused on bullying in schools (Cowie & Myers, 2018), whereas the current book has a broader focus.

Children's and young people's mental health and wellbeing has become of increasing concern in recent years. For example, the UK government recently reported that 10% of young people aged between 5 and 16 years had a clinically significant mental health problem, while only 25% of those in need were receiving appropriate support and treatment (Cooper & Hornby, 2018). This is of critical importance to schools because, for 50% of those who go on to develop mental illness, the symptoms are clearly evident before the age of 14, so schools have a key role to play in identifying and addressing the early signs of mental illness, and the book considers how they can best do this.

Teachers and other professionals who work with young people in schools need to be equipped with up-to-date theory, research and skills, based on knowledge of effective practical interventions, in order to optimise children's mental health and help them manage the challenges that they face (Atkinson & Hornby, 2002; Hornby & Atkinson, 2003). This book focuses on the theory, research and skills that are needed.

The book addresses the strong connection between social and emotional development and academic learning and therefore reinforces the need for schools to focus more broadly than just on academic learning. It thereby clarifies the role of social and emotional learning in academic success and elaborates on the key components of programs for social and emotional learning and the benefits of whole of school approaches to the promotion of mental health and wellbeing.

The critical role of schools in the identification of mental health problems and in the provision of safe environments for the development of wellbeing and academic learning is discussed. The elements of excellent teaching, including formative assessment and constructive feedback, are considered along with the need for effective behaviour management and intervention programs promoting the development of positive mental health.

The importance of including a wide range of diversity of children and young people, and of being aware of the impact of achievement grouping on children, is discussed. Also, partnerships with professionals and families, and of attention to teacher stress as well as their own mental health and wellbeing, are considered. Guidance is provided on how schools can cope with traumatic events at the family, school and community levels. Finally, the need to optimise the implementation of evidence-based practices and to collect practice-based evidence is emphasised.

This book makes a strong case for the critical role of schools in facilitating the mental health and wellbeing of children and young people and provides useful guidelines for how schools can do this effectively. It is therefore considered to be essential reading for teachers, school leaders and other professionals who work in or with schools.

Emeritus Professor Garry Hornby,
University of Plymouth

References

Atkinson, M., & Hornby, G. (2002). *Mental health handbook for schools*. London: RoutledgeFalmer.
Cooper, P., & Hornby, G. (2018). Facing the challenges to mental health and wellbeing in schools. *Pastoral Care in Education, 36*(3), 173–175.
Cowie, H., & Myers, C-A. (Eds.). (2018). *School bullying and mental health*. London: Routledge.
Hornby, G., & Atkinson, M. (2003). A framework for promoting mental health in schools. *Pastoral Care in Education, 21*(2), 3–9.

Chapter 1

Alice's story

In many parts of the world, the scope of education is becoming increasingly narrow. Educational decisions are typically driven by expectations about student performance in high stakes national tests and the need to achieve or surpass school and national achievement benchmarks. In the seemingly constant pursuit of academic outcomes, opportunities to enhance important objectives are lost, including the promotion of student wellbeing.

Predominately focusing teaching efforts and resources on academic outcomes comes at a cost, to staff as well as student wellbeing. Alice's story, which is outlined in detail below, highlights the ways in which schools not only miss opportunities to enhance wellbeing but also, in many ways, actively mitigate against it.

Like most children, Alice was very happy to start school, as she says:

> I think I was a pretty excited kid . . . I absolutely wanted to go. Yeah, I was ready for that. I was looking forward to it . . . I absolutely adored primary school. I loved it. I just remember being just a typical prep kid.

In many ways, Alice shined at primary school and was engaged in learning.

> I really wanted to learn, yeah. I was really interested in learning. I was – I was interested in doing a good job. I liked every subject.

However, she learnt early on that she was not like the other kids, though she simultaneously worked out ways to accommodate what she later discovered to be a diagnosis of dyslexia.

> I noticed I was always a bit slower at reading, especially around grade 3. Two friends of mine – they'd begun to excel at reading, and they would be reading chapter books as a race with each other, like sitting there next to each other, flipping pages as fast as they could. And that sort of – it never interested me because I just knew I couldn't keep up with that. Even by grade 3 I realised I didn't actually know how to spell my middle name – one of them. I never got taught how to spell it. So – and I think I used to write my name backwards.

Alice's self-identified accommodations seemed to work, for a while at least.

> And so, it didn't really seem like it was a problem in primary school. I just knew I was not great at spelling but I always had a trick up my sleeve just to sound words out and try and spell things phonetically. I had lots of strategies. Instead of learning how to spell words I would just learn the shape of the words – like the image of it and write that again. That was how I got by mostly.

Moving into high school was an entirely different experience. A spiral of events, including not getting on with friends, not being able to play sport and not being able to complete homework on time, led to feeling depressed and constantly tired.

> So, after that I tried my hardest to keep going at school and keep my head above water. But I just sort of slowly begun to sink under the weight of more school work and just the depression and not caring anymore.

She started to "wag" (an Australian term for truancy).

> I began to wag around year 10. And it wasn't that I was really wagging because I would say, okay, I'm getting up, I'm going to school. I'd put my uniform on, my mum would go out, I would then go out the back fence to where I was meant to go catch the bus, circle around the block and sneak back into the house and just hop back into bed. And I would be there until at least 2:00pm and Mum would come and find me because she got the text from the school saying I wasn't there.

Alice was eventually diagnosed with depression, then anxiety.

> All I wanted to do was go to sleep. I didn't care about anything at all. So, it was sort of like Mum was just – she would put in so much work to get me to school. Or if she realised I just couldn't do school that day, she would then say, okay, well, at least just get out of bed or just get dressed for the day or just shower. But I ultimately didn't – I spent about – I spent months not going to school. . . . I was still checking up on my emails from teachers and things like that, but I just couldn't do it. And then somehow amongst all of that, I begun to develop some extreme anxiety and so sometimes when Mum would – she'd have to drive me to school. And it would be, maybe, 11:00am by the time we get there. And she'd be pulled up at the front and I'd be sitting in the car and she goes, "Okay, get out of the car. It's okay. Time to go." And I would just sit there. I go, "No, I can't. I can't. I can't." And I burst into tears. And I would just have this horrible anxiety. I couldn't go to school.

Her focus at school understandably turned from learning to "surviving" day by day.

> And basically, just the whole thought of doing school work was just completely out of my mind. It was the last thing I was focusing on. All I was trying to focus on was just surviving. Just trying to stay rested and able to function just a little bit

When she was at school, she did try to ask for help, but when the help was not forthcoming she ended up being "disruptive":

> I remember [when I used to go to English class] I used to sit there and say [to the teacher], "Okay, so I actually can't understand this. Is there another way you can explain it to me? A different way?" And she would get frustrated because she's explained it twice and she wants to move on with the class. And so – okay. I was – I was really – I hate asking for help, but I really put myself up there and I just went, I can't understand this . . . after a while I realised that she wasn't going to help me. And so, I decided just to go, well, f# you then. And I was just a disruptive nuisance in the class.

Alice continued by describing how she reacted:

> Cheeky little one liners, chatting to the person next me. Not like full riots in the class or anything like that – not shouting or dancing or doing stupid things – standing on tables – but just – I wasn't there to learn anymore. And I wasn't respecting the teacher because she – I felt like she wasn't respecting me, or she was – I was – I felt like I was completely ignored by her.

The school did try to make allowances for Alice. In Year 11, she was enrolled in a graphic design subject delivered from a TAFE (vocational) College along with other school-based subjects:

> One day a week I got to go to Melbourne for my course. And even though I had to get up at 5:00am and get a train, I never missed – I never missed one unless I was ridiculously sick with the flu or something. So, it was sort of a big change around. I was – yeah – surrounded by people I liked, I was happy and so I just – I was doing kind of well at school. I was – I was doing the classes, I was doing the work – I'd picked some pretty easy subjects though. I was – I was doing food tech, I was doing graphics, I was doing another art – studio art. I wasn't doing any sciences. I don't think I was even doing maths.

Things did not go to plan, however, with her school subjects:

> I couldn't see the point . . . When are we actually going to put this into practice. . . ? It's just all – there was just all print outs [work sheets]. And I just went, f# this. It wasn't engaging at all.

Alice rationalised her learning and place at school in the following way:

> In my mind, I was in charge of my own education from here. I had been, sort of, that whole year. And so, I think I just went, you're [teacher] in charge of the class, but I'm just here in charge of myself and I'm going to be doing my own thing. And once they [teachers] knew that I wasn't in their class to be learning what they were teaching me – well, I was still learning, but I just wasn't in their class to be taught by them – they sort of went, oh, that's not right.

This mindset helped Alice but, perhaps unsurprisingly, it did not go down well with all of her teachers.

> [I began] to feel much more relaxed and happy that school – I'd begun to sort of slow down and sit back in classes because I wasn't there tentatively taking notes. And I'd sit back and actually listen to what they were saying and realise, no, that's actually not right. Or that's – I don't agree with this. And if they would ask for an opinion and I'd put my hand up and give the opinion of who thinks this, who thinks that – but if they didn't like my opinion, they would sort of skip over it. And then so I'd go, whoa, whoa, whoa, whoa, whoa, hold on, I've given my opinion on this topic, which you've left open for discussion, at least tell me why you think my opinion isn't correct or where I've gone wrong . . . And they went, oh wait, so she does want to learn with us but, oh, she's being a little bit rude about it because I was getting frustrated at this point and I had sort of stopped using all my manners. So, after a while I was wagging school a lot too. I just wouldn't turn up to class or I'd just leave. And I got caught a few times, but I just didn't really care.

She continued to wag and, on this basis, was expelled from school and "never went back". Three years later, Alice is now enrolled in a Science Diploma at a city university with plans to go into nutrition, though as she is quick to point out, she failed science all through school. She concluded the interview, excited for the future:

> And the thing is that I'm excited about learning because I know it's going to be challenging because one thing that I sort of – it didn't get taught to me, but it just sort of – it was never said directly, but it just sort of felt like it

was all around me that I'm not smart enough. I'm failing because I'm not smart enough. When really, no, I was just depressed. But I've sort of slowly learnt that I actually am bright, and I am – I always thought that science was something that I could never do because I wasn't smart enough. Then I realised, no actually – so, encouragement helps a lot.

Alice most definitely **had** a problem – in the first instance, her diagnosis of dyslexia followed by depression and anxiety. She certainly **became** a problem as can be seen by her "disruptive" behaviour in class, truancy and eventual expulsion. But was Alice **the** problem? I don't think so. Instead, I would suggest that the problem was a mismatch between her unique, though not uncommon, learning needs and an overstretched, under-resourced educational system that was not able to support and challenge her and accommodate her particular learning and mental health needs. This distinction is important, as it moves from trying to "fix" or otherwise change Alice to instead concentrating efforts on teaching and learning practices and resourcing. Like many other children, she started off happy to go to school, but then, slowly but surely over time, her experience of school became increasingly negative. It is thus incumbent on educators and administrators to change the course of learning for children such as Alice to prevent the downward spiral into academic failure and despair that too many children currently experience.

The following book is written for and about young people such as Alice. It is based on the premise of putting children at the forefront of decision making. Once we place children at the centre of our thinking, we start to ask hard questions about the established order and the way that things have always been done, even if we do not always have the answers. For instance, how do we decide at what age should children start school? In many European countries it is 7 years of age, while in other countries it is 5. Why, and in whose best interest? Other questions should also be asked. For example, why does sitting down equal learning? Why is play undervalued? What is the best physical layout of schools? Why are art, music and movement undervalued? Can teachers be both authoritative and caring? Why do teachers have to be called Mr or Ms to show respect? Why don't we celebrate mistakes? Why do schools give out printed stickers/certificates to reward children? These are not necessarily easy questions, but if we are genuine about supporting children's learning and mental health, it is critical that we start to explore what works, for which student groups and when.

Children's learning, emotional wellbeing and mental health will be enhanced if we find the right answers to these questions. This book intends to answer some of these questions but, ultimately, aims to reflect on ways in which children's academic learning and mental health can be simultaneously promoted. By engaging in these questions and supporting a holistic approach, schools can create a safe, interactive and positive environment that allows all children to be fully engaged and actively involved in their own learning journey.

Chapter 2

The role of schools in promoting children's mental health

Introduction

This chapter provides a rationale for promoting children's mental health in schools. Though the core business of schools will always be the promotion of academic learning, a strong rationale will be made that schools need to address children's mental health and wellbeing as a necessary co-requisite for literacy, numeracy and other areas of academia. Terms often used in this field will be defined, including mental health, mental illness and wellbeing. It is not the sole responsibly of schools to address young people's mental health. Nonetheless, given the high prevalence of mental illness in children and the inseparable relationship between mental health, behaviour and learning, it is critical that schools work with students and their families in a holistic way, as part of a broader societal response and an important stakeholder of the "village" that helps nurture its young.

The role of schools

What is the role of schools? There appears to be some urgency in many parts of the world to refocus school efforts back to academic learning, as the following headlines suggest:

> Schools under pressure as crowded curriculum and programs swamp literacy and numeracy
> (Hore, writing for the *Herald Sun*, 2017)

> National curriculum overcrowded and too advanced, say principals
> (Knott, writing for the *Sydney Morning Herald*, 2014)

> Decluttered curriculum allows the right focus
> (Butterfield, writing for *The Age*, 2018)

Likewise, there are reports that a Chinese high school has removed chairs from its cafeteria to encourage students to eat faster so they have more time to devote to study (The Age, 13 September 2018). Much of this urgency is based on the perceived need to prepare students for standardised national testing. Accordingly, many believe that there is limited or no class time to implement universal mental health and wellbeing programs and that such strategies are unrelated to academic success. In sum, that schools play little or no role in the promotion of young people's mental health.

Schools have a powerful influence on children's development. Children spend up to 15,000 hours at school (Rutter, Maugham, Mortimore, Ouston & Smith 1979), arguably making schools more influential on children's development than any other social institution besides their family. Due to external pressures, some schools neglect to implement mental health initiatives and instead concentrate time, resources and teacher efforts on enhancing academic learning and success. Some schools, often unintentionally, cause or make worse young people's mental illness through the demands of the learning environment and school culture. Thus, regardless of intent, all schools play a role in young people's mental health and wellbeing and may either promote it or actively mitigate against it in the way the learning environment is structured.

Around the world, schools are social institutions where children are taught basic academic knowledge and various learning skills. However, schools do more than transmit academic and informal knowledge. Explicitly employing a holistic view of the child, the United Nations Convention on the Rights of the Child (2001) states that the aims of education should be directed to:

(a) The development of the child's personality, talents and mental and physical abilities to their fullest potential;
(b) The development of respect for human rights and fundamental freedoms;
(c) The development of respect for the child's parents, his or her own cultural identity, language and values, for the national values of the country in which the child is living, the country from which he or she may originate, and for civilisations different from his or her own;
(d) The preparation of the child for responsible life in a free society, in the spirit of understanding, peace, tolerance, equality of sexes, and friendship among all peoples, ethnic, national and religious groups and persons of indigenous origin; and
(e) The development of respect for the natural environment.

The UN Charter makes it clear that schools need to consider children's cognitive, emotional, social and physical needs, within the context of their background and culture. We know that healthy and happy children learn better; accordingly, it is in the interests of schools to ensure children are healthy, both physically and psychologically. Rather than an additional burden, mental health promotion, prevention and intervention should be part of core business in schools and integral to the business of teaching and learning, regardless of subject discipline or year level. Fostering children's hearts as well as their minds is critical to their success, and therefore to society as a whole, and accordingly needs to be at the forefront of educational practice, policy and research.

A question of priorities

Compulsory national and state curriculum tests that exist in many parts of the world have meant that academic instruction takes precedence over funding and time for supporting children's mental health and fostering their social and emotional wellbeing. According to the US National Education Association (2015), teachers spend an average of 54 school days, or 29% of their total work time for the school year, on tasks related to testing. Furthermore, over 40% of teachers reported that an emphasis on improving standardised test scores has had a negative impact on their classrooms. Likewise, in Australia, 40% of 568 parents reported that their child exhibited signs of stress or anxiety as a result of standardised testing (Whitlam Institute, 2013). For some children, standardised testing creates anxiety and a sense of exclusion and failure, especially for those with existing literacy and numeracy concerns (Whitlam, 2013).

While standardised testing is purported to measure a child's individual progress and the effectiveness of educational programs, questions continue to be asked whether such testing is in the best interests of children and a good use of teachers' time. Teaching to the test may lead to a narrowing of the school curriculum, a focus on what is easily measurable and the standardisation of teaching and learning strategies that do not consider individual students' learning styles and needs. Walker (2014) summarised these sentiments when he writes

> Over the past decade, the high stakes testing regime has squeezed out much of the curriculum that can make schools an engaging and enriching experience for students, and teachers have been forced to dilute their creativity to teach to the test.

There are many things that schools are tasked with, and it can be challenging to prioritise what is and is not required. As well as preparing students for high stakes assessments, there are repeated calls, as seen in the media, for schools to tackle obesity, substance use, character, civics, conflict resolution, sex education, road safety – the list goes on – as well as children's competencies across traditional academic domains. The risk of curriculum overload is high, and school efforts to address these issues are often piecemeal and delivered via a category-by-category approach, where separate health-related behaviours are addressed independently.

The public has their own views as to what schools should be doing. In the USA, the 49th 2017 Annual PDK Poll of the public's attitudes toward public schools found that the public overwhelmingly wanted schools to do more than educate students in academic subjects. Specifically, over 80% of Americans say that it is important for schools to help students develop interpersonal skills, such as being persistent, cooperative and respectful of others; again, over 80% supported career readiness classes, even if that means students spend less time in academic classes. Only 13% say that performance on standardised tests is a highly important indicator of school quality, although 39% indicate that developing students' interpersonal skills is extremely important. Similarly, businesses want employees who possess strong communication skills, perseverance and the ability to work in teams (National Network of Business and Industry Association, 2014). Likewise, over 2,000 Australians indicated that though schools need to promote basic literacy and numeracy as a priority, they also highlighted other priorities around life skills such as financial management, job preparation and cooking or, in the words of one participant "learning to adult" (Leahy & Selwyn, 2019, p. 15). Such data suggest that schools need to focus on more than children's cognitive domains.

Indeed, children's mental health and academic learning are inextricably connected (as will be detailed further in Chapter 2), though schools do not always acknowledge this in how and what they teach. Faupel (2006, pp. 167–168) argued that

> schooling has fundamentally lost its way. Traditionally, we have distinguished between the head (thinking), the heart (feelings) and behaviour (action). It seems we have lost sight of that essential human wholeness in embracing a narrow view of what education (schooling) is all about, focusing exclusively on academic and behavioural aspects of human development.

Thus, children's social, emotional and cognitive domains need to be integrated throughout the learning process, and schools need strategies and initiatives that simultaneously improve students' mental health, social–emotional capacities and their academic achievement in a holistic, integrative manner.

Key terms and concepts

It is important from the outset to be clear about what we mean by mental health, mental illness and other commonly employed terms in the field. Such a discussion is particularly pertinent in the education context, where mental illness is often seen as negative and stigmatising (Humphrey, 2016).

Mental illness

According to the American Psychiatric Association (2018), mental illnesses are defined as "health conditions involving changes in thinking, emotion or behaviour (or a combination of these) associated with distress and/or problems functioning in social, work or family activities". In childhood, mental health problems primarily consist of internalising problems (such as anxiety, depression and somatic complaints) and externalising problems (including, for example, aggressiveness, oppositional defiance and hyperactivity). When faced with stress, children with internalising problems tend to turn inward, while those with externalising problems direct their behaviour outward, typically towards other people or objects.

Some children may experience a relatively short-lived mental illness, and their health may improve with or without intervention. However, there are other children who experience more complex and severe difficulties which affect their ability to enjoy life and meet age appropriate developmental milestones.

Mental health

Mental health is more than the absence of mental illness. The World Health Organization (2014) defined mental health as "a state of well-being in which the individual realizes his or her own abilities, can cope with the normal stresses of life, can work productively and fruitfully, and is able to make a contribution to his or her community". The terms mental health and wellbeing are often used interchangeably and indicate a sense of "flourishing" or feeling good about and functioning well in life (Jeste, Palmer, Rettew & Boardman, 2015). For children, mental health typically refers to a sense of identity and self-worth, strong family and peer relationships, an ability to learn and a capacity to use cultural resources to maximise development.

However, mental health and mental illness are not opposite ends of the same construct. This "dual factor" approach recognises that someone with a mental illness might well report optimal mental health and feel good about themselves, maintain positive relationships and work towards goals (Humphrey, 2016). This approach also means that an individual with no mental illness might have difficulty coping with stresses and hence experience poor mental health. The dual factor approach recognises that some children may not be ill but may nonetheless require support in coping with stress. Thus, we need to focus on building students' strengths rather than simply tackling their academic, behavioural, social and emotional "problems" or "difficulties".

Social and emotional wellbeing

Mental health and illness are both broad concepts and, accordingly, may include other related concepts, such as emotional and social competence, especially when referring to children's mental health.

Social and emotional wellbeing involves acquiring the knowledge, skills and attitudes necessary to understand and manage emotions (one's own and others), set and achieve positive goals, feel and show empathy for others, establish and maintain positive relationships and make responsible decisions. In particular, social competence refers to those skills required to initiate and sustain positive relationships with peers and adults and may include, for example, taking turns, joining in, listening to others and "reading" other people's facial expressions and gestures, being able to initiate social interactions, asking for help and communicating appropriately with peers and adults (Illinois Early Learning Project, n.d.). For children, emotional competence includes the ability to identify and understand one's feelings, accurately read and understand emotional states in others, manage strong emotions and express these in a constructive and positive manner, regulate one's own behaviour and develop empathy for others (National Scientific Council on the Developing Child, 2004).

Social wellbeing and emotional wellbeing (or competence) are unusually combined, as it is critical to be able to identify and express one's own and other emotions in order to establish and maintain relationships with others. Collectively, social and emotional wellbeing includes a child's experience, expression and management of his or her emotions and the ability to establish positive and rewarding relationships with others (Cohen, Onunaku, Clothier & Poppe, 2005).

Mental health promotion, prevention and intervention

Mental health promotion consists of those efforts that seek to improve social and physical environments and enhance an individual's ability to achieve and maintain mental health. In comparison, mental illness prevention works to reduce the impact or prevent the initial onset of a mental illness, especially directed to "at-risk" populations, including those who may experience multiple childhood adversities such as parental mental illness or exposure to violence (Reupert, Maybery, Nicholson, Göpfert & Seeman, 2015). Finally, mental illness intervention aims to remedy a mental illness or lessen the ill effects caused; such interventions can be intensive or relatively minor (World Health Organization, 2014).

Why should schools be involved in promoting children's mental health?

There are many reasons why schools should be involved in promoting children's mental health, including the prevalence of children's mental illness, the intertwined relationship between children's mental health and academic success, the economic burden of not intervening and, finally, the right for all children to have access to appropriate support.

Prevalence of children's mental illnesses

Mental illness is common for people of all ages. Goodman et al. (2017) argued that for most of us, having a mental illness is like having influenza or bronchitis – all conditions which are highly prevalent and where sufferers may experience impaired functioning in social and occupational roles, but will mostly recover.

Goodman et al. (2017) drew on data from over 1,000 New Zealander participants who had been repeatedly assessed for common mental disorders by trained professionals over close to three decades. They found that only 17% reached midlife (age 38) without experiencing mental illness symptoms. In other words, experiencing a diagnosable mental disorder at some point during the life course is normal, not an extraordinary event.

Moreover, the onset of many mental health issues start in childhood and adolescence. Copeland, Shanahan, Costello and Angold (2011) employed a prospective, population-based study to assess 1,420 participants up to nine times from 9 through 21 years of age in the USA. They found that by 21 years of age, 82.5% of participants had met criteria for a diagnosed mental illness. Males had higher rates of substance and disruptive behaviour disorders compared with females. Similar to others in this field, they conclude by suggesting that mental illness, like other medical illnesses, is a nearly universal experience for young people.

In regard to the prevalence of mental illness in school-aged children, Merikangas et al. (2010) used a face-to-face survey with over 10,000 adolescents aged 13–18 years in the USA and found that 40% of participants experienced some form of mental illness, with anxiety disorders being the most common (31.9%), followed by behaviour disorders (19.1%), mood disorders (14.3%) and substance use disorders (11.4%). Female adolescents were more likely than males to have mood and anxiety disorders, but less likely to have behavioural and substance use disorders. Just over 11% experienced a severe mental illness, a figure that, the authors point out, is higher than the most frequent major physical conditions in adolescence such as asthma or diabetes. The median age of onset was earliest for anxiety (6 years), followed by 11 years for behaviour, 13 years for mood and 15 years for substance use disorders. Similarly, according to WHO (2018), globally, depression is the top cause of illness and disability among adolescents, and suicide is the third highest cause of death.

Notwithstanding the current high prevalence of mental illness in young people, there are varying reports regarding whether the prevalence of mental illness in young people is increasing and getting worse. In one nationally represented study of young people aged 6–17 years in Australia, Sawyer, Reece, Sawyer, Johnson and Lawrence (2018) presented data on the stability of the 12-month prevalence of major depression, Attention-Deficit/Hyperactivity Disorder (ADHD) and conduct disorder (CD) at two time points more than 15 years apart. Using parents' reports to assess the symptoms and associated features of these three conditions at both time points, they found little overall change in their prevalence across the 15-year period. This is confirmed by Baxter et al. (2014), who also found no evidence for increasing rates of childhood mental disorders over the past two decades, and Bor, Dean, Najman and Hayatbaksh (2014) in a systematic review, who found that children and toddler cohorts did not show increased rates between the twentieth and twenty-first centuries and instead found rates of externalising problems to be stable. They did, however, identify an increase in internalising problems in adolescent girls (Bor et al. 2014). In comparison, Collishaw (2015) found that the diagnosis and treatment of many child and adolescent disorders has increased, but concluded that this increase might be due to better recognition of health professionals. Though Collishaw (2015) did not find evidence to suggest an increased rate of ADHD, his findings indicate a substantial increase in emotional problems and antisocial behaviour for adolescents in high-income countries at least.

What does mental illness in students look like?

As argued in the above, all children and adolescents experience emotional and behavioural difficulties to various degrees. Though mental illness might be "normal", its consequences can be distressing and adversely impact school performance. Moreover, students may present with more than one problem, as one may lead to or be associated with other problems, including any combination of other mental illnesses, behavioural concerns and academic problems. Mental illness concerns might well vary as children develop, where for example, a simple phobia such as a fear of dogs might be common in young children, and fears about relationships become more common in adolescence. Different mental health issues will emerge in line with developmental milestones and will be influenced by cultural factors in regard to what is considered normal or abnormal development.

As noted earlier, children's mental health concerns are usually classified in two ways, "internalising" and "externalising". Children with internalising difficulties present with behaviours that are reserved and over-controlled. These children may be constantly worried, pessimistic, fearful and nervous and may withdraw from social situations. Such behaviours may lead to a diagnosis of an anxiety disorder or depression. In comparison, children with externalising difficulties present with behaviours that are impulsive or reactive, typically leading to problems with attention, oppositional behaviour or aggression, with subsequent potential diagnoses being ADHD or an oppositional disorder. Some children may present with both internalising and externalising patterns of behaviour.

Notwithstanding the distress inherent in many mental illnesses, how we view and judge the symptoms involved in certain mental illnesses may need to be challenged. For example, the concept of neurodiversity builds on the premise that conditions like autism are natural brain variations, not brain malfunctions, and should accordingly be recognised as a social category such as ethnicity, sexual orientation or disability and not an illness per se (Singer, 1999). Likewise, some have argued that ADHD may be a useful attribute to have. White and Shah (2006) found that ADHD may be associated with better performance on certain types of creativity tasks, specifically those that involve divergent thinking or "thinking outside the box". It is how we judge and interpret presenting behaviours and emotions, not necessarily the presentation per se, that might be the "problem".

Moreover, mental illness diagnoses tend to provide descriptions of symptoms and ignore or do not acknowledge the social context and adversities faced by the child. It is within this broad context that the causes of mental illness need to be examined, and for young people, the role of schools in creating or sustaining mental health concerns considered.

Causes of mental illness

There are many causes of mental illness. A combination of factors may be involved, including genetics, psychological trauma, certain stressful developmental phases (such as starting school or moving to high school) and societal and cultural expectations and restrictions. Social media and cyberbullying are also increasingly suggested as possible causes for the rise in mental health concerns in young people. It is usually a combination of genetic and environmental stressors that may precipitate a mental illness episode. Goodman et al. (2017) identified several childhood factors that clearly differentiated between those who experienced enduring, serious mental illness in adulthood and those who did not, including fewer emotional difficulties, social support during childhood (especially having strong friendship groups), and higher levels of childhood self-control.

Since the 1990s, an organising principle for determining risk, health and well-being in children has been adverse childhood experiences (ACEs), including for example exposure to abuse, neglect and intimate partner violence, or growing up with a parental mental illness or substance misuse. ACEs tend to be any issue that creates inescapable stress and disrupts key early relationships for children. Persistent and multiple ACEs lead to progressively increased risk of poor developmental outcomes. Blodgett and Langian (2018) found that the number of ACEs was associated with high risk of poor school attendance, behavioural issues and failure to meet grade-level standards in mathematics, reading or writing. Blodgett (2012) found that 45% of students had experienced at least one ACE and 22% had experienced multiple, while one in 16 had been exposed to four or more ACEs. He found that the more ACEs experienced by students, the more students struggled at school. For example, a student with one adverse childhood experience was 2.2 times more likely than was a student with no ACEs to have serious attendance issues; a student with two ACEs was 2.6 times more likely to have school-related struggles; and a student with three or more ACEs was 4.9 times more likely to have these issues. It is too simplistic to say that ACEs cause mental illness, as many people exposed to one or more ACEs do not necessarily develop a mental illness; conversely, those without exposure to an ACE may nonetheless develop a mental illness. We do know, however, that ACEs increase the risk of developing mental illness, so efforts need to be made to address, buffer or minimise the impact of these on children.

As well as acknowledging those factors that children bring with them to school that might impact adversely on their mental health, we also need to consider how the school environment may contribute to children's stress and ill health. Repeated academic failure, bullying, social isolation and harsh discipline measures including exclusion and suspension can all impact negatively on children's mental health and wellbeing. Additionally, the stress of high stakes testing potentially negatively impacts young people. Writing from Hong Kong, Sharp (2013) argued that:

> There are clear indications however, that the pressure to perform in an increasingly micro-managed, accountable education system may be playing a part in developing mental health problems and in suicidal behaviour.
> (p. 10)

Thus, mental illness might be considered a normal reaction to unrealistic academic pressures or negative and harmful learning environments. Instead of locating the "problem" within the child, the broad structural or organisational systems of schools may need attention. For instance, features of ADHD may present with many symptoms, some of which may not be inherent to the child but are instead a normal and understandable reaction to one's environment. See Figure 2.1 for the multiple possible causes that might result, for example, in the presentation of inattentiveness, one of the key symptoms of ADHD.

Moreover, what is considered normal and abnormal (or in other words, appropriate or inappropriate) is heavily influenced by cultural biases and assumptions. In respect to appropriate classroom behaviour, Gillies (2011) argued that

> the central place accorded to judgements of right and wrong in the classroom leaves little room for teachers to comfortably engage with the alternative moral frameworks that might structure some young people's lives without pathologising or misinterpreting.
> (Gillies, 2011, p. 193)

She points out that what are considered to be appropriate classroom behaviours are typically based on Western cultural viewpoints, which reproduce normative assumptions about development, autonomy and personal expression. Such attitudes assume a "white, privileged standpoint, in which 'difficult feelings' rarely involve anything more testing than rowing with friends or feeling left out" (Gillies, 2011, p. 193) and may not reflect the daily realities of students, especially those living in violent communities. Thus, what might be considered pathological, immature or inappropriate behaviour could instead be reframed and interpreted as behaviour that challenges the status quo. It is this positioning of how we perceive, value and act on children's behaviour in the context of their learning behaviours that is critical here. Such reflections demonstrate how schools might contribute to young people's academic failure and stress,

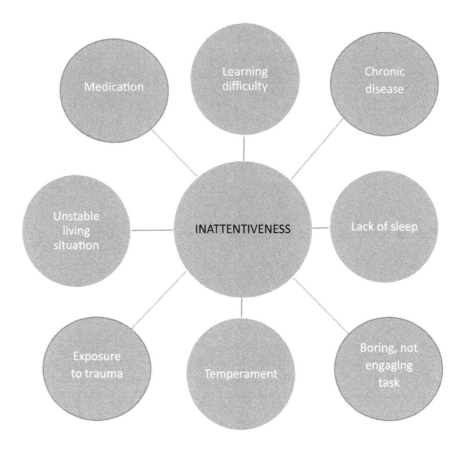

Figure 2.1 Possible causes for student inattentiveness

but also where and how we might successfully intervene to at least minimise young people's distress.

Lack of support for children's mental health concerns

Notwithstanding the high prevalence of mental illness, most young people with a mental health issue do not receive professional support for their symptoms. Using data from Grade 7 and 8 Canadian students, Brownlie et al. (2018) found that while internalising and/or externalising problems exceeded 30% of those surveyed, fewer than half had received mental health services in the past 12 months. Similar figures have been found elsewhere. For example, in Germany, Hintzpeter (2015) collected data from close to 3,000 young people aged 7–17 years and found that among those with general mental health problems, only 29.5 % sought professional help. Likewise, Merikangas et al. (2011) found that 36.2% of adolescents with mental disorders received services for their illness. While severity was associated with increased likelihood of receiving treatment, half of those adolescents with severely impairing mental disorders had never received mental health treatment for their symptoms. Among those who received mental health treatment, a substantial proportion reported receiving relatively few visits (six or less visits). They also found that Hispanic and non-Hispanic black adolescents were less likely than their white peers to receive services for mood and anxiety disorders, even when such disorders were associated with severe impairment. Fewer than one in five affected adolescents received services for anxiety, eating or substance use disorders. In comparison, service rates for those with ADHD were 59.8% and for those with behaviour disorders, 45.4%. While it is not clear why this is the case, it could be that in these cases children's behaviour was more disruptive and so relatively easier to identify than an internalising disorder. Alternatively, it may be that ADHD symptoms created more of a problem for teachers and parents than internalising disorders and so were more readily referred to services.

Often those young people with the most need for mental health services are the ones least likely to access or be offered support. In a review of service use, Elster, Jarosik, VanGeest and Fleming (2003) found that in six out of nine studies, African American adolescents received fewer mental health services than their Caucasian counterparts. Whether and how young people obtain community mental health services does not appear to be based on need but may instead relate more to factors such as access and family income. However, in a national survey of students in Grades 7 to 12, Slade (2002) found that access to school-based mental health services did not differ based on race, possibly because, in the USA at least, school-based services are not dependent on insurance status as community-based mental health care is. Regardless of the availability (or lack thereof) of external support services, schools are often in the first line of defence for meeting the needs of students with mental health concerns.

As well, parents may not always be in the best position to support their children's mental health concerns. Though young people rely on their parents or caregivers to obtain appropriate help, caregivers may not appreciate what is happening for their children. Teagle (2002) found that only 39% of parents in her sample of 1,420 youth–parent pairs were aware of their child's mental health difficulties, while Reardon et al. (2017) found that many parents did not believe that their child needed help or believed that the problem would be resolved over time. There are other structural issues that impede caregivers from accessing help for their children; Reardon et al. (2017) found that the amount of time that caregivers had to wait to access support for their children was a significant barrier to seeking help, and some parents may not know where or how to access help.

Though many people experience some form of mental health distress during their lifetime, the onset for these concerns usually begins in childhood or adolescence. Students with mental health problems are present in every school, regardless of their socio-economic background. Helping young people, as well as their teachers and carers, manage difficulties early in life may prevent the development of mental illnesses as adults. Once mental illness develops, it may become a regular part of a child's behaviour and may be more difficult to treat. Thus, efforts and interventions aimed at prevention or early intervention need to focus on children and their environments, including schools.

School-based mental health support may address gaps in current services, irrespective of family resources. Indeed, parents look to schools to address these gaps. In a national survey of children and young people in Britain, Green, McGinnity, Meltzer, Ford and Goodman (2005) found that a third of parents worry about their child's mental health, and of the 93% who had sought help, 70% had first approached a teacher, in contrast with a quarter who had first met up with their family doctor.

Overall, problems at school and other adverse childhood experiences tend to be accumulative and may remain undetected and therefore untreated. Regardless of the cause of the mental illness, it is commonplace for many students in our schools today to present with some form of mental illness or mental health concern. Hence, responding to children is not just a mental health problem but also an educational one. Schools need to promote healthy environments in which children can learn and address any present barriers that children may have to learning. In other words, there can be no learning without adequate mental health support.

Schools can make a positive difference

Schools have the potential to initiate or worsen children's mental illnesses or, alternatively, buffer the impact of adverse childhood experiences and promote a healthy school environment that encourages mental health and wellbeing.

Mashburn et al. (2008) found that after adjusting for various background variables, including family characteristics, teachers' instructional and supportive interactions predicted children's social skills in their first year of school. Moreover, the impact of delivering effective programs that focus on children's social and emotional wellbeing extends beyond childhood. Campbell et al. (2014) found that high-quality early childhood programs have substantial benefits in that young people exposed to these programs had increased earnings, fewer instances of crime and significantly lower prevalence of risk factors for cardiovascular and metabolic diseases in their mid-30s.

Indeed, social and emotional wellbeing can be taught and actively developed throughout the schooling years. Numerous systematic reviews and meta-analyses (Durlak, Weissberg, Dymnicki, Taylor & Schellinger, 2011; Taylor, Oberle, Durlak & Weissberg, 2017; Sancassiani et al. 2015; Sklad, Diekstra, De Ritter, Ben & Gravesteijn, 2012) conclusively demonstrate that schools can improve young people's mental health, social and emotional skills and attitudes to school as well as their academic performance. Indeed, efforts may be especially effective when targeting high-risk children (due to existing mental health concerns or academic concerns) (Greenberg, Kusche, Cook & Quamma, 1995). Thus, policies, program development and professional development efforts that improve school environments and teacher–child interactions can facilitate children's school readiness and later success in adulthood across multiple health and wellbeing domains.

Inseparable relationship between school success and mental health

As will be further detailed in Chapter 3, children's mental health and how they feel about themselves is inseparable from whether, how and what they learn. Children with greater wellbeing and lower levels of mental health problems achieve higher achievement scores, have better attendance and drop out of school less often than children with significant mental health difficulties (Weare, 2015). A focus on children's mental health and wellbeing not only fosters happy and healthy school environments but also explicitly supports effective teaching and learning environments – the two are inseparable. As succinctly summarised by Jones and Kahn (2017, p. 4), the "major domains of human development – social, emotion, cognitive, academic – are deeply intertwined in the brain and in behavior, and all are central to learning". Likewise, as pointed out by Brackett (2015), "the neural pathways in the brain that deal with stress are the same ones that are used for learning".

Spending time on students' wellbeing does not take time away from academic learning – on the contrary, it enriches children's learning abilities and experiences. Wang, Haertel and Walberg (1997) investigated 28 categories of influences on learning and found that eight of the 11 most influential categories involved social and emotional factors, such as student–teacher social interactions, classroom climate and positive support from the peer group. Conversely, among the major reasons cited for students dropping out of school were not getting along with teachers (35%), not getting on with peers (20.1%), feeling left out (23.2%) and not feeling safe (12.1%) (National Center for Education Statistics, 2002). Thus, students' mental health can have a profound impact on school success, in regard to academic outcome, their behaviour and how they relate to peers and school staff.

Economic arguments

There is an economic cost for society as a whole if schools do not act on young people's mental health concerns. As outlined in an editorial by Insel (2008), there are direct costs of treating someone with a mental illness, including medication and clinic visits, and indirect costs related to a reduced labour supply, public income support payments and costs associated with consequences such as incarceration or homelessness. Kessler et al. (2008) estimated that serious mental illness is associated with an annual loss of earnings totalling $193.2 billion. These costs will continue to climb, and so questions need to be asked as to the most effective means of spending a finite mental health budget.

Investment in schools, especially in the early years of schooling, can reap multiple rewards and deliver substantial returns on investment (Campbell et al. 2014; García, Heckman, Leaf & Prados, 2016). For example, the Caring School Community, a program which promotes prosocial behaviour and a school-wide feeling of community, yielded $28.42 for each dollar spent (Schaps, Battistich & Solomon, 2004). Belfield et al. (2015) examined the weighted average benefit–cost ratio of six, evidence based social and emotional learning (SEL) interventions and found that identified benefits outweighed the costs by a factor of 11:1, with an average net present value per 100 participants of $618,380. While cautioning against inconsistencies in the measurement of impacts and hence benefits, the authors conclude that such programs can "easily pass a benefit–cost test" (p. 46).

A consensus document, signed off by 28 members of the Council of Distinguished Scientists and complied by Jones and Kahn (2017), convincingly argued that supporting children's social, emotional and cognitive development is financially sound and hence a wise use of public resources that delivers benefits not only to individuals but also to society as a whole. They highlighted research that shows that individuals with higher social and emotional competencies have higher labour market earnings, long-term employment and taxable earnings. Sound social and emotional competence also means a reduction in violence, drug use and mental health problems and thus less government funding required for incarceration and mental health services (Jones & Kahn, 2017).

At the same time, US government investment in mental health, child and adolescent services and intervention research has reduced by 42% from 2005 to 2015 (Hoagwood et al. 2018). While it is not solely the role of schools to pick up these pieces, they do play an important but often unfulfilled role in this field.

Equality

Success at school is important from a societal perspective because a nation's ability to increase its standard of living, compete in global markets and promote participation in civic affairs all require an educated citizenry. Simultaneously, mental health and wellbeing have a profound effect on an individual's quality of life, physical and social wellbeing and economic productivity (WHO, 2003). Jones and Kahn (2017) argued that building all children's social and emotional wellbeing, regardless of their background, can be part of achieving a more equitable society. Strategies and interventions designed to promote children's wellbeing and social and emotional competence can make a difference to all children, and especially those exposed to adverse experiences, including poverty, parental substance use/parental mental illness and violence (Jones &

Kahn, 2017). Well-designed and -delivered wellbeing programs can "buffer" the impact of various adverse childhood experiences and ensure all children are provided with opportunities to learn and succeed (Jones & Kahn, 2017). Due to poverty and many adverse childhood experiences, there are a significant number of young people who enter school already at risk of educational failure. There is an important role for schools to offset this vulnerability and, along with other community and political forces, to support children's mental health as well as academic learning.

Finally . . .

No single institution or professional discipline has all the tools to understand or intervene in the course of a child's development. Accordingly, collaborations across a range of services are needed for integrating children's education, mental and physical health needs and supports. Nonetheless, many of children's developmental milestones, especially around academic and social competence, are achieved (or not) within the context of schools. Thus, although schools cannot be expected to address all the problems that children may experience, they can provide, through their climate and curriculum, an opportunity to promote wellbeing and prevent mental health problems. Notwithstanding their important role in this field, educational responses are not straight-forward and will vary depending on the broad cultural and political context in which they operate.

The universal nature of schooling, which most children attend from an early age, provides a focal point to promote children's mental health and wellbeing and intervene early if necessary. Thus, schools can and should play an important role in the development of young people, including their affective and cognitive domains. There are many competing demands and barriers for this work, emulating from policy, professional development opportunities, time and resourcing. The central aim of this book is to prompt and support those working in, and for, schools and to incorporate mental health promotion, prevention and intervention initiatives and strategies as a core part of business as usual. How schools might deliver mental illness prevention, early intervention, mental health treatment and positive social and emotional skill development and simultaneously target academic learning, monitoring and success is at the heart of this book.

References

American Psychiatric Association (2018). *What is mental illness?* Retrieved January 7, 2019, from www.psychiatry.org/patients-families/what-is-mental-illness

Baxter, A., Scott, K. M., Ferrari, A. J., Norman, R. E., Vos, T., & Whiteford, H. (2014). Challenging the myth of an "epidemic" of common mental disorders: Trends in the global prevalence of anxiety and depression. *Depression and Anxiety*, *31*(6), 506–516.

Belfield, C., Bowden, B., Klapp, A., Levin, H., Shand, R., & Zander, S. (2015). The economic value of social and emotional learning. *Journal of Benefit-Cost Analysis*, *6*(3), 508–544.

Blodgett, C. (2012). *Working paper: Adopting ACEs screening and assessment in child serving systems*. Retrieved January 7, 2019, from https://del-public-files.s3-us-west-2.amazonaws.com/Complex-Trauma-Research-ACE-Screening-and-Assessment-in-Child-Serving-Systems-7-12-final.pdf

Blodgett, C., & Lanigan, J. D. (2018). The association between adverse childhood experience (ACE) and school success in elementary school children. *School Psychology Quarterly, 33*(1), 137–146.

Bor, W., Dean, A. J., Najman, J., & Hayatbaksh, R. (2014). Are child and adolescent mental health problems increasing in the 21st century? A systematic review. *Australian & New Zealand Journal of Psychiatry, 48*(7), 606–616.

Brackett, M. (2015). Teaching peace in elementary school. *The New York Times*. Retrieved July 27, 2018, from www.nytimes.com/2015/11/15/sunday-review/teaching-peace-in-elementary-school.html

Brownlie, E., Beitchman, J. H., Chaim, G., Wolfe, D. A., Rush, B., & Henderson, J. (2018). Early adolescent substance use and mental health problems and service utilisation in a school-based sample. *The Canadian Journal of Psychiatry, 64*(2), 116–125.

Butterfield, N. (2018). Education: Decluttered curriculum allows the right focus. *The Age*, December 11, 2018. Retrieved June 18, 2019, from https://www.theage.com.au/national/education-decluttered-curriculum-allows-the-right-focus-20181210-h18yso.html

Campbell, F., Conti, G., Heckman, J. J., Moon, S. H., Pinto, R., Pungello, E., & Pan, Y. (2014). *Early childhood investments substantially boost adult health*. Retrieved August 12, 2017, from www.ncbi.nlm.nih.gov/pmc/articles/PMC4028126/

Cohen, J., Onunaku, N., Clothier, S., & Poppe, J. (2005). *Helping young children succeed. Strategies to promote childhood social and emotional competence*. Retrieved August 11, 2017, from www.buildinitiative.org/WhatsNew/ViewArticle/tabid/96/ArticleId/396/Helping-Young-Children-Succeed-Strategies-to-Promote-Early-Childhood-Social-and-Emotional-Developmen.aspx

Collishaw, S. (2015). Annual research review: Secular trends in child and adolescent mental health. *Journal of Child Psychology and Psychiatry, 56*(3), 370–393.

Copeland, W., Shanahan, L., Costello, E. J., & Angold, A. (2011). Cumulative prevalence of psychiatric disorders by young adulthood: A prospective cohort analysis from the Great Smoky Mountains Study. *Journal of the American Academy of Child & Adolescent Psychiatry, 50*(3), 252–261.

Durlak, J. A., Weissberg, R. P., Dymnicki, A. B., Taylor, R. D., & Schellinger, K. (2011). The impact of enhancing students' social and emotional learning: A meta-analysis of school based universal interventions. *Child Development, 82*(1), 474–501.

Elster, A., Jarosik, J., VanGeest, J., & Fleming, M (2003). Racial and ethnic disparities in health care for adolescents: A systematic review of the literature. *Archives of Pediatrics and Adolescent Medicine, 157*(9), 867–874.

Faupel, A. (2006). Promoting emotional literacy: Its implications for school and classroom. In M. Hunter-Carsch, Y. Tiknaz, P. Cooper, & R. Sage (Eds.), *The handbook of social emotional, and behavioural difficulties* (pp. 167–175). London: Continuum.

García, J., Heckman, J., Leaf, D. E., & Prados, M. J. (2016). *The life-cycle benefits of an influential early childhood program*. The National Bureau of Economic Research. Retrieved January 7, 2019, from www.nber.org/papers/w22993

Gillies, V. (2011). Social and emotional pedagogies: Critiquing the new orthodoxy of emotion in classroom behaviour management. *British Journal of Sociology of Education, 32*(2), 185–202.

Goodman, S., MacDonald, A. W., Schaefer, J. D., Caspi, A., Belsky, D. W., Harrington, H. . . . Moffitt, T. E. (2017). Enduring mental health: Prevalence and prediction. *Journal of Abnormal Psychology, 126*(2), 212–224.

Green, H., McGinnity, A., Meltzer, H., Ford, T., & Goodman, R. (2005). *Mental health of children and young people in Great Britain, 2004.* Retrieved January 7, 2019, from https://sp.ukdataservice.ac.uk/doc/5269/mrdoc/pdf/5269technicalreport.pdf

Greenberg, M. T., Kusche, C. A., Cook, E. T., & Quamma, J. P. (1995). Promoting emotional competence in school-aged children: The effects of the PATHS curriculum. *Development and Psychopathology, 7*(1), 117–136.

Hintzpeter, B., Klasen, F., Schön, G., Voss, C., Hölling, H., Ravens-Sieberer, U., & the BELLA study group (2015). Mental health care use among children and adolescents in Germany: Results of the longitudinal BELLA study. *European Child & Adolescent Psychiatry, 24*(6), 705–713.

Hoagwood, K. E., Atkins, M., Kelleher, K., Peth-Pierce, R., Olin, S., Burns, B., Landsverk, J., & McCue Horwitz, S. (2018). Trends in children's mental health services research funding by the National Institute of Mental Health from 2005 to 2015: A 42% reduction. *Journal of the American Academy of Child & Adolescent Psychiatry, 57*(1), 10–13.

Hore, M. (2017). Victorian schools under pressure as crowded curriculum and programs swamp literacy and number. *Herald Sun*, September 1, 2017. Retrieved June 18, 2019, from https://www.heraldsun.com.au/news/special-features/news-in-education/victorian-schools-under-pressure-as-crowded-curriculum-and-programs-swamp-literacy-and-numeracy/news-story/d0cc7a661d6f7341b81bd717bb6a2ef3

Humphrey, N. (2016). The role of schools in promoting children's mental health. In S. Campbell, D. Morley, & R. Catchpole (Eds.), *Critical issues in child and adolescent mental health* (pp. 129–147). Palgrave: London.

Illinois Early Learning Project (n.d.) *The Illinois early learning project*. Retrieved August 7, 2017, from https://illinoisearlylearning.org/

Insel, T. R. (2008). Assessing the economic costs of serious mental illness. *American Journal of Psychiatry, 165*(6), 663–665.

Jeste, D. V., Palmer, B. W., Rettew, D. C., & Boardman, S. (2015). Positive psychiatry: Its time has come. *The Journal of Clinical Psychiatry, 76*, 675–683.

Jones, S., & Kahn, J. (2017). *The evidence base for how we learn. Supporting students' social, emotional, and academic development. Consensus statements of evidence from the Council of Distinguished Scientists*. The Aspen Institute. Retrieved January 7, 2019, from https://assets.aspeninstitute.org/content/uploads/2017/09/SEAD-Research-Brief-9.12_updated-web.pdf

Kessler, R. C., Heeringa, S., Lakoma, M. D., Petukhova, M., Rupp, A. E., Schoenbaum, M., . . . Zaslavsky, A. M. (2008). Individual and societal effects of mental disorders on earnings in the United States: Results from the National Comorbidity Survey Replication. *American Journal of Psychiatry, 65*, 703–711.

Knott, M. (2014). National curriculum overcrowded and too advanced, say principals. *The Sydney Morning Herald*, March 11, 2014. Retrieved June 18, 2019, from https://www.smh.com.au/politics/federal/national-curriculum-overcrowded-and-too-advanced-say-principals-20140310-34hxw.html

Leahy, D., & Selwyn, N. (2019). *Pubic opinions on Australian schools and schooling*. Education Futures, Monash University. Retrieved February 25, 2019, from www.monash.edu/__data/assets/pdf_file/0005/1653548/Education-Futures-Research-Report-Public-Opinions.pdf

Mashburn, A. J., Pianta, R. C, Hamre, B. K., Downer, J. T., Barbarin, O. A., Bryant, D., ... Howes, C. (2008). Measures of classroom quality in prekindergarten and children's development of academic, language and social skills. *Child Development, 79*(3), 732–749.

Merikangas, K. R., He, J. P., Burstein, M., Swanson, S. A., Avenevoli, S., Cui, L., ... Swendsen, J. (2010). Lifetime prevalence of mental disorders in U.S. adolescents: Results from the National Comorbidity Survey Replication – Adolescent Supplement (NCS-A). *Journal of the American Academy of Child & Adolescent Psychiatry, 49*(10), 980–989.

Merikangas, K. R., He, J., Burstein, M., Swendsen, J., Avenevoli, S., Case, B., ... Olfson, M. (2011). Service utilization for lifetime mental disorders in U.S. adolescents: Results of the National Comorbidity Survey – Adolescent Supplement (NCS-A). *Journal of the American Academy of Child & Adolescent Psychiatry, 50*(1), 32–45.

National Center for Education Statistics. (2002). *Dropout rates in the United States 2000.* Washington, DC: U.S. Department of Education, Offices of Educational Research and Improvement. Retrieved January 7, 2019, from https://nces.ed.gov/pubs2002/2002114.pdf

National Education Association (2015). *Excessive high-stakes testing has negative effects on students, teachers.* Retrieved January 7, 2019, from www.nea.org/assets/docs/TestingMemberSurvey(RES)0215.pdf

National Network of Business and Industry Associations (2014). *Common employability skills. A foundation for success in the workplace: The skills all employees need, no matter where they work.* Retrieved January 7, 2019, from https://s3.amazonaws.com/brt.org/archive/Common%20Employability_asingle_fm.pdf

National Scientific Council on the Developing Child (2004). *Children's emotional development is built into the architecture of their brains.* Working paper 2. Retrieved August 7, 2004, from http://developingchild.harvard.edu/wp-content/uploads/2004/04/Childrens-Emotional-Development-Is-Built-into-the-Architecture-of-Their-Brains.pdf

Reardon, T., Harvey, K., Baranowska, M., O'Brien, D., Smith, L., & Creswell, C. (2017). What do parents perceive are the barriers and facilitators to accessing psychological treatment for mental health problems in children and adolescents? A systematic review of qualitative and quantitative studies. *European Child and Adolescent Psychiatry, 26,* 623–647.

Reupert, A., Maybery, D., Nicholson, J., Göpfert, M., & Seeman, M. (2015, Eds.). *Parental psychiatric disorder: Distressed parents and their families.* Cambridge, UK: Cambridge University Press.

Rutter, M., Maugham, B., Mortimore, P., Ouston, J., & Smith, A. (1979). *Fifteen thousand hours: Secondary schools and their effects on children.* Cambridge, MA: Harvard University Press.

Sancassiani, F., Pintus, E., Holte, A., Paulus, P., Moro, M. F., Cossu, G., ... Lindert, J. (2015). Enhancing the emotional and social skills of the youth to promote their wellbeing and positive development: A systematic review of universal school-based randomized controlled trials. *Clinical Practice and Epidemiology in Mental Health, 11*(Suppl. 1), 21–40.

Sawyer, M. G., Reece, C. E., Sawyer, A. C. P., Johnson, S. E., & Lawrence, D. (2018). Has the prevalence of child and adolescent mental disorders in Australia changed between 1998 and 2013 to 2014? *Journal of the American Academy of Child & Adolescent Psychiatry, 57,* 343–350.e5.

Schaps, E., Battistich, V., & Solomon, D. (2004). Community in school as key to student growth: Findings from the child development project. In J. E. Zins, R. P. Weissberg, M. C. Wang, & H. J. Walberg (Eds.), *Building academic success on social and emotional learning: What does the research say?* (pp. 189–205). New York: Teachers College Press.

Sharp, A. (2013). Exam culture and suicidal behaviour among young people. *Education and Health, 31*(1), 7–11.

Singer, J. (1999). Why can't you be normal for once in your life? In M. Corker, & S. French (Eds.), *Disability discourse* (pp. 59–67). Buckingham: Open University Press.

Sklad, M., Diekstra, R., De Ritter, M., Ben, J., & Gravesteijn, C. (2012). Effectiveness of school-based universal social, emotional, and behavioral programs: Do they enhance students' development in the area of skill, behavior, and adjustment? *Psychology in the Schools, 49*(9), 892–909.

Slade, E. P. (2002). Effects of school-based mental health programs on mental health service use by adolescents at school and in the community. *Mental Health Services Research, 4*(3), 151–166.

Taylor, R. D., Oberle, E., Durlak, J. A., & Weissberg, R. P. (2017). Promoting positive youth development through school-based social and emotional learning interventions: A meta-analysis of follow up effects. *Child Development, 88*(4), 1156–1171.

Teagle, S. E. (2002). Parental problem recognition and child mental health service use. *Mental Health Services Research, 4*(4), 257–266.

The 49th Annual PDK Poll (2017). *The 49th Annual PDK Poll of the public's attitudes toward the public schools.* Retrieved January 7, 2019, from https://journals.sagepub.com/doi/pdf/10.1177/0031721717728274

UN Convention on the Rights of the Child (2001). *Article 29(1). The aims of education.* Retrieved January 7, 2019, from www.refworld.org/docid/4538834d2.html

Walker, T. (2014). NEA Survey: Nearly half of teachers consider leaving profession due to standardised testing. *NEA Today.* Retrieved July 27, 2018, from http://neatoday.org/2014/11/02/nea-survey-nearly-half-of-teachers-consider-leaving-profession-due-to-standardized-testing-2/

Wang, M. C., Haertel, G. D., & Walberg, H. J. (1997). Toward a knowledge base for school learning. *Review of Educational Research, 63,* 249–294.

Weare, K. (2015). *What works in promoting social and emotional well-being and responding to mental health problems in schools?* National Children's Bureau, London. Retrieved January 7, 2019, from www.mentalhealth.org.nz/assets/ResourceFinder/What-works-in-promoting-social-and-emotional-wellbeing-in-schools-2015.pdf

White, H., & Shah, P. (2006). Uninhibited imaginations: Creativity in adults with attention-deficit/hyperactivity disorder. *Personality and Individual Differences, 40*(6), 1121–1131.

Whitlam Institute (2013). *Senate Inquiry into the effectiveness of the National Assessment Program – Literacy and Numeracy (NAPLAN).* Retrieved January 7, 2019, from www.whitlam.org/publications/2017/10/17/naplan-senate-inquiry-submission

WHO (2003). *Investing in mental health. Evidence for action.* Retrieved January 7, 2019, from http://apps.who.int/iris/bitstream/handle/10665/87232/9789241564618_eng.pdf;jsessionid=18A79BA6FFACFC2AE6297A4864F39C1D?sequence=1

WHO (2014). *Mental health: A state of wellbeing.* Retrieved January 7, 2019, from www.who.int/features/factfiles/mental_health/en/

WHO (2018). *Adolescents: Health risks and solutions.* Retrieved January 7, 2019, from www.who.int/news-room/fact-sheets/detail/adolescents-health-risks-and-solutions

Chapter 3

The relationship between mental illness, wellbeing and academic achievement

How students perform in school will impact their mental health and, in turn, how they feel about themselves will impact on their learning; the two are inseparable. However, when resources are scarce, or when children's standardised assessment scores fall, schools are criticised for spending time and effort on promoting children's mental health and wellbeing rather than on what many consider to be schools' core responsibility of teaching children reading, writing and mathematics. In this chapter, the relationships between successful school adjustment and performance, mental health and social and emotional competence will be highlighted. Such information is important as it sheds light on when and how schools might intervene and support children in their learning and wellbeing. Additionally, this discussion provides a strong rationale for why schools need to deliver an integrated model of teaching and learning that promotes young people's mental health, wellbeing and academic progress.

What is academic success and failure?

In many parts of the world, a child's academic success is limited to his or her performance on a given test. Nonetheless, children's development across social, emotional and academic domains is necessary for a child's successful adaptation and long-term prosperity. In a slightly different approach, Suldo, Gormley, DuPaul and Anderson-Butcher (2014) suggested that school success can be defined in relation to students' skill and knowledge in specific areas (e.g. literacy, grade point average or some other assessment score), their behaviour (such as engagement, drop out and attendance) and attitudes (including, for example, perceptions of their own abilities and how much they feel they belong to the school). Studies regarding academic success tend to provide very specific, measurable academic outcomes such as grade repetition/progression, a reading or other test score.

School failure depends on who is doing the evaluation and the system (rubric, assessment, criteria) used. Nonetheless, what constitutes a failure for one person might well be seen differently for another. Typically, however, failure is characterised by low marks or falling behind other same-age peers. Interestingly, the OECD (2010) defined school failure in terms of when school systems fail to provide services leading to successful student learning, putting the onus back on schools rather than blaming or otherwise targeting the individual student and his or her learning difficulties or shortcomings.

Overall, academic performance has implications that play out across life stages and on multiple levels. On the individual, student level, academic struggles are associated with disengagement and school dropout, both of which have the potential to derail educational and occupational trajectories into adulthood. Students who struggle with the demands of the academic program may disrupt the teaching and learning process by impacting negatively other students as well as the teacher. On the population level, widespread academic failure negatively influences rates of mortality and unemployment (Najimi, Sharifirad, Amini & Meftagh, 2013). Accordingly, it is important to examine what influences academic performance and arguably more importantly to consider what this means for schools and how and when to intervene. Ascertaining the reasons why some children thrive at school while others struggle is complex but important to understand in order to intervene appropriately.

Why do some children fail at school?

In a seminal study, Wade and Moore (1993) asked teachers to list what they believed to be the causes of student failure. Over 60% of teachers blamed the child, while 32% blamed the students' home situation; only 3% blamed teachers or the school system for learning problems. In a similar vein, Nuthall (2004, p. 274) wrote that

> Within the professional culture of teaching, it is commonly believed that if something is taught (which usually means explained or demonstrated), it is automatically learned. If it is not learned, then the problem lies in the inadequacy of the student's ability, motivation, or persistence, *not* in the ineffectiveness of the instruction.

> (italics added)

Alessi (1988, cited in Hempenstall, 2013) listed five areas that explain a child's learning or behaviour difficulties in school:

1. The curriculum does not meet the needs of the student.
2. The teacher may not be implementing effective teaching and/or behaviour management practices.
3. The principal and other school administrators may not be implementing effective school management practices.
4. Parents may not be providing the home-based support necessary for effective learning.
5. The child may have physical and/or psychological problems that may be contributing to his or her learning problems.

This list was sent to school psychologists, who agreed that all five factors played a role in children's learning or behavioural difficulties (Alessi, 1988, cited in Hempenstall, 2013). The psychologists were then invited to examine the reports they had written on students who had been referred for learning or behavioural issues and consider, from their reports, why this might be the case. Psychologists' responses were matched against the initial list, and out of 5,000 cases, Alessi (1988, cited in Hempenstall, 2013) found that in relation to psychologists' beliefs about academic failure;

1. None were related to curriculum factors
2. None were related to inappropriate teaching practices
3. None were related to factors associated with school administration
4. 10–20% was related to parent and home factors
5. 100% was related to factors pertaining to the individual child

Jokingly, Alessi (1988, as cited in Hempenstall, 2013) summarised the results of his survey by suggesting: "If only these districts had better functioning children with a few more supportive parents, there would be no educational difficulties". If only it were so simple. Clearly, it is more complex than blaming the individual student or his or her family for school failure.

A sequence of experiences

Contrary to the studies highlighted above, there are many variables related to the child, family, school and community that influence a child's risk of academic failure and/or mental illness. These variables tend to set into motion a sequence of experiences that eventually become a dynamic cascade. Developmental cascade models demonstrate how (mal)adaption in one domain of functioning can ripple into other areas of functioning and identify the steps along that progression (Masten & Cicchetti, 2010). Cascade models resonate with the view that child development is a dynamic process in which the skills and abilities acquired in one stage of the life cycle affects learning in the next step.

Developmental cascades may be positive or negative in terms of adaptive outcomes. Generally, early advantage or competence will influence later development in positive ways, or in other words, "success in earlier tasks build skills for success in later tasks" (Masten & Cicchetti, 2010, p. 493). Conversely, problems or delays can lead to subsequent problems in other domains; for example, children who start school with existing behaviour problems might then experience problems with learning and social interactions at school (Masten & Cicchetti, 2010). Demonstrating further the snowballing impact of negative developmental cascades, Masten et al. (2005) found that externalising problems of children aged 8–12 years undermined academic achievement by adolescence, which in turn contributed to internalising problems in young adulthood. In other words, the negative cascade progressed over time from externalising problem behaviours to academic difficulties to internalising problem behaviours. Moreover, they found that this negative pattern was consistent after controlling for the students' cognitive ability and socio-economic background and applied to both girls and boys.

According to Masten and Cicchetti (2010), developmental cascade effects may present across levels, among domains at the same level and across different systems or generations. An important characteristic of developmental cascade models is their dynamic nature, whereby the various developmental steps offer opportunities to disrupt the negative cascade or alternatively exacerbate its process (Dodge, Malone, Lansford, Miller, Pettit & Bates, 2009). Hence, developmental cascade models are important as they have the potential to tell us which domains might predict later adaptive outcomes, psychopathology or resilience and accordingly provide some guidance as to when and how to intervene. As summarised by Dodge et al. (2009), there are opportunities for change in each new domain.

Various theoretical models that further detail the relationships between mental health and academic performance, are summarised below and then further elaborated.

- How a child's mental health impacts on academic achievement is often referred to as the *adjustment erosion* model (see Moilanen, Shaw & Maxwell, 2010; Panayiotou & Humphrey, 2017; Wigglesworth, Qualter & Humphrey, 2017)
- How achievement achievement/failure impacts on mental health is sometimes referred to as the *academic incompetence* model (see Moilanen et al. 2010; Panayiotou & Humphrey, 2017; Wigglesworth et al. 2017)
- The third model, referred to as *shared risk*, postulates that it is an accumulation of several risk factors, such as poverty, inadequate parenting and low intellectual ability, that might impact on both mental health and academic achievement (see Moilanen et al. 2010; Panayiotou & Humphrey, 2017; Wigglesworth et al. 2017).

The adjustment erosion model

In the adjustment erosion model, a child's mental health concerns, typically represented by externalising or internationalising symptoms, adversely impact academic competence, then exacerbate the original mental health concern and/or influence other domains of development.

Much of the evidence for this model can be seen in the ripple effect of a child's externalising behaviours. Moilanen et al. (2010), for example, found that high levels of externalising problems in middle childhood predicted low levels of academic competence in early adolescence. This can perhaps be best explained by the way in which externalising behaviours play out in the classroom. For example, externalising behaviours such as inattention, impulsivity, hyperactivity or aggressiveness may limit a child's opportunities for learning and so impact adversely on academic attainment. Taken further, very disruptive and/or aggressive behaviour can also lead to suspension or exclusion and hence remove children from learning opportunities (Moilanen et al. 2010). Likewise, Suldo et al. (2014) found that students' externalising problems were strongly linked to reduced attendance and increased misbehaviour and were associated with students' poor academic performance. Finally, externalising behaviour may alienate some peers and teachers and thus impede academic progress.

Other research has examined the impact of internalising behaviours such as anxiety and depressive symptoms on academic performance. These internalising symptoms may limit classroom participation and engagement and so impact adversely on academic progress (Roeser, van der Wolf & Strobel, 2001). Roeser et al. (2001) found that negative moods affected adolescents' learning and achievement by discouraging learning strategies such as rehearsal, summarising ideas and organising study materials as well as through general avoidance in class activities such as class discussions and asking for help. In addition, young people with anxiety and depression tend to avoid school. Suldo et al. (2014) found that internalising symptoms were a risk factor for poor attendance, though surprisingly the results of their study found that internalising problems did not predict academic achievement. Similarly, Moilanen et al. (2010) found no pathways between internalising problems and subsequent externalising behaviours or academic competence. Though Masten and colleagues (2005) showed that high levels of internalising symptoms at ages 15–19 were indicative of fewer externalising problems at ages 18–22, they did not find data to support the theory that internalising symptoms affected subsequent academic competence. As summarised by Moilanen et al. (2010) it is possible that emotional problems may have small impacts on academic competence, but these small effects do not emerge when longitudinal stability in academic competence is controlled.

Suldo, Thaljia and Ferron (2011) examined the role of young people's wellbeing as well as psychopathology and found that even after accounting for students' family characteristics, those with a greater wellbeing at the beginning of the one-year study were more likely to experience gains in subsequent grades. They also found that students who identified as average to high on wellbeing but who were also identified with high psychopathology (described as students who were "symptomatic but content"; p. 27) did not experience a greater decline in grades than students without clinical levels of psychopathology, perhaps because, as the authors suggest, students' wellbeing enabled them to draw on their internal resources when dealing with school demands. Their findings demonstrate that the absence of psychopathology alone is not always the best predictor of later academic performance, and it is also important to identify and promote students' strengths and overall wellness.

The academic incompetence model

As highlighted by Harpine (2008), academic failure is more than an educational problem; it is also a psychological problem. The impact of school failure on children can be profound and, over time, self-fulfilling. Failure is accumulative, as students who experience failure lose confidence, become discouraged, disengaged and are more likely to fail again. Overall, children who fail in school are more likely to engage in subsequent risk behaviours such as smoking, drinking and drug abuse (Byrd, 2005).

In terms of cascade models, the academic competence model posits that failure at school can instigate a child's mental health concerns or exacerbate current symptoms (Moilanen et al. 2010). There is much support for this model. Morgan, Farkas, Tufis and Sperling (2008) found that children with reading problems in first grade were significantly more likely to display poor task engagement, poor self-control, externalising behaviour problems and internalising behaviour problems in third grade. In a UK longitudinal study, Wigglesworth et al. (2017) found that higher levels of conduct problems at 11 years of age were associated with poorer academic attainment at 13 years of age. Another longitudinal study conducted by Metsäpelto et al. (2015) found that low academic performance in Grades 1 and 2 was associated with high externalising problems in Grades 3 and 4.

Other studies have highlighted the ripple down effect of this hypothesis. Moilanen et al. (2010) found that low levels of academic competence were associated with high levels of internalising problems in middle childhood, and with high levels of externalising problems during the transition from elementary school to middle school. Their explanation for this result is that as a result of low academic attainment, boys may receive negative feedback from teachers, which may then lead to negative mood and poor self-image, which in turn may lead to symptoms of anxiety and depression.

Shared risk model

The shared risk model speculates that ripple or cascade effects may be a product of other variables, such as inadequate parenting, poverty or low cognitive ability, and it is these variables that place young people on a path underlying low academic competence and/or high levels of externalising or internalising symptoms. Moilanen et al. (2010) found that shared risk factors, including neighbourhood adversity and intelligence, played a minimal role in developmental cascade models. Likewise, Wigglesworth et al. (2017) found that shared risk variables, including socio-economic status and special education status, did little to alter the magnitude or statistical significance of any of the established pathways for cascade models. Accordingly, these studies would suggest that the cascade developmental pathway exists, irrespective of SES background or intelligence.

Socio-economic factors, academic performance and mental illness

Notwithstanding what developmental cascade research tells us, there is an association (not necessarily causative) for socio-economic status and school achievement as well as between socio-economic status and mental illness. Indeed, school failure is not equal. Reardon, Greenberg, Kalogrides, Shores and Valentino (2013) found that children from economically disadvantaged families enter high school with average literacy skills five years behind those of high-income students, while the success rate of low-income students in science, technology, engineering and mathematics disciplines is much lower than that of students who do not come from under-represented backgrounds (Doerschuk et al. 2016). Likewise, unemployment, poverty and housing unaffordability have been found to be associated with mental illness and psychiatric hospitalisation (Hudson, 2005).

Money makes a difference. The SAT (Scholastic Assessment Test) is a standardised test widely used for college admissions in the United States. The US College Board data for the SATs in 2016 shows that SAT scores go up with $20,000-dollar family income amounts with similar trends apparent over the last five years. See Table 3.1 with data on SAT scores in relation to family income, collected by the College Board (2016).

It perhaps makes sense that money makes a difference to educational opportunities, as those with financial resources are able to purchase computers, books, learning materials and extra curricula activities that can promote academic engagement and performance. The above SAT scores might suggest, however, that those with more money can therefore buy more educational advantages and, indeed, that the SAT is merely a proxy for socio-economic influence and therefore power.

Table 3.1 Students' family income and SAT scores

SAT	Test takers		Critical reading		Mathematics		Writing	
	Number	%	Mean	SD	Mean	SD	Mean	SD
All test takers	1,637,589	100	494	117	508	121	482	115
Family income								
Less than $20,000	124,290	13	435	104	453	115	426	101
$20,000-$40,000	158,909	16	465	102	477	109	452	99
$40,000-$60,000	132,182	14	488	101	495	107	471	99
$60,000-$80,000	115,998	12	503	101	509	105	485	99
$80,000-$100,000	119,593	12	517	100	527	106	501	100
$100,000-$140,000	146,434	15	530	101	539	105	513	101
$140,000-$200,000	93,275	10	542	102	553	106	528	103
More than $200,000	87,482	9	569	105	586	107	562	108

Source: College Board (2016).

However, it is not only wealth that makes a difference to a child's mental health or school performance. For example, a high income is often associated with social capital, namely connections to networks who might provide access to opportunities that might otherwise not exist, such as invitations to summer internships or work experience opportunities, as well as human capital, for example, having parents who provide a rich and stimulating language environment for their children (Willingham, 2012). Moreover, low SES is often associated with long-term physical and mental illness, the stress of which can negatively impact parenting and children's maturing brains (Willingham, 2012), making it difficult to provide a cognitively stimulating environment (Yeung, Linver & Brooks-Gunn, 2002).

Schools also play a role in the relationship between socio-economic status and school performance. Schools in disadvantaged communities are often under-resourced (Aikens & Barbarin, 2008) and less likely to have access to a stimulating and rigorous academic curriculum (Lamb, Hogan & Johnson, 2001) and qualified teachers (Akiba, LeTendre & Scribner, 2007). Pribesh, Gavigan and Dickinson (2011) found that schools in disadvantaged communities have fewer library resources to draw on (fewer staff and opening hours) compared to schools in more middle-class areas. There is also evidence that their teachers are less likely to have high expectations for them (Auwarter & Aruguete, 2008). For example, mathematics teachers emphasise basic computations rather than advanced procedures when working with children from low SES backgrounds (Willingham, 2012).

Whether it is the advantages that having wealth brings, the stresses associated with being poor or both, no one single theory appears to conclusively explain the association between socio-economic status, mental illness and school achievement. We do, however, know that socio-economic status is associated with children's mental health and how well they perform at school.

Children's social and emotional competence and academic achievement

Further establishing the intertwined nature of wellbeing, mental illness and school success, other research has specifically examined the social and emotional skills that children require in order to adapt to the routine and demands of school and succeed in learning. For example, Wigglesworth et al. (2017) found that in early adolescence, those with higher emotional self-efficacy (defined as emotion regulation and social problem solving skills) were found at a later age, to have lower levels of conduct problem and higher academic attainment. They argue that for adolescents, emotional self-efficacy influences school engagement, perseverance and resilience to normal social and academic stressors, all skills that young people require to succeed at school.

Children need to acquire a range of skills in order to be efficient learners and to succeed in managing the demands of school routines. Self-regulation and social competence in particular are two skills that contribute to academic success, especially in the early years. McClelland, Acock and Morrison (2006) examined how children fared throughout elementary school on reading and math depending on various learning skills, including self-control, staying on task, organisation, working independently, listening and following directions and participating appropriately in groups (such as taking turns). They found that learning-related skills predicted growth in reading and math between kindergarten and second grade. In addition, children with poor learning-related skills performed lower than their higher-rated peers on measures of reading and mathematics between kindergarten and sixth grade, with the gap widening between kindergarten and second grade. Such findings help to explain how social skills in primary students predict performance on Australia's national achievement test (Kettler, Elliott, Davies & Griffin, 2011).

Self-management skills, for example, planning, deliberating and learning from feedback, are important skills for everyday life as well as for learning in schools – they are also key skills actively taught in many social and emotional learning programs (Lopes & Salovey, 2004). As well, many social and emotional learning programs teach children to stop and think when confronted with social (or other) problems, and generate different strategies for resolving problems (Lopes & Salovey, 2004). This problem solving process can be applied not only to social difficulties but also to academic challenges. Zins, Weissberg, Wang and Walberg (2004) found that students who were more self-aware and confident about their learning abilities tried harder, and that students who set goals, are organised and manage their stress perform better. These research papers provide strong evidence that success at school requires competences across social and emotional domains.

A remaining question is whether social and emotional competencies should be important for school attainment and success. We know that certain social and emotional competencies, for example listening, following directions, compliance, working independently, attentiveness and being organised, are skills that are needed in the classroom in order to successfully learn. To this end, some make a distinction between "learning-related" skills and "interpersonal" skills (McClelland et al. 2006). But the question needs to be asked: should they be? There is some evidence to suggest that children with ADHD can have high intelligence though they still experience problems at school (Brown, Reichel & Quinlan, 2011). Another way of looking at this is to consider whether it is the child's disability (e.g. ADHD) or the environment in which he or she is placed and the expectations that others have (to sit still and listen) that may be the source of the problem. Could it be that teachers value students who behave appropriately and are organised and attentive, rather than those who are intelligent and do things in a different, albeit challenging, manner? Likewise, should it be that a child's behaviour determines how well they do at school?

The cascade models presented earlier demonstrate that young people with behavioural issues do not do as well in school as those without behavioural issues, but is this because their behaviour impacts adversely on their cognitive ability, or is it due to how teachers perceive, manage and respond to these behaviours or both? McLeod, Uemura and Rohrman (2012) found that attention problems, delinquency and substance use were significantly associated with diminished achievement, but depression was not. Esch et al. (2014) found that mood and anxiety disorders had a less consequential direct effect on early school leaving than substance use and disruptive behaviour disorders. These findings suggest that the social consequences of mental health problems are not the inevitable result of diminished functional ability but rather reflect negative social responses. It has been found, for example, that teachers provide disruptive students with less positive feedback and instruction than other students (McEvoy & Welker, 2000; Shores & Wehby, 1999). People react differently to different types of illness, and this applies to school staff as well, with comparatively more understanding shown for some disorders (such as depression) than other problems such as behavioural disorders (Reupert & Maybery, 2015). Thus, what are considered to be appropriate social and emotional competencies is culturally informed and historically positioned.

Additionally, we need to be cautious about overstating the value of social and emotional learning programs and what they can and cannot achieve. Ecclestone (2015), in a provocative article titled "Well-being programmes in schools might be doing children more harm than good", argued that

> supporters . . . claim that it's essential to teach emotional well-being to all children and young people. Skills such as emotional expression, empathy, resilience, determination, self-esteem and mindfulness, hope and humour, have become a non-negotiable foundation to combat a widening array of deep-seated problems – from teenage pregnancy, obesity and poor parenting to mental ill-health, unemployment and low educational achievement.

Influence of schools on mental health and academic achievement

Schools can make a positive difference to the lives of children when they deliver programs that aim to promote both social and emotional competence and academic performance.

For example, Jones, Brown and Lawrence Aber (2011) described the 4Rs Program (Reading, Writing, Respect and Resolution), a school-based intervention that combines literacy development and social and emotional learning for children in grades K–5. They found that building social and emotional skills and simultaneously enriching literacy practices can promote positive development in both social–emotional and academic domains.

A seminal meta-analysis by Durlak et al. (2011) found that compared to a control group, children who had participated in social and emotional learning programs demonstrated significantly improved social and emotional skills, attitudes, behaviour and academic performance (reflecting an 11-percentile-point gain in achievement). A more recent meta-analysis reviewed 82 school-based, universal social and emotional learning interventions involving 97,406 kindergarten to high school students (Taylor et al. 2017). They found that children who participated in these programs fared significantly better than controls in social–emotional skills, attitudes and indicators of wellbeing as well as academic performance (measured by high school graduation rates). Benefits were similar regardless of students' race, socio-economic background or school location.

It is evident that what we think and feel about ourselves and others cannot be separated from how and what we learn. See Figure 3.1 for a visual guide to the iterative interactions between these different domains, when one domain impacts and is impacted by other domains. The complex interactions that influence children's development over time calls for collaborative approaches and interventions that are embedded in the many environments in which children live. Schools are central in this response.

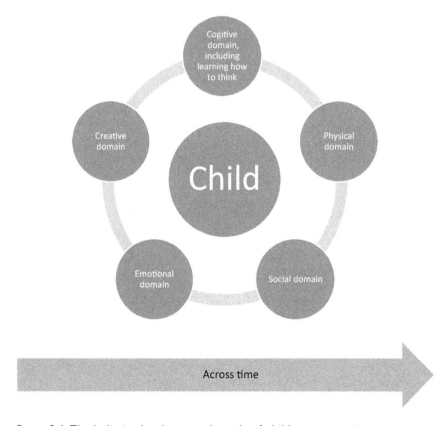

Figure 3.1 The holistic, developmental needs of children across time

What does this mean for schools?

A common critique of wellbeing programs is that they demand time and attention that would otherwise be directed to academic learning. The assumption is that academic achievement and wellbeing are two separate entities and that schools must choose between the two. The evidence presented in this chapter highlights the inextricably connected links between mental health and academic performance. As was detailed here, the interrelationship between a child's mental health, learning and behaviour is intertwined and positioned within his or her community, family and the school (see Figure 3.2). In particular, the research suggests that there are multiple pathways to most mental illness concerns and that different combinations of risk factors may lead to the same outcome. As children often present with both mental health concerns and academic problems, efforts are needed to reduce multiple risk factors rather than focus on a single

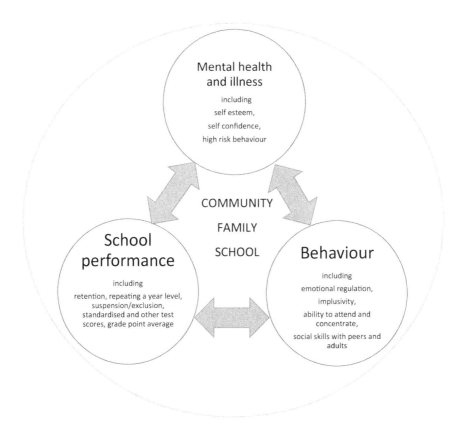

Figure 3.2 The interrelationships between mental health, illness, school performance and behaviour

Source: adapted from Geierstanger & Amaral, 2004.

factor. Hence, schools cannot focus their attention on narrowly defined domains of development, such as academic performance, to the exclusion of children's social–emotional development and wellbeing. On this basis, there are several, other implications for schools in terms of identification and intervention.

Developmental cascade research in particular illuminates the crucial bi-directional relationship between wellbeing and children's functioning at school, where children with social and emotional difficulties often show declining performance, while students experiencing difficulties at school tend to present with social and emotional difficulties over time. Additionally, schools are often the first to identify a student who presents with a mental health or academic concern, which, as can be seen in the developmental cascade research, represents risk factors for difficulties in the same and other domains at later times.

Knowing when to intervene is another important question. The evidence is clear that it is critical to intervene early. Jones, Greenberg and Crowley (2015) found that a kindergarten measure of social and emotional skills was highly predictive of young adult outcomes across education, employment, criminal activity, substance abuse and mental health. Thus, initiatives that promote social–emotional development and improve behavioural self-regulation in the early years have potential long-term impacts on cognitive development and wellbeing (Bierman, Nix, Greenberg, Blair & Domitrovich, 2008). Although genetic factors contribute to individual differences in children's attention skills and emotional regulation, children's socialisation and educational experiences play an important role in determining outcomes (Vandell, Burchinal & Pierce, 2016). Hence, the importance of investment in the early years has been argued from both economic and health perspectives (Campbell et al. 2014; García, Heckman, Leaf & Prados, 2016).

Similarly, there are other key milestones where it may be critical to intervene, including when children start formal schooling. For instance, students who start school with high levels of externalising problems at 8 years of age often present with poor academic competence and internalising problems (Moilanen et al. 2010). Another period is at the ages of 10 and 12 years, and where low academic competence is associated with subsequent internalising problems. Roeser et al. (2001) showed that low levels of academic competence during the transition to adolescence was associated with subsequent higher levels of internalising and externalising behaviour. It is perhaps of no surprise that key school transition points (starting school, moving into high school) represent critical at-risk times.

One way to prevent a problem may be to intervene earlier in another domain (Masten et al. 2005). As can be seen, problems with academic progress appear to be a consistent precursor to aggressive behaviours and subsequent internalising concerns. This means that concerted and early efforts need to be made to address difficulties that children may be experiencing in managing school work. There are several strategies that might be employed to support children who are at risk of academic failure e.g. use of formative feedback, providing clear goals, normalisation of mistakes as part of the learning process and cooperative learning principles (Roeser et al. 2001). Helping teachers instruct effectively and build learning communities designed to develop academic skills as well as students' sense of efficacy will likely ensure students do not fail and will benefit students' mental health and wellbeing. Even with this early emphasis on academics, it is nonetheless still important for schools to ensure that students feel safe, cared for and confident in their learning abilities. In sum, keeping mental health and wellbeing programs separate from academics does a disservice to educators, families and, more importantly, students.

References

Aikens, N. L., & Barbarin, O. (2008). Socioeconomic differences in reading trajectories: The contribution of family, neighborhood, and school contexts. *Journal of Educational Psychology, 100*, 235–251.

Akiba, M., LeTendre, G. K., & Scribner, J. P. (2007). Teacher quality, opportunity gap, and national achievement in 46 countries. *Educational Researcher, 36*(7), 369–387.

Auwarter, A. E., & Aruguete, M. S. (2008). Effects of student gender and socioeconomic status on teacher perceptions. *The Journal of Educational Research, 101*(4), 242–246.

Bierman, K. L., Nix, R. L., Greenberg, M. T., Blair, C., & Domitrovich, C. E. (2008). Executive functions and school readiness intervention: Impact, moderation, and mediation in the Head Start REDI Program. *Development and Psychopathology, 20*, 821–843.

Brown, T., Reichel, P. C., & Quinlan, D. M. (2011). Executive function impairments in high IQ children and adolescents with ADHD. *Open Journal of Psychiatry, 1*(2), 56–65.

Byrd, R. S. (2005). School failure: Assessment, intervention, and prevention in primary pediatric care. *Pediatrics in Review, 26*(7):233–243.

Campbell, F., Conti, G., Heckman, J. J., Moon, S. H., Pinto, R., Pungello, E., & Pan, Y. (2014). *Early childhood investments substantially boost adult health*. Retrieved August 12, 2017, from www.ncbi.nlm.nih.gov/pmc/articles/PMC4028126/

College Board (2016). *2016 College-bound seniors. Total group profile report*. Retrieved January 9, 2019, from https://secure-media.collegeboard.org/digitalServices/pdf/sat/total-group-2016.pdf

Dodge, K., Malone, P., Lansford, J., Miller, S., Pettit, G. S., & Bates, J. E. (2009). A dynamic cascade model of the development of substance-use onset. *Monographs of the Society for Research in Child Development*. Serial Number 294, 74(3), vii–119.

Doerschuk, P., Bahrim, C., Daniel, J., Kruger, J., Mann, J., & Martin, C. (2016). Closing the gaps and filling the STEM pipeline: A multidisciplinary approach. *Journal of Science Education and Technology, 25*, 682–695.

Durlak, J. A., Weissberg, R. P., Dymnicki, A. B., Taylor, R. D., & Schellinger, K. B. (2011). The impact of enhancing students' social and emotional learning: A meta-analysis of school based universal interventions. *Child Development, 82*(1), 405–432.

Ecclestone, K. (2015). *Well-being programmes in schools might be doing children more harm than good*. The Conversation. Retrieved January 9, 2019, from https://theconversation.com/well-being-programmes-in-schools-might-be-doing-children-more-harm-than-good-36573

Esch, P., Bocquet, V., Pul, C., Couffignal, S., Lehnert, T., Graas, M., ... Ansseay, M. (2014). The downward spiral of mental disorders and educational attainment: A systematic review on early school leaving. *BMC Psychiatry, 14*, 237.

García, J., Heckman, J., Leaf, D. E., & Prados, M. J. (2016). *The life-cycle benefits of an influential early childhood program*. The National Bureau of Economic Research. Retrieved January 7, 2019, from www.nber.org/papers/w22993

Geierstanger, S. P., & Amaral, G. (2004). *School-based health centers and academic performance: What is the intersection?* April 2004 Meeting Proceedings. White paper. Washington, DC: National Assembly on School-Based Health Care. https://files.eric.ed.gov/fulltext/ED539815.pdf

Harpine, E. C. (2008). *Group interventions in schools: Promoting mental health for at-risk children and youth*. New York: Springer Science + Business Media.

Hempenstall, K. (2013). *Failure to learn: Causes and consequences*. Retrieved January 9, 2019, from www.nifdi.org/news-latest-2/blog-hempenstall/397-failure-to-learn-causes-and-consequences-dr-kerry-hempenstall

Hudson, C. G. (2005). Socioeconomic status and mental illness: Tests of the social causation and selection hypotheses. *American Journal of Orthopsychiatry, 75*(1).

Jones, D. E., Greenberg, M., & Crowley, M. (2015). Early social-emotional functioning and public health: The relationship between kindergarten social competence and future wellness. *American Journal of Public Health, 105*(11), 2283–2290.

Jones, S. M., Brown, J. L., & Lawrence Aber, J. (2011). Two-year impacts of a universal school-based social-emotional and literacy intervention: An experiment in translational developmental research. *Child Development, 82*(2), 533–554.

Kettler, R. J., Elliott, S. N., Davies, M., & Griffin, P. (2011). Testing a multi-stage screening system: Predicting performance on Australia's National Achievement Test using teachers' ratings of academic and social behaviors. *School Psychology International, 33*(1), 93–111.

Lamb, S., Hogan, D., & Johnson, T. (2001). The stratification of learning opportunities and achievement in Tasmanian secondary schools. *Australian Journal of Education, 45*(2), 153–167.

Lopes, P., & Salovey, P. (2004). Toward a broader education: Social, emotional and practical skills. In J. E. Zins, R. P. Weissberg, M. C. Wang, & H. J. Walberg (Eds.), *Building academic success on social and emotional learning* (pp. 76–93). New York: Teachers College Press.

Masten, A., Roisman, G., Long, J. D., Burt, K. B., Obradovic, J., Riley, J. R., ... Tellegen, A. (2005). Developmental cascades: Linking academic achievement and externalizing and internalizing symptoms over 20 years. *Developmental Psychology, 41*(5), 733–746.

Masten, A. S., & Cicchetti, D. (2010). Developmental cascades. *Development and Psychopathology, 22*(3), 491–495.

McClelland, M., Acock, A. C., & Morrison, F. J. (2006). The impact of kindergarten learning-related skills on academic trajectories at the end of elementary school. *Early Childhood Research Quarterly, 21*(4), 471–490.

McEvoy, A., & Welker, R. (2000). Antisocial behavior, academic failure, and school climate: A critical review. *Journal of Emotional and Behavioral Disorders, 8*(3), 130–140.

McLeod, J. D., Uemura, R., & Shawna, R. (2012). Adolescent mental health, behavior problems and academic achievement. *Journal of Health and Social Behaviour, 53*(4), 482–497.

Metsäpelto, R-L., Pakarinen, E., Kiuru, N., Poikkeus, A-M., Lerkkanen, M-K., & Nurmi, J-E. (2015). Developmental dynamics between children's externalizing problems, task-avoidant behavior, and academic performance in early school years: A 4-year follow-up. *Journal of Educational Psychology, 107*(1), 246–257.

Moilanen, K., Shaw, D. S., & Maxwell, K. L. (2010). Developmental cascades: Externalizing, internalizing, and academic competence from middle childhood to early adolescence. *Developmental Psychopathology, 22*(3), 635–653.

Morgan, P., Farkas, G., Tufis, P. A., & Sperling, R. A. (2008). Are reading and behavior problems risk factors for each other? *Journal of Learning Disabilities, 41*(5), 417–436.

Najimi, A., Sharifirad, G., Amini, G. M., & Meftagh, S. D. (2013). Academic failure and students' viewpoint: The influence of individual, internal and external organizational factors. *Journal of Education & Health Promotion, 2*(22), 1–4.

Nuthall, G. (2004). Relating classroom teaching to student learning: A critical analysis of why research has failed to bridge the theory-practice gap. *Harvard Educational Review, 74,* 273–306.

OECD (2010). *Overcoming school failure: Policies that work.* Retrieved January 9, 2019, from www.oecd.org/education/school/45171670.pdf

Panayiotou, M., & Humphrey, N. (2017). Mental health difficulties and academic attainment: Evidence for gender-specific developmental cascades in middle childhood. *Developmental Psychopathology, 30*(2), 523–538.

Pribesh, S., Gavigan, K., & Dickinson, G. (2011). The access gap: Poverty and characteristics of school library media centers. *The Library Quarterly, 81*(2), 143–160.

Reardon, S. F., Greenberg, E. H., Kalogrides, D., Shores, K. A., & Valentino, R. A. (2013). *Left behind? The effect of no child left behind on academic achievement gaps.* Retrieved January 9, 2019, from www.apa.org/pi/ses/resources/publications/education.aspx

Reupert, A. E., & Maybery, D. J. (2015). Stigma and families where a parent has a mental illness. In A. Reupert, D. Maybery, J. Nicholson, M. Gopfert, & M. Seeman (Eds.), *Parental psychiatric disorder: Distressed parents and their families* (pp. 51–60). Cambridge: Cambridge University Press.

Roeser, R. W., van der Wolf, K., & Strobel, K. R. (2001). On the relation between social – emotional and school functioning during early adolescence: Preliminary findings from Dutch and American samples. *Journal of School Psychology, 39*(2), 111–139.

Shores, R. E., & Wehby, J. H. (1999). Analyzing the classroom social behavior of students with EBD. *Journal of Emotional and Behavioral Disorders,* 7(4), 194–199.

Suldo, S. M., Gormley, M. J., DuPaul, G. J., & Anderson-Butcher, D. (2014). The impact of school mental health on student and school level academic outcomes: Current status of the research and future directions. *School Mental Health, 6*(2), 84–98.

Suldo, S., Thaljia, A., & Ferron, J. (2011). Longitudinal academic outcomes predicted by early adolescents' subjective well-being, psychopathology, and mental health status yielded from a dual factor model. *The Journal of Positive Psychology, 6*(1), 17–30.

Taylor, R. D., Oberle, E., Durlak, J. A., & Weissberg, R. P. (2017). Promoting positive youth development through school-based social and emotional learning interventions: A meta-analysis of follow up effects. *Child Development, 88*(4), 1156–1171.

Vandell, D. L., Burchinal, M., & Pierce, K. M. (2016). Early child care and adolescent functioning at the end of high school: Results from the NICHD Study of Early Child Care and Youth Development. *Developmental Psychology, 52,* 1634–1645.

Wade, B., & Moore, M. (1993). *Experiencing special education.* Buckingham: Open University Press.

Wigglesworth, M., Qualter, P., & Humphrey, N. (2017). Emotional self-efficacy, conduct problems, and academic attainment: Developmental cascade effects in early adolescence. *The European Journal of Developmental Psychology, 14*(2), 172–189.

Willingham, D. (2012). Why does family wealth affect learning? *American Educator,* 33–39.

Yeung, W. J., Linver, M. R., & Brooks-Gunn, J. (2002). How money matters for young children's development: Investment and family process. *Child Development, 73,* 1861–1879.

Zins, J. E., Weissberg, R. P., Wang, M. C., & Walberg, H. J. (Eds.). (2004). *Building academic success on social and emotional learning: What does the research say?* New York: Teachers College Press.

Chapter 4

Towards a school-wide model for supporting students' mental health and academic learning

In this chapter, the various ways that schools might adopt a whole school approach to supporting and fostering children's mental health alongside academic learning will be presented. Currently, many schools provide a categorical approach to prevention and early intervention, where programs are delivered for different problems – for example, with separate and seemingly unrelated programs targeting bullying, literacy, violence prevention or obesity. This singular focus is costly (financially and in staff time) and runs the risk of overloading the curriculum, administrative systems and school and class procedures. Given that schools are pressed for time and resources, the issue for schools is knowing how to accommodate, connect and integrate all these demands without having to decide between academics or mental health. Nonetheless, though recent research has progressed our understanding in this area, finding a definitive, evidence-based model is not possible based on research collected to date. Instead, this chapter presents an attempt to document the journey *towards* an integrated, evidence-based, whole school model that focuses on the whole child. Hence, this discussion serves to provide some direction to school leaders, teachers and other school personnel when developing whole school approaches to supporting children's mental health and academic learning.

Programs to support students' mental health and academic learning

There are many programs that schools might employ to support students' mental health and academic learning. These vary in terms of foci (social and emotional learning, behaviour, academic progress) as well as range (classroom, school-wide and school–community partnerships), and can also be a combination thereof. The following are a selection of some of the commonly applied, evidence-based programs in this area.

Social and emotional learning (SEL) programs

PATHS (Promoting Alternative Thinking Strategies)

Promoting Alternative Thinking Strategies (PATHS) is a program designed to increase students' social and emotional competence, prevent aggression and other behaviour problems, improve critical thinking skills and enhance the classroom climate (Greenberg, Kusché & Mihalic, 1998). The theoretical framework of PATHS postulates that social competence is achieved when affect, behaviour and cognition are aligned (Greenberg, Kusché & Riggs, 2004). In the PATHS program, teachers deliver lessons on self-control, social problem solving and emotional awareness and understanding. PATHS also includes lessons on recognising and expressing feelings (Greenberg et al. 1995).

RULER (Recognising, Understanding, Labelling, Expressing and Regulating emotions)

Another commonly employed program in this area is RULER. The premise of RULER is emotional literacy, which posits that being able to recognise, understand, label, express and regulate emotions (i.e. the RULER skills) is critical to academic engagement and achievement as well as life success (Rivers & Brackett, 2011). It is a school-wide approach for use in kindergarten through eighth grade that also includes workshops for families so that emotions become central to learning, teaching and parenting. RULER uses a skill-based approach and integrates formal lessons and opportunities to practice skills during regular classroom instruction.

Academic learning programs

Response to Intervention (RtI)

Response to Intervention (RtI) is a multi-tier approach that aims to provide high quality instruction and interventions that are matched to student needs, and where progress is monitored and teaching and learning decisions are made by applying child response data to important educational decisions (Batsche et al. 2005). The RtI approach begins with high-quality instruction in the classroom and universal screening. Struggling learners are identified and subsequently provided with interventions at increasing levels of intensity to accelerate their rate of learning. Educational decisions about the intensity and duration of interventions are based on individual student response to instruction as their progress is closely monitored. Parents are kept informed about the program and their child's progress.

Programs that target student behaviour

Positive Behavioural Interventions and Supports (PBIS)

Based on behaviour analytic foundations, Positive Behavioural Interventions and Supports (PBIS) involves a school-wide application of behavioural systems and interventions to change the behaviour of teachers and students in schools (Horner, Sugai & Anderson, 2010). PBIS provides a three tier approach including (i) a universal primary service for all students, (ii) selective, secondary supports for some students (for example, group interventions for students with risky behaviours) and (iii) indicated interventions for a small proportion of students with very high-risk behaviours. The universal level is the tier most commonly implemented component of the model (Bradshaw, Bottiani, Osher & Sugai, 2014) and is commonly based on school-wide expectations of behaviour and taught to all students and staff. The PBIS framework provides structures and routines to support all school staff, so that consistency, predictability and positive relations are promoted across a variety of school contexts such as classroom, corridors and buses (Bradshaw et al. 2014). A key element of the PBIS approach is the use of multiple sources of data, which informs decision making.

Programs to promote a positive school environment

Responsive Classroom approach

The Responsive Classroom approach aims to foster a collaborative, caring approach to classroom organisation and management processes by respectful social interactions and academically engaging instruction. The approach includes running morning meetings for children to practise prosocial skills, collaborative work between teachers and students to develop and apply classroom rules and instructional practices that foster students' social interaction as well as their academic choice (Rimm-Kaufman et al. 2014).

The Child Development Project

The Child Development Project aims to foster the social and moral development of children through systematic changes in the classroom, school and home. The program incorporates class meetings, a cross-age buddy scheme, cooperative learning activities and open-ended discussions on literature to enhance students' social, ethical and intellectual development. The central tenet of the CDP is to help schools become "caring communities of learners" by creating caring and supportive environments and collaborative relationships (Battistich, Schaps, Watson, Solomon & Lewis, 2000; Solomon, Battistich, Watson, Schaps & Lewis, 2000)

One to one counselling services

Many schools, in the Western world at least, offer some form of one to one counselling support. These tend to follow primarily humanistic (Pybis, Cooper, Hill, Cromarty, Levesley, Murdoch & Turner, 2014) and/or cognitive behavioural approaches (Mychailyszyn, Brodman, Read & Kendall, 2012). Often services are provided by external, specialist staff (e.g. psychologists or those with specialist skills in the particular program) who deliver their services on school grounds. Such services may be difficult for some school communities to access and fund.

The evidence base

Overall, repeated evaluation studies for the many of the above-mentioned programs report positive effects. The seminal systematic review from Durlak et al. (2011) examined 213 studies covering school-wide SEL programs impacting more than 270,000 kids from kindergarten through to Year 12. They found that SEL programs significantly increased children's social and emotional skills; positive attitudes toward oneself and others; and prosocial behaviours in children of all ages, while at the same time reducing children's problem behaviours and emotional distress; they also reported that these positive changes were sustained six months after the program. Pertinently, for students exposed to SEL programs, academic achievement increased by 11 percentage points. More recently, Corcoran, Cheung, Kim and Xie (2018) confirmed and extended the Durlak et al. (2011) review and found that SEL programs had a positive effect on attainment in reading, mathematics and science.

Though there is clear evidence that high-quality programs can make a difference, effect sizes tend to be small to moderate (e.g. Jones et al. 2011). Evaluation results show that high-risk students tend to benefit most, as effects are usually larger for high-risk students than low- to moderate-risk students for universal populations (see for example Jones et al. 2011). Likewise, though two studies failed to demonstrate the expected impact of PATHS on children's outcomes, those children identified from the outset as having emotional difficulties reported significant improvements in schools that delivered PATHS, than in control schools (Malti, Ribeaud & Eisner, 2011; Berry et al. 2015).

Additionally, not all evaluation studies report positive outcomes. Challen, Node and West (2011) evaluated a UK program (based on the Penn Resiliency Program) that aimed to build students' resilience and promote wellbeing with Year 7 students in 22 schools. They found that the program did have a small average impact on students' depression scores, school attendance and numeracy and literacy grades, but these improvements were not sustained at the two-year follow up. Students involved in the program were doing no better than those who had not been involved. As per Jones et al. (2011), some students, especially those identified with worse psychological health and lower academic attainment, did benefit substantially more and for longer. The program was delivered to "universal" or mixed workshop groups, not to groups consisting entirely of targeted students. Hence, it cannot be assumed that the same impact might have been obtained if classes were targeted to at risk student groups.

There are several methodological issues in many of these studies. Corcoran et al. (2018) suggested that, due to conservative cut-off points, some of the traditional interventions over the last few decades might not have reported meaningful effects in reading, mathematics and science for pre-K–12 students. Additionally, it can be challenging to find schools that serve as valid "control" schools, as most schools employ some, albeit informal, SEL approaches in their classrooms. Thus, students in the comparison schools may have benefited from some form of SEL instruction even if they did not receive a formal intervention. Another potential methodological problem relates to researcher allegiance. Haaga and Stiles (2000) suggest that allegiance affects may account for a greater proportion of the outcome variance in intervention studies than differences between treatments. Barkham, Stiles, Lambertd and Mellor-Clark (2010, p. 33) succinctly summarise this sentiment when they argued that "it is invariably the case that research attesting to the benefits of a candidate therapy is typically carried out by researchers with an allegiance to that specific therapy", which may, perhaps inadvertently, lead to positive, albeit biased results.

Moreover, the traditional gold standard of intervention effectiveness tends to be viewed as research evidence obtained in randomised controlled trials (RCTs), with manuals to ensure fidelity, and the provision of clearly specified student characteristics, replicated in multiple sites with large sample groups (Weiss, 1998). However, there is robust debate about how best to evaluate the type of complex interventions that schools typically deliver (Moore et al. 2014). While some argue that randomised controlled trials are the gold standard, others argue that more nuanced approaches are needed that examine not only if but also how and why an intervention works. Context becomes key, as what works in one site or with one population or under one system may not work in another. The multiple paths of influence and diversity of students, schools and communities may mean that complex evaluation procedures are not always appropriate, especially where some groups are placed in a wait-list control group (and provided with no intervention). Alternative evaluation approaches may need to be sought using more community-oriented or participatory models of evaluation (see the final chapter of this book).

Finally, the quality of the implementation in delivering any given program plays a major role in moderating the impact of that program on student outcomes. In public health evaluation, implementation is typically considered in terms of fidelity (the degree to which a program is delivered as intended) and program dosage (how much of the program was delivered, for example whether all ten of the classes were delivered or not). Perhaps unsurprisingly, Durlak and DuPre (2008) found that better implementation is typically associated with better outcomes. Accordingly, it is difficult to ascertain whether evaluations demonstrating no or unsustainable positive impact is due to the intervention per se, or rather because the program was not delivered correctly (for example, where staff are not provided with the correct resources and time).

And, indeed, not all programs are implemented appropriately. One evaluation of the PATHS program found that while the program did not have the expected positive impact on students, teachers reported that due to a lack of time, they were only able to deliver half of the recommended lessons. Likewise, Challen et al. (2011) described evidence of what they called "program drift", where programs were delivered by school auxiliary staff, rather than trained facilitators. Finally, there is something to be said for "talking the talk" (i.e. delivering a particular lesson according to the program guidelines) and "walking the talk" where a teacher might be actively and purposively promoting specific social and emotional skills, not only during class time as a program might stipulate but also across other school settings such as in hallways, lockers and sportsgrounds (Hirschstein, Edstrom, Frey, Snell & MacKenzie, 2007). Many SEL programs tend to be delivered in short lessons, with little effort made to integrate them as part of the general curriculum or to generalise the skills learnt outside of the classroom (Jones & Bouffard, 2012).

Overall, when reviewing these programs, it is critical to remember that we are working with children who have developmental needs across many interrelated domains (see Figure 3.1 in previous chapter). A holistic approach is based on the premise that children's competencies cannot be compartmentalised and are instead interrelated parts of a whole child, encompassing psychological, social and emotional growth. Efforts are needed that target or incorporate each of these domains. It is on this basis that the following rationale is offered for developing a model that simultaneously supports children's mental health and academic learning.

The rationale for developing a whole school, integrated approach for supporting children's academic learning and mental health needs

There are many reasons for integrating evidence-based approaches into a whole school approach for supporting children's academic learning and mental health needs. There is abundant research to show that school and classroom organisation and teacher–student interactions are not only correlates of student mental health and wellbeing but are also associated with classroom behaviour, attendance and academic attainment (Banerjee, Weare & Farr, 2016). Domitrovich et al. (2010) pointed out that even though programs will vary according to targets (e.g. violence or substance use), age of children and setting (playground, classroom), they share many similar components, including creating a sense of community or promoting emotional regulation. The pedagogy for evidence-based programs may also share some commonalities. Durlak et al. (2011) found four practices were associated with effective skill training, using the acronym SAFE: namely when teachers provided Sequenced, Active and Focused lessons with an Explicit teaching of skills.

A whole school, integrated approach may be less demanding on staff time and effort and hence less vulnerable to staff turnover and duplication of efforts. Such approaches are also more likely to become part of the overall mission and fabric of the school environment through the use of a common language, logic, structure and systems (Bradshaw et al. 2014). An integrated model which targets mental health, behavioural and social and emotional competencies into one single program has the advantage of producing better outcomes that might be achieved from the one program (Cook, Frye, Slemrod, Lyon & Renshaw, 2015).

Such foci draw on the strengths of different programs rather than duplicate any one program component and ideally should be theoretically consistent (Cook et al. 2015; Domitrovich et al. 2010).

Moreover, such a model has the potential to build on and reinforce individual program components for all children and at-risk children in particular and to compensate for gaps in any one program (Domitrovich et al. 2010). Schools that assume a whole school approach can potentially target multiple individual risk factors as opposed to single pronged interventions which may not address all the underlying mechanisms of a given problem (Domitrovich et al. 2010). Likewise, given the heterogeneous nature of a student population where skills and needs vary, it may be beneficial to target a range of competencies. As different risk factors may lead to the same problem, an integrated model may deliver a broad approach that can improve the impact of any one intervention in an efficient and effective manner.

Banerjee et al. (2016) argued that schools are already engaged in multiple activities designed to address multiple outcomes. Even if they do decide to deliver one particular program, such as PATHS or RULER, they will need to make links with other school programs that staff are already delivering. In this way, rather than doing more and more, in delivering a whole school approach schools could be "doing less in a more effective, efficient and relevant manner" (Bradshaw et al. 2014, pp. 114–115). A careful integration of evidence-based strategies provides the potential to positively impact children's social, emotional and behavioural development, and academic learning and indirectly impact, through enhanced program implementation, school communication and efficiency (Bradshaw, et al. 2014).

Tiered approaches

One framework for the integration of services and supports is a tiered approach to prevention and early intervention. In the mental health field, public health approaches incorporate the full spectrum of interventions designed to promote wellbeing and address all levels of risk in a population, and these have also been applied to educational settings.

Mrazek and Haggerty (1994) outlined three levels or tiers of intervention. *Universal approaches* aim to improve the mental health of the general public or population group, such as a school community or student body. There are different types of universal approaches. Some aim to change the ethos of the whole school; others are class-based and aim to deliver a particular curriculum; others combine whole school and class-based interventions. *Selected interventions* target individuals or subgroups who are at increased risk of mental health or academic problems. For students, this might be because of social risk factors including various adverse childhood experiences (exposure to trauma, poverty) or key developmental stages such as transitioning into high school, which we know can be a stressful time for many young people. The final and third tier is *indicated interventions*, which targets individuals who are identified as already presenting with signs of mental health distress, behavioural problems or academic difficulties.

Children's basic learning, behavioural and mental health needs should all be addressed within universal programs (see Figure 4.1), and all children, regardless of their other needs, need to receive these universal supports. Those students whose learning, behavioural and mental health needs are not fully met by a universal program would then also receive targeted and/or individually tailored interventions based on a systematic assessment of their needs. Though efforts need to be directed at prevention, all tiers are important as there will always

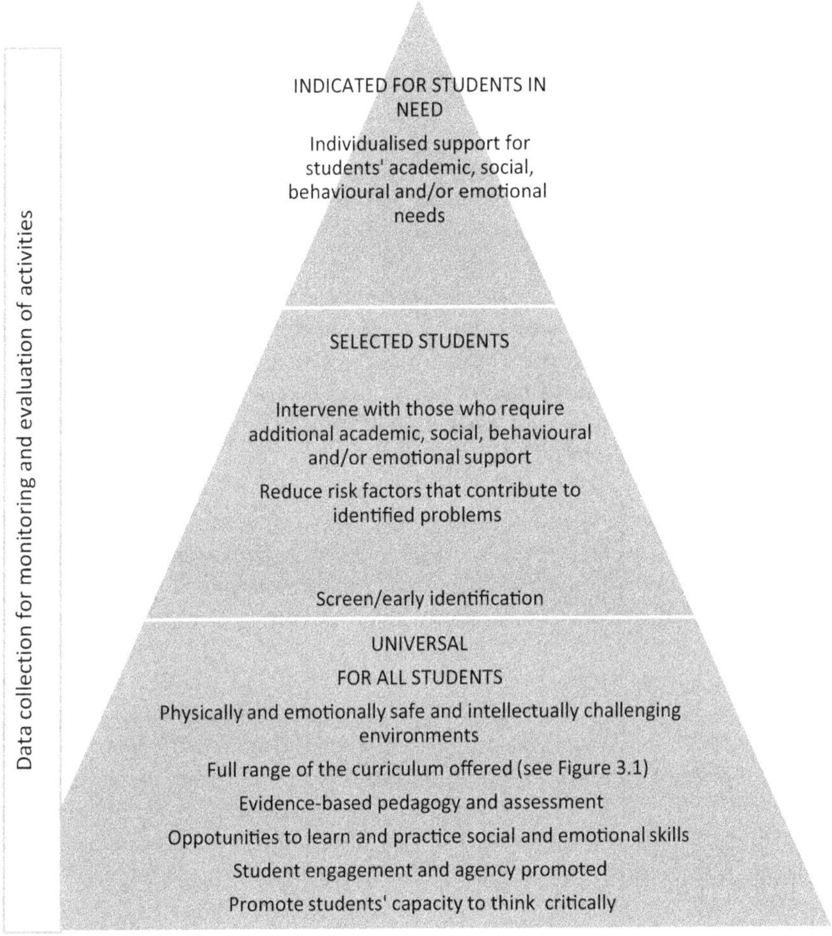

Figure 4.1 A three-tiered approach for supporting children's mental health and academic learning needs

be some children whose needs are not fully accommodated within a universal approach.

Stice, Bohon, Marti and Rohde (2009) found that the effects of depression prevention programmes were larger when the programs targeted high-risk individuals (such as those starting with higher levels of depressive symptoms). Efforts at program integration can be horizontal where, for example, different universal programs might be integrated at that level, and/or vertical where programs at different levels (e.g. a universal program and a tier two program) are integrated.

Examples of whole school, integrated approaches

Increasingly there are calls to organise and deliver a continuum of school services to prevent mental health problems, promote social and emotional competencies and academic success and reverse and minimise the impact of mental health problems (Cook et al. 2015). These calls have led to attempts to provide whole school approaches in this area.

Many of these approaches integrate PBIS, with its focus on behaviour across a tiered framework, with one or more SEL programs into different tiers and so target children's behaviour and social and emotional competencies across universal, selective and indicative levels. For example, Bradshaw et al. (2014) synthesised PBIS, PATHS and another program called Coping Power, an intervention for aggressive children. They suggested that the PATHS curriculum would be more likely to meet some of the social and emotional deficits displayed by those who do not respond to the universal PBIS approach. They also argued that PBIS would lower disruptive behaviour and so increase the likelihood that teachers will have more time to deliver PATHS. Cross-over points were identified between the two approaches, for example, using the PBIS reinforcement systems to reward SEL skills learnt in the PATHS lessons across all contexts. The three-tiered PBIS approach, along with data collected (for example, on discipline breaches), was used to identify children who could then be referred to the relatively more behaviourally intensive Coping Power program.

Another approach has been to integrate attempts to address children's academic and behavioural needs. Sandomierski, Kincaid and Algozzine (2007) showed how the tiered approaches of RtI and PBIS can be combined to provide a continuum of interventions and resources, appropriate to students' level of need (either academic or behavioural) and then monitor their progress. However, though it is not the intention of these developers, it often feels like the approach is an additive one – that is, one program simply added to the other.

Positive Action (PA) was developed as an integrative program from the outset. It aims to promote positive actions across children's physical, intellectual, emotional and social domains. PA consists of training and materials for schools, families and communities, including a pre-K–12 classroom curriculum, kits for school preparation and teacher training, school-wide climate development, a counsellor's kit and parent and community involvement manuals. It incorporates active learning, positive classroom management, SEL development, role play, a detailed curriculum, school-wide reinforcement of positive behaviours and family and community involvement. Flay and Allred (2003) found that participation in the Positive Action program improved student behaviour, school involvement and academic achievement in the selected primary or elementary schools. In their systematic review and meta-analysis of 40 SEL programs (including the PATHS program reviewed earlier), Corcoran et al. (2018) found that across the five previous evaluations of Positive Action on reading, involving 11,370 students, the mean effect size was +0.78, a relatively large and important number. Averaged across the four evaluations of Positive Action on mathematics, involving 10,380 students, the mean effect size for mathematics was +0.45, again significant and substantial. Positive Action also delivered promising improvements in science achievement with a mean effect size of +0.2. In a ranking of programs, Corcoran et al. (2018) found that the Positive Action program to be the strongest in terms of impact on children's reading, mathematics and science.

Incorporating aspects of both physical and social health, the WHO (1998) developed the Health Promoting Schools Framework, which aims to foster health and learning across multiple domains and targets. The concept of a healthy schools framework has been picked up by the Schools for Health in Europe Network Foundation (SHE: see www.schools-for-health.eu/she-network), which defined a health-promoting school as one which delivers a structured and systematic plan for the health and wellbeing of all students as well as teaching and other school staff. Accordingly, the activities of a health-promoting school is more than just offering "health education" in the curriculum (Langford et al. 2014). SHE provides six components that designate a whole school approach to health promotion:

- **Healthy school policies** that are part of the school plan and designed to promote health and wellbeing of the entire school community. Reflecting the broad nature of the remit of "healthy schools", policies might include what foods can be served at the school as well as policies to prevent and address school bullying.
- **School physical environment**, including classroom rooms, sportsgrounds and school surroundings. This ensures that the school environment is safe and encourages recreation and physical activity.
- **School social environment** relates to the quality of the relationships among and between school community members that is between students, staff, school leaders and the community.
- **Individual health skills and action competencies** can be promoted through the curriculum including social and emotional competencies so

that students can make their own informed decisions around health, wellbeing and educational attainment.
- **Community links** between the school, family and community are made to support the school community in their health promoting actions.
- **Appropriate health services** are available and accessible in the community and within the school.

Langford et al. (2014) sought to assess whether a health-promoting framework could improve students' wellbeing, academic attainment and health (across a broad range of physical domains). In a review of programs in 1,345 schools, a wide range of health topics were covered, including physical activity, nutrition, substance use (tobacco, alcohol and drugs), bullying, violence, mental health, sexual health, hand-washing, cycle-helmet use, sun protection, eating disorders and oral health. They found that interventions using the health-promoting schools framework reduced students' body mass index (BMI), increased physical activity and fitness levels, improved fruit and vegetable consumption, decreased cigarette use and reduced reports of being bullied. However, little evidence of effectiveness was found on fat intake, alcohol and drug use, mental health, violence and bullying others. There was insufficient data to draw conclusions about the effectiveness of the approach for sexual health, hand-washing, cycle-helmet use, eating disorders, sun protection, oral health or academic outcomes. The researchers point out that the quality of evidence was low to moderate, with several methodological problems indicated (e.g. relying on students' accounts of their own behaviours rather than these being measured objectively) and high numbers of students dropping out of studies. It needs to be said that the absence of evidence does not necessarily mean that the healthy schools framework is not effective, just that more research needs to be conducted to ascertain what works, for what schools, when and under what conditions.

A tiered system of common evidence-based practices

While the evidence for many available programs is mixed, unclear or emerging, I believe that we do not need more programs or interventions. Instead, what is required are unifying systems that have the capacity to pull together the common elements associated with efficiently promoting young people's mental health and academic learning. What this will look like, however, will vary depending on the school environment and community. Nonetheless, Cook et al. (2015) suggested that there are different ways of going about this, including (i) delivering interventions side by side without making theoretical links, (ii) making alterations to core practices to remove duplicates across programs, (iii) considering how evidence-based practices in one intervention might complement or enhance the other/s programs or (iv) systematically blending interventions by highlighting differences and emphasising the theoretical similarities between them, removing duplicate practices and specifying those practices that complement and extend each other. By far the most theoretically sound approach is the final option, but it is still not clear what this looks like in practice. Nonetheless, integration in this sense is not simply implementing two or more models side by side, in an additive way, but instead creating something altogether new. Bradshaw et al. (2014) continued by suggesting that integration can occur horizontally, in terms of a whole school focus, and/or vertically, where integration might occur across universal, selected and indicated tiers.

In making a case for an integrated approach, Jones and Bouffard (2012) apply a food metaphor and advocate for schools to move away from packaged, branded products (such as specific programs) and instead consider necessary vitamins and minerals that are required from foods, namely the essential, beneficial strategies that all schools need to adopt. At the same time, they concede that little research has been conducted to identify and evaluate the essential ingredients associated with positive changes in students and learning environments.

Looking to simplify interventions, overcome implementation difficulties, limit cost and deliver a broad-range impact, Embry and Biglan (2008, p. 75) put forward the notion of evidence-based kernels, defined as "fundamental units of behavioral influence that appear to underlie effective prevention and treatment for children, adults, and families". Kernel units are core components of programs that cannot be removed if the program is to still be effective. While they caution that not all programs can be irreducible, they do suggest that it may still be possible to identify various mechanisms of influence that can influence the "acquisition, rate or duration of behaviour" (p. 78). Due to their influence, kernels can be used as standalone strategies or within programs.

When attempting to identify those "kernels of influence", it needs to be pointed out that the conditions for effective learning necessitate attention not only to effective instruction but also to addressing children's social, emotional and physical needs. As Berg, Osher, Moroney and Yoder (2017) illuminated, when aggression in school is reduced, students are less fearful and interact more effectively, inclusively and, importantly, productively. Subsequently, there are fewer behavioural problems and disruptions of learning, which promotes better conditions for teaching and learning. Hence, any identification of common elements or "kernels" needs to incorporate and attend to both learning and mental health needs.

Based on the research reviewed for this chapter, the lists at the end of this chapter are some of these "kernels" of influence (acknowledging that the evidence base is emerging and somewhat unclear) at different levels of the school environment. This overview is positioned within a three-tiered approach (Figure 4.1), and the whole school community rather than being limited to a set of curriculum lessons or discrete activities. Implicit in this overview is the assumption that any school model for supporting young people's academic learning and mental health needs to be ecologically and developmentally informed. Given the dynamic influences of the environment on children, ranging from more proximal influences of the family, to more distal factors such as the school or community, efforts need to be targeted at multiple levels. While the complexity implied by developmental cascade models and ecological models of child development may be daunting, these multiple paths of influence do allow for consideration of a variety of intervention targets and processes. Consequently, there are many opportunities for intervention development that offer promise for the improved outcomes for children across a range of domains.

An ecological approach also means that any resulting guide or framework needs to move away from a purely individualised focus. Instead, meeting the educational and psychological needs of students must incorporate the class and school environment. If for example, a large number of students are identified as experiencing academic difficulties, then instruction and curriculum may need attention, rather than the children themselves. Likewise, if large numbers of students are reported with behavioural concerns, then attention needs to be directed at the teaching and learning environment. Thus, within these principles, the list at the end of the chapter, together with Figure 4.1, is one attempt that seeks to "move towards" an integrated approach to supporting young people's mental health and academic learning. It should be noted that in Figure 4.1, levels 2 and 3 are not offered in isolation but instead are offered simultaneously with level 1 so that services are not separated from the regular school business. Moreover, it is critical that services are labelled according to the tiers, and children are not labelled according to their allocated service type (e.g. children are not seen as tier one children, etc.). Across all three tiers, the same language, philosophy and competencies need to be consistently labelled and promoted.

What this tiered, evidence-based kernel approach looks like in practice and whether a "program" can be developed that incorporates and integrates each of these elements remains to be seen. Rather than a manualised program per se, it is more likely that these components will need to be adapted, contextualised and then operationalised into practice guidelines for each individual school and community. Many of these strategies align with characteristics associated with "good schools" (Lipsitz & West, 2006) and provide a vision or template for what schools might deliver – rather than a "how to" guide or explicit programs. Given the different types of schools (primary/elementary, high, middle, specialist) and demographics (according to community and location), how these elements are interpreted and more importantly applied will differ. In this way, each school community will need to consider how best to integrate these elements into daily interactions and practices with students in a way that is time efficient, low cost and integrated with (and not in competition with) academic curricula.

Overall, the relationships between mental health and learning highlight the need for an approach that is integrated and embedded in every aspect of the school culture and ethos. It means we need to move past formal programs to instead, or also, reflect on what is happening in and outside the classroom, daily interactions, routines and social norms. These "kernels" can be differentiated according to different target groups, as outlined below.

For students

- A comprehensive, quality curriculum, including dedicated lessons on mental health issues and social and emotional learning, that is engaging and relevant – where children are challenged but also experience success; accommodations are made as required to make instruction accessible to all students
- Both formative and summative assessment is provided
- Instructional strategies are evidence-based
- Non-stigmatising strategies for identifying and supporting students who are experiencing academic, behavioural and/or social and emotional difficulties.

For staff

- Systematic and ongoing staff development opportunities (including induction) to enable staff to effectively implement a wide range of strategies (pedagogy and curriculum in academic subjects as well as social and emotional competency, including assessment processes) and relationship building
- Staff wellbeing is promoted and monitored
- Leaders who model self-care and wellbeing
- Active, engaged, supportive leadership that promotes academic learning and mental health promotion, early intervention and prevention.

School systems and environment

- A physically safe environment that promotes respect for cultural diversity and inclusion
- Opportunities for students to generalise the skills learnt in class to a range of settings and interactions
- An environment that encourages and supports positive relationships between range of stakeholders
- Positive, supportive and prevention-based school systems and strategies for managing student (mis)behaviour that aim to promote motivation and engagement rather than punish or isolate students
- Connections are made with families and the wider community, including specialist services
- A data-driven approach to assess student, class and school needs, identify appropriate interventions or programs and monitor progress.

Problems and future opportunities for whole school approaches for supporting children's academic learning and mental health

The above list of individual "kernels of influence" may well have (emerging) evidence for the effectiveness of their individual components, but further research is required to confirm a formalised unified model and to articulate what this might look like in practice and policy. Cook et al. (2015) argued that there is little evidence that highlights what elements are needed to achieve prevention-focused goals. Though an integrated, multi-systems approach is gaining traction, we still do not know what is scientifically validated for supporting children's instructional, social and emotional needs nor how they might work collectively, especially for tier two approaches (Fuchs & Fuchs, 2007). Moreover, Domitrovich et al. (2010) argued that integrating or synthesising different singular elements may be just as labour intensive and time consuming as delivering numerous programs. They also point out, given the lack of an evidence base, that such an approach may be iatrogenic to students. An integrated, holistic approach to supporting children's mental health and academic learning is not easy, and as Durlak et al. (2011) noted, complex initiatives that intend to impact on multiple stakeholders such as parents and the school-wide curriculum approach are more likely to encounter implementation difficulties, even if they do allow greater scope for problems to be addressed and generalised. A final question is determining which components of an integrated model to implement first or whether to introduce massive changes at the same time. These questions all present future research and practice opportunities.

References

Banerjee, R., Weare, K., & Farr, K. (2016). Working with social and emotional aspects of learning (SEAL): Associations with school ethos, pupil social experiences, attendance, and attainment. *British Educational Research Journal, 40*(4) 718–742.

Barkham, M., Stiles, W., Lambert, M., & Mellor-Clark, J. (2010). Building a rigorous and relevant knowledge base for the psychological therapies. In M. Barkham, G. E. Hardy, & J. Mellor-Clark (Eds.), *Developing and delivering practice-based evidence: A guide for the psychological therapies* (pp. 21–61). London: Wiley.

Batsche, G., Elliott, J., Graden, J. L., Grimes, J., Kovaleski, J. F., Prasse, D., . . . Tilly, W. D. (2005). *Response to intervention: Policy considerations and implementation*. Alexandria, VA: National Association of State Directors of Special Education, Inc.

Battistich, V., Schaps, E., Watson, M., Solomon, D., & Lewis, C. (2000). Effects of the Child Development Project on students' drug use and other problem behaviors. *Journal of Primary Prevention, 21*(1), 75–99.

Berg, J., Osher, D., Moroney, D., & Yoder, N. (2017). *The intersection of school climate and social and emotional development*. American Institute for Research (AIR). Retrieved January 11, 2019, from www.air.org/sites/default/files/downloads/report/Intersection-School-Climate-and-Social-and-Emotional-Development-February-2017.pdf

Berry, V., Axford, N., Blower, S. L., Taylor, R. S., Edwards, R., Tobin, K., . . . Bywater, T. J. (2015). The effectiveness and micro-costing analysis of a universal, school-based, social – emotional learning programme in the UK: A cluster-randomised controlled trial. *School Mental Health*, *8*(2), 238–256.

Bradshaw, C. P., Bottiani, J., Osher, D., & Sugai, G. (2014). Integrating positive behavioral interventions and supports (PBIS) and social emotional learning. In M. D. Weist, N. A. Lever, C. P. Bradshaw, & J. Owens (Eds.), *Handbook of school mental health: Advancing practice and research* (2nd ed., pp. 101–118). New York: Springer.

Challen, A., Node, P., West, A., & Machin, S. (2011*). UK resilience programme evaluation: Final report*. Research Brief. Retrieved January 9, 2019, from https://assets.publishing.service.gov.uk/government/uploads/system/uploads/attachment_data/file/197313/DFE-RB097.pdf

Cook, C. R., Frye, M., Slemrod, T., Lyon, A. R., & Renshaw, T. L. (2015). An integrated approach to universal prevention: Independent and combined effects of PBIS and SEL on youths' mental health. *School Psychology Quarterly*, *30*(2), 166–183.

Corcoran, R. P., Cheung, A. C. K., Kim, E., & Xie, C. (2018). Effective universal school-based social and emotional learning programs for improving academic achievement: A systematic review and meta-analysis of 50 years of research. *Educational Research Review*, *25*, 56–72.

Domitrovich, C. E., Bradshaw, C. P., Greenberg, M. T., Embry, D., Poduska, J. M., & Ialongo, N. S. (2010). Integrated models of school-based prevention: Logic and theory. *Psychology in the Schools*, *47*(1), 71–88.

Durlak, J. A., & DuPre, E. P. (2008). Implementation matters: A review of research on the influence of implementation on program outcomes and the factors affecting implementation. *American Journal of Community Psychology*, *41*, 327–350.

Durlak, J. A., Weissberg, R. P., Dymnicki, A. B., Taylor, R. D., & Schellinger, K. B. (2011). The impact of enhancing students' social and emotional learning: A meta-analysis of school based universal interventions. *Child Development*, *82*(1), 405–432.

Embry, D. D., & Biglan, A. (2008). Evidence-based kernels: Fundamental units of behavioral influence. *Clinical Child & Family Psychological Review*, *11*, 75–113.

Flay, B. R., & Allred, C. G. (2003). Long-term effects of the positive action program. *American Journal of Health Behavior*, *27*, 6–21.

Fuchs, L. S., & Fuchs, D. (2007). A model for implementing responsiveness to intervention. *TEACHING Exceptional Children*, *39*(5), 14–20. https://doi.org/10.1177/004005990703900503Greenberg, M., Kusché, C., & Mihalic, S. (1998). *Blueprint for violence prevention, book ten: Promoting alternative thinking strategies (PATHS)*. Boulder: COL Centre for the Study and Prevention of Violence.

Greenberg, M. T., Kusche, C. A., Cook, E. T., & Quamma, J. P. (1995). Promoting emotional competence in school-aged children: The effects of the PATHS Curriculum. *Development and Psychopathology*, *7*, 117–136.

Greenberg, M. T., Kusché, C. A., & Riggs, N. (2004). The PATHS curriculum: Theory and research on neuro-cognitive development and school success. In J. E. Zins, R. P. Weissberg, M. C. Wang, & H. J. Walberg (Eds.), *Building academic success on social and emotional learning: What does the research say?* (pp. 170–188). New York: Teachers College Press.

Haaga, D. A. F., & Stiles, W. B. (2000). Randomized clinical trials in psychotherapeutic research: Methodology, design and evaluation. In C. R. Snyder, & R. E. Ingram (eds.), *Handbook of psychological change: Psychotherapy processes and practices for the 21st century* (pp. 14–39). New York: Wiley.

Hirschstein, M. K., Edstrom, L. S., Frey, K. S., Snell, J. L., & MacKenzie, E. P. (2007). Walking the talking bullying prevention: Teacher implementation variables related to initial impact of the Steps to Respect Program. *School Psychology Review, 36*(1), 3–21.

Horner, R. H., Sugai, G., & Anderson, C. M. (2010). Examining the evidence base for school-wide positive behavior support. *Focus on Exceptional Children, 42*(8), 1–14.

Jones, S. M., & Bouffard, S. (2012). Social and emotional learning in schools: From programs to strategies. *Social Policy Report, 23*(4), 1–33.

Jones, S. M., Brown, J. L., & Lawrence Aber, J. (2011). The longitudinal impact of a universal school-based social- emotional and literacy intervention: An experiment in translational developmental research. *Child Development, 82*(2), 533–554.

Langford, R., Bonell, C. P., Jones, H. E., Pouliou, T., Murphy, S. M., Waters, E., ... Campbell, R. (2014). The WHO health promoting school framework for improving the health and well-being of students and their academic achievement. *Cochrane Database of Systematic Reviews*, 4. Art. No.: CD008958. Retrieved January 11, 2019, from www.cochrane.org/CD008958/BEHAV_the-who-health-promoting-school-framework-for-improving-the-health-and-well-being-of-students-and-their-academic-achievement

Lipsitz, J., & West, T. (2006). What makes a good school? Identifying excellent middle schools. *Phi Delta Kappan, 88*(1), 57–66.

Malti, T., Ribeaud, D., & Eisner, M. P. (2011). The effectiveness of two universal preventive interventions in reducing children's externalizing behavior: A cluster randomized controlled trial. *Journal of Clinical Child & Adolescent Psychology, 40*(5), 677–692.

Moore, G., Audrey, S., Barker, M., Bond, L., Bonell, C., Cooper, C., ... Baird, J. (2014). Process evaluation in complex public health intervention studies: The need for guidance. *Journal of Epidemiology and Community Health, 68*, 101–102.

Mrazek, P. J., & Haggerty, R. J. (Eds.). (1994). *Reducing risks for mental disorders: Frontiers for preventive intervention research*. Institute of Medicine (US) Committee on Prevention of Mental Disorders. Washington, DC: National Academies Press.

Mychailyszyn, M. P., Brodman, D. M., Read, K. L., & Kendall, P. C. (2012). Cognitive-behavioral school-based interventions for anxious and depressed youth: A meta-analysis of outcomes. *Clinical Psychology: Science and Practice, 19*(2), 129–153.

Pybis, J., Cooper, M., Hill, A., Cromarty, K., Levesley, R., Murdoch, J., & Turner, N. (2014). Pilot randomised controlled trial of school-based humanistic counselling for psychological distress in young people: Outcomes and methodological reflections. *Counselling and Psychotherapy Research, 15*(4), 241–250.

Rimm-Kaufman, S. E., Larsen, R. A. A., Baroody, A. E., Curby, T. W., Ko, M., Thomas, J. B., . . . DeCoster, J. (2014). Efficacy of the responsive classroom approach: Results form a 3-year longitudinal randomised controlled trial. *American Educational Research Journal, 51*(3), 567–603.

Rivers, S. E., & Brackett, M. A. (2011). Achieving standards in the English language arts (and more) using The RULER Approach to social and emotional learning. *Reading & Writing Quarterly, 27*(1/2), 75–100.

Sandomierski, T., Kincaid, D., & Algozzine, B. (2007). Response to intervention and positive behavior support: Brothers from different mothers or sisters with different misters? *Positive behaviorial interventions and supports newsletter*. Retrieved January 11, 2019, from www.pbis.org/common/cms/files/Newsletter/Volume4%20Issue2.pdf

Solomon, D., Battistich, V., Watson, M., Schaps, E., & Lewis, C. (2000). A six-district study of educational change: Direct and mediated effects of the child development project. *Social Psychology of Education, 4*(1), 3–51.

Stice, E., Bohon, C., Marti, C. N., & Rohde, P. (2009). A meta-analytic review of depression prevention programs for children and adolescents: Factors that predict magnitude of intervention effects. *Journal of Consulting & Clinical Psychology*, 77(3), 486–503.

Weiss, C. H. (1998). *Evaluation* (2nd ed.). Englewood Cliffs, NJ: Prentice-Hall, Inc.

WHO (1998). *Health promoting schools*. Retrieved January 11, 2019, from www.who.int/school_youth_health/media/en/92.pdf

Chapter 5

School culture and climate

This chapter provides a research-informed discussion about the different functions of school culture and climate and how these can be used to promote students' academic learning as well as mental health. It further extends the formal structures outlined in the previous chapter to discuss more broadly the impact of school ethos. This discussion will cover several core elements associated with a positive school climate, such as how a school might be organised, how children are identified or screened for academic and/or mental health difficulties, leadership attributes, school policy, the social environment and the physical layout of the school environment. A key component of school culture is the feeling of connectedness and belonging, and this will also be covered. Finally, the importance of relationships as a critical component in promoting children's learning and mental health will be discussed.

School culture and climate shape every aspect of how a particular school functions. While clearly related, there are differences between school culture and school climate. School culture includes a school's shared beliefs, values and assumptions and "the way things are done around here" (Hemmelgarn, Glisson & James, 2006, p. 75). Culture is driven by the school's history, values and expectations, which are embedded (or some might say entrenched) in structures and practices and shape a school's particular identity. The ceremonies the school routinely engages in, the stories they tell and the trophies they value and put out on display are all key elements of a school's culture. In comparison, school climate refers to the feel of the school environment from the perspective of different stakeholders. Freiberg and Stein (1999, p. 11) defined school climate as "the heart and soul of the school... [the] essence of a school that leads a child, a teacher and an administrator to love the school and to look forward to being there each school day". How new staff and students are welcomed, what behaviour is expected, how behavioural transgressions are managed and what extra curriculum activities are provided all provide examples of school culture. In sum, culture is the end result of the relational history of a school, while climate focuses on how people perceive those relationships in the present. Along with its institutional history and the community and political context in which it is positioned, students, parents, teachers, school leaders and other school staff all play a role in forming a school's culture and climate.

School size

Smaller is better. Though the research evidence is tentative at best, overall it would appear that smaller schools have advantages over larger schools in terms of their impact on school culture and climate. In larger schools, there is a higher incidence of violence; student are less engaged and teachers less happy with school climate (Garrett et al. 2004). At the same time, costs per student decrease as school size increases, which perhaps explains why approximately 70% of US high school students are enrolled in schools with 1,000 or more students (Office of Career, Technical and Adult Education, 2009). Large high schools, especially those attended by minority students, result in students with disproportionately lower achievement scores, while in comparison, students attending smaller schools are more academically productive and less likely to drop out (Office of Career, Technical and Adult Education, 2009). In smaller schools, students feel more connected to their school and cared for by their teachers, and concurrently, teachers feel that they have more opportunity to get to know and support their students (Bryk & Schneider, 2002; Felner et al. 1997; McNeely, Nonnemaker & Blum, 2002). Compared to larger schools, those with 900 or fewer students are more likely to have high teacher sense of self-efficacy and sense of responsibility for student learning, thus having an indirect impact on student learning (Office of Career, Technical & Adult Education, 2009).

Likewise, there is an optimal size for classes. Zyngier (2014) reviewed 112 research papers on class sizes written between 1979 and 2014 and found that reducing class size in the first four years of school can have an important and lasting effect on school culture, climate and ultimately student achievement. He found that the longer students spend in small classes during the early years of schooling, the longer the benefits for achievement last during grades 4–8, especially for children who come from disadvantaged families (low income and minority students). While acknowledging that class size is among a range of variables that impact on learning, it is nonetheless important to how children learn. Generally class sizes between 15 and 18 are recommended, but this may vary by subject matter (Mathis, 2017). There are cultural considerations, however. Hattie (2005) argued that smaller classes may be more beneficial in Western cultures where autonomy is valued, though larger classes may be more accepted in Eastern cultures that value collectiveness.

Nonetheless, to be effective, smaller class sizes need to be accompanied by a change in pedagogy. Zyngier's (2014) paper is important as it shows not only that class size matters but also what teachers can do when working with smaller groups of children to be most effective. In sum, teachers working with small classes are able to develop their lessons in depth, move through curricula more quickly and provide additional enrichment activities, manage their classes more efficiently and, arguably most importantly, provide more individualised attention to students, including more encouragement, counselling and monitoring. It is not surprising that as a result, students are then more attentive to their classwork (Zyngier, 2014).

Screening

Schools are ideal sites not only to deliver universal prevention initiatives but also to identify and address problems that children might be experiencing in their learning and/or mental health. School culture and climate will inform what schools screen for (and what they do not) as the foci of the screening process reflects what school administrators think is important among their student population. Ikeda, Neessen and Witt (2007) pointed out that as a rule schools do not screen students for music, athletic or artistic performance because proficiency in these areas is not considered a necessity but more of an elective. When provided, screening measures generally tap into academic learning (primarily literacy), while other screening tools gauge students' mental health and wellbeing. Only 2% of schools in the US provide universal screening of mental health, however, likely due to stigma, fiscal reasons and the lack of socially acceptable and valid screening tools (Humphrey & Wigelsworth, 2016).

Universal screening approaches allow schools to intervene early before problems (either academic or mental health) become entrenched and severe. Screening approaches also offer a systematic approach to making data-informed decisions about the provision of learning, behavioural and mental health services in schools. Ikeda et al. (2007) emphasised that screening provides a sample of a particular skill in one point of time only, which should not be used as a sole indicator for selection into a particular program or intervention. Further diagnostic tests are required to better appreciate the problems that students are presenting with.

Universal screening procedures not only identify potential learning or mental health problems in children but should also be used to identity instructional problems and evaluate the effectiveness of teaching and learning practices. If, for example, a large majority of children are identified as having literacy problems that are not found in other classrooms, efforts may need to be made to provide support and guidance to the teacher. Relatedly, when examining screening data, Ikeda et al. (2007) suggest that schools need to ask themselves whether data indicate a large or small group problem or an individual problem, and on that basis make decisions about resource allocation, differentiation activities and professional development needs of staff.

Screening measures need to be sufficiently sensitive to identify at-risk students, as well as inform the development and offering of effective interventions (Messick, 1989). Screening measures can be also be used to monitor how an at-risk student is progressing before providing more intensive specialised support (Jenkins, Hudson & Johnson, 2007). The screening measures employed and school assessments, curricula, instruction and professional development activities for staff need to be aligned and integrated so that one can inform the other, in a cyclical manner.

Screening measures are not without problems, especially when applied universally. False positives occur when a child is identified as needing support but in reality does not require it. This may lead to children being given inappropriate diagnostic labels, with implications for stigma and a wasteful use of resources. More importantly, it may lead to unnecessary or perhaps even harmful treatments. Merten, Cwik, Margraf and Schneider (2017) found that children born close to school cut-off dates (and so young compared to their classmates) are between 30–60% more likely to be diagnosed with ADHD and receive mediation twice as often as children born after the cut-off date. In these cases, children's developmentally normal behaviour was considered to be problematic (diagnosis of ADHD) rather than immature. Other potential problems arising from screening measures occur when children are not identified as needing support but in reality require further intervention (false negatives). Moreover, though it is relatively easy to collect data, time is needed for staff to understand screening data and its implications. Finally, most screening measures focus on students' deficits and symptomatic concerns rather than their competencies and strengths.

Another, significant issue concerning screening approaches is when a child is identified as being at-risk but there is no available support or follow-up. One new initiative to identify mental distress and, arguably more importantly, act on any resulting concerns, comes from the Black Dog Institute in Australia. Called Smooth Sailing, the program is delivered in the high school classroom using a mobile or desktop device (Subotic-Kerry, King, O'Moore, Achilles & O'Dea, 2018). Students are invited to complete a series of clinically validated measures and on the basis of their responses are then allocated to different "treatment groups". Youth reporting with mild to moderate symptoms are offered low intensity interventions they can do in their own time and on their own devices (e.g. Web-based psycho-education), whereas more intensive face-to-face interventions (such as school counselling) are reserved for those whose scores indicate high distress. Students who report suicidal ideation trigger an automatic email alert to the school counsellor, who responds within 48 hours and then conducts a risk assessment and, on that basis, decides whether to proceed with an external referral.

At-risk students

Related to screening initiatives in schools, it is important to understand what we mean by "at-risk" students, who they are and how to capture them. See Figure 5.1 for what at-risk might refer to, noting that risk may potentially include learning, mental health and/or behavioural concerns.

Though there are various systematic measures, as outlined earlier for screening mental health and learning difficulties, no one measure can sufficiently

Figure 5.1 The different meanings of "at risk"

capture all possible at-risk students. Other ways are needed to identify students presenting with problems, for example by noting changes in attendance, behaviour, academic progress, peer and family relationships. Informal processes for identifying students who need additional support may come from caregiver reports, student self-referrals or other forms of data schools routinely collect, such as behavioural reports, changes in academic progress and attendance patterns. Often someone knows when something is wrong with a student, and generally that someone is the teacher.

A help-seeking school

Schools can increase their likelihood of identifying at-risk students by ensuring that there are supportive teachers who will listen to young people and help them obtain more intensive support. However, it is not uncommon for young people to believe that they should be able to sort out their problems on their own. Also, some young people may be too embarrassed to talk to someone about their and some may be worried about the confidentiality of information they give a professional. Many would prefer to talk to friends rather than a professional (Rickwood, Deane, Wilson & Ciarrochi, 2005). Overall, young people need to believe that the benefits of seeking help outweigh the fears they have about seeking help from a professional.

According to Walcott and Music (2012), a help-seeking school is one where students and parents know where to turn to at school and in the community for assistance; peers support each other and promote help-seeking behaviour; and staff discuss with relevant personnel any concerns they might have about a student. Such a school has strong links with external agencies and where communication channels are formally established with clear referral guidelines (that includes referral processes to and from school). Help-seeking schools are those where parents and teachers encourage and assist young people to seek professional help.

Leadership

School leaders can have a profound impact on school climate and culture. Several large-scale systematic reviews have found that leadership has the second biggest impact on student outcomes after classroom teaching (Leithwood & Jantzi, 2008). The relationship between student outcomes and school culture is seen in a study which found that leaders' efforts to enhance staff capacities impacted students' motivation, engagement and achievement (Day, Gu & Sammons, 2016).

In the performance-driven culture that can be found in many schools, there is much emphasis on instructional leadership. Instructional leadership is largely concerned with efforts to promote student learning (Flath, 1989) and accordingly focuses on setting clear teaching and learning goals, allocating resources to instruction, managing the curriculum, collecting and monitoring assessment data and evaluating teachers. Attesting to the whole school instructional focus of these leaders, Hattie (2015, p. 37) described the work of instructional leaders as those who

> focus more on students. They're concerned with the teachers' and the school's impact on student learning and instructional issues, conducting classroom observations, ensuring professional development that enhances student learning, communicating high academic standards, and ensuring that all school environments are conducive to learning.

Hallinger (2003) proposed three dimensions of instructional leadership: defining the school's mission, managing the instructional program and promoting a positive school learning climate. He continues by asserting that all three dimensions prompt principals to ensure the school has clear measurable goals focused on the academic progress of students. While important, the emphasis here is on effective teaching for student academic achievement. Nonetheless, each of these three dimensions can be related to student wellbeing and mental health, as further extrapolated in Table 5.1.

Table 5.1 Extending Hallinger's (2003) instructional leadership functions to wellbeing and mental health

Hallinger instructional leadership (2003)		
Dimensions	Functions	Applicability to staff and student wellbeing and mental health
Defining the school mission	Frames the school's goals around the importance of a learning culture Communicates the school's goals around quality teaching; high expectations about student achievement	Includes goals related to staff and student mental health and wellbeing
Managing the instructional program	Coordinates the curriculum	The curriculum is integrated with social and emotional skills and mental health topics
	Supervises and evaluates instructions	Supervises and evaluates the instruction and promotion of mental health and wellbeing
	Monitors students' progress	Monitors staff and student wellbeing and social and emotional competencies
Developing the school learning and climate program	Protects instructional time, including the allocation of resources	Ensures instruction times includes instruction on wellbeing, mental health and social and emotional competency Ensures adequate resources are allocated to a wellbeing curriculum
	Promotes professional development in teaching and learning	Promotes professional development in wellbeing and mental health
	Maintains high visibility	Models wellbeing Ensures there are senior leadership roles in wellbeing

Thus, school leaders are instrumental in finding a balance between improving student achievement and responding to a range of other demands, including delivering a creative, engaging curriculum and promoting young people's wellbeing. Overall, their actions and attitudes are key to establishing warm and inclusive school climates and promoting student wellbeing, raising staff morale and providing opportunities for staff to support students' wellbeing needs.

Leaders would be wise to "walk the walk" and "talk the talk". If they advocate for students' wellbeing and mental health, leaders need to also consider this for their staff. If they support the inclusion of wellbeing programs, they need to ensure staff are given adequate resources and time to do so. If they want teachers to have an "open door" policy with students, they also need to ensure they have the availability to do this as well, for students, caregivers and staff. In addition to relational skills such as team building and communication, the skill set of leaders includes the ability to set a vision for the direction of the school that highlights the values and principles upon which decisions are made and establishes a positive school climate.

Vision and policies

Every school requires a strong, shared vision, to provide purpose and direction and ensure everyone is working together (Gabriel & Farmer, 2009). A well-considered, comprehensive school vision presents an understood, agreed sense of purpose that can be used to filter or decode policies and inform decision making. An effective school vision tends to be collaboratively developed, reflect a broad consensus about what is important regarding the direction of the school and its culture. Inevitably, any school that values academic achievement and wellbeing needs to install a vision around valuing individual students.

One of the most important roles of a school leader is to share in the development of a school vision with others and then explicitly and repeatedly communicate that school vision to the student body, staff, families and community (Heffernan, 2018). The vision allows the school to articulate and plan for clearly articulated goals and for what the school community as a whole wants their student to acquire, by way of twenty-first-century minds, hearts, knowledge and skills. This then informs what leaders and their colleagues require from the curriculum and how it might be organised and delivered.

While important, policies are not always nor necessarily integrated into practice. Another significant component of a leader's role is working out how a particular policy might be applied in their specific community and context in a process that Heffernan (2018) called "policy enactment" (2018). In this process, leaders do not just apply policies into their schools "as is", but instead make a number of critical decisions. In the first instance, they "decode" policies by considering whether and how it fits within their school vision. If or when a decision is made that it does align, they then consider the resources, relationships and local expertise available to them alongside the needs of students, staff and the community in terms of how it might be enacted within their particular school (Heffernan, 2018).

Overall, school policies are needed that promote safety, equity and respect, and these should be reflected across specific learning and wellbeing policies, anti-bullying policies and behaviour programs. There is a plethora of policies that schools may (or need to) draw on, from the national to the local level. Below is an example of one policy, around school uniforms, that has been controversial in countries such as Australia and the UK. This example clearly highlights the association between policy enactments and school culture.

Some school policies in the UK and Australia ban trousers for girls; others stipulate skirt lengths, arguing that short school skirts are too distracting to male students and teachers, while other schools ban shorts for boys. Dresses can be physically restricting for girls and discouraging to activity, yet many schools in the UK, Australia and elsewhere still insist on girls wearing dresses and offer no alternative. Dunn (2018) pointedly notes:

> Surely one of the first considerations in a school uniform should be whether students are comfortable and equal before they start each learning day. So how about this for a solution: get rid of the skirts and dresses and just have gender neutral uniforms. . . . If they [schools] were to devise a uniform, with the input of students, that was comfortable and adaptable to the weather, it would nullify clothes as an issue and allow students to concentrate on learning. Importantly, it would allow them to run and play and do whatever they wanted to do without self-consciousness. And it would ameliorate the problem that not all kids fit neatly into gender categories – something schools are increasingly having to deal with.

If schools value the autonomy of students, we need to ensure that they have input into what they wear. Their views and opinions, including those of their parents, should be reflected in uniform codes and policies. It in this way that policies should reflect the school's core values, with actions that then follow accordingly.

In regard to mental health promotion, prevention, early intervention and treatment, there is some debate whether these domains are included in the remit of schools, with concerns that attention to these matters will compromise valuable instructional time (Dowdy, Quirk & Chin, 2012). Given the intertwined relationship between mental health and academic success (outlined in 3), it is critical that schools adapt a unified and cohesive school policy where school mental health services are provided to students who require them. Adelman and Taylor (2003) argued that policy approaches in this area are especially pertinent when a student's mental health directly impacts on their learning. Policy is also required in those cases where a student's learning experiences impact on mental health and where policy attention is required on how and what is taught and assessed with these students.

School connectedness

School connectedness, sometimes referred to as school belonging or school bonding, includes relationships between children and their peers, teachers and other school staff; children's satisfaction with school experiences; their sense of membership in the learning community; and their participation and voice (Gray, Galton, McLaughlin, Clarke & Symonds, 2011). Goodenow and Grady (1993, p. 80) defined school connectedness as the "the extent to which students feel personally accepted, respected, included, and supported by others in the school social environment". Similarly, according to Allen, Kern, Vella-Brodrick, Hattie and Waters (2016), conceptualisations of school connectedness emphasise school-based relationships and experiences, student–teacher relationships and students' general feelings about school as a whole.

When students feel a sense of belonging and connection with adults and other students at school, they more readily use adults as social models, accept feedback and navigate and persevere through academic and other school-related challenges (Osher, Sprague, Weissberg, Axelrod, Keenan, Kendziora & Zin, 2008). Students' sense of belonging has been positively associated with academic success (Pittman & Richmond, 2007), academic motivation (Gillen-O'Neel & Fuligni, 2013), less absenteeism, less truancy and less misconduct (Allen et al. 2016). It is also positively associated with various psychosocial outcomes, including happiness, adjustment and self-esteem (Allen et al. 2016).

However, approximately one in five students does not have a sense of belonging to their school (Australian Council for Educational Research, 2018). In the US, Wang and Eccles (2011) found that students' sense of belonging declined from Year 7 through to Year 11 along with their educational aspirations. The authors suggest that this decline may be attributed to a mismatch between secondary school students' need for autonomy and interaction and the demands of their learning environment. Another study, this time in Finland, found that students' sense of belonging weakened at the end of Year 8 (Ulmanen, Soini, Pietarinen & Pyhältö, 2016). In that study, the authors suggested the decline may be the result of moving from primary/elementary to secondary school and being surrounded by a largely unknown social network of peers and teachers. Similarly, an Australian study found students' engagement in learning and sense of belonging decreased in the middle of secondary school, a phenomena referred to as the "year 9 dip" (Centre for Education Statistics & Evaluation, 2015a). These problems are not country specific: data across 42 countries, 8354 schools and 224,058 15-year-olds found that on average, one in four adolescents reported low feelings of belongingness and approximately one in five reported low levels of academic engagement (Willms, 2003).

There is much that schools can do to promote school connectedness. The Wingspread Declaration on School Connections (2004) suggested that school connectedness was fostered when schools provide academic support to students, apply fair and consistent disciplinary policies, create trusting relationships among students, teachers and staff, work closely with families and ensure that every student feels close to at least one supportive adult at school. Another review (Centers for Disease Control and Prevention, 2009) add to this list by suggesting that the school's commitment to education, the physical environment and the psychosocial climate of the school environment contribute to school belonging.

Cultural competence and sensitivity

For students to feel that they belong, it is important for school staff to be culturally competent. Cultural competence refers to the behaviours, attitudes and policies employed by schools that enable staff to work effectively in bicultural and multicultural settings and interactions (King, Sims & Osher, 1998). Staff who are culturally competent are aware of their own privilege, possible biases, and daily or routine interactions which may further perpetuate disadvantage (Osher & Berg, 2017).

Teachers can use their knowledge of students to be instructionally responsive in terms of what and how they teach. As outlined by Osher and Berg (2017), culturally responsive instructional approaches are engaging, participatory, draw on students' prior knowledge to teach new concepts and work at connecting learning experiences between the classroom and the community. In this way, culturally sensitive approaches and practices can build students' confidence and counter the negative stereotypes often held towards certain cultural groups. Explicit connections between the cultural backgrounds of students and topics taught in history and the social sciences are another way of promoting cultural respect and competency.

Safe schools

When students feel emotionally and physically safe, they are more willing to focus on learning and take academic risks. A physically safe school is one that does not lead to harm or injury for students. Physical safety is concerned with the school building and grounds, furniture, the use of chemicals and surrounding environment such as air and water (Centre for Education Statistics and Evaluation, 2015b) and protection from exposure to weapons. An emotionally safe environment is positive, free from negative behaviours such as bullying and negative or judgmental reactions when mistakes are made. In emotionally safe schools, students feel safe to express emotions and have the confidence to take risks and try something new. In these schools, students feel safe knowing they will be supported on an emotional level should they encounter any issues.

Hot spot mapping is a process where students are invited to map out their entire school by highlighting areas where they feel safe and those where they do not. Hot mapping allows schools to make more effective decisions and work with students in an empowering way to support each other. Safe spaces tend to be those that are supervised, while unsafe spaces tend to be areas with minimal lighting and minimal staff supervision, such as bathrooms or gyms. Unsafe spaces may not necessarily require more supervision but instead may highlight a need to practice social and emotional skills taught in class, and consider issues such as social inclusion, exclusion and bullying (Astor, Meyer & Pitner, 2001).

Feeling safe at school is an important component of school culture and is necessary for students to feel that they belong. How schools promote a feeling of safety varies. One measure has been the employment of School Resource Officers (SRO). The number of SROs assigned to North American schools has increased during the past two decades, with other countries such as Australia also following the trend. In the US, SROs were specifically employed to protect children and reduce gun violence in schools. Other related measures sometimes employed by schools have been security measures (metal detectors, cameras) and policies (visitor sign in, locked doors) (Perumean-Chaney & Sutton, 2013).

According to Theriot and Orme (2016), SROs assume various tasks, including patrolling the school property, investigating delinquency complaints, mentoring students, assisting with student discipline and educating students and staff about safety and violence prevention. Usually armed and in uniform, their presence has an immediate impact on students' feelings of safety. Juvonen (2001, p. 3) suggested that SROs might "breed a sense of mistrust among students" and hence negatively impact school climate. Indeed, aggressive SRO actions such as threatening to arrest a student who is already being disciplined may lead to increased school disorder and misbehaviour (Bracy, 2011; Mayer & Leone, 1999). Likewise, Perumean-Chaney and Sutton (2013) found that metal detectors and the number of visible security measures employed in schools were associated with a decrease in students' feelings of safety. They found that students who were male, white and reported feeling safe in their neighbourhood were more likely to report feeling safe at school, in comparison to students who experienced prior victimisations, were placed in larger classes and who attended schools that had disorder problems. These results were confirmed by a later study from Theriot and Orme (2016), who found African American students and victimised students felt less safe in the presence of SROs. These results speak to the inherent conflict between law enforcement and positive school culture, especially where security measures are focused on control and domination.

Relationships

Efforts need to be made to ensure that interactions between staff, between students and staff and between students themselves are trusting, respectful and appreciative. Thus, staff relationships should ideally be collegial, respectful and productive, with all staff are held to the highest professional standards.

Student–student relationships

With regard to school culture and climate, it is important to consider how students relate to each other. Positive peer friendships can develop a sense of belonging and provide a buffer for students against the challenges and pressures of school (Pittman & Richmond, 2007). Additionally, students' supportive relationships with their peers can promote participation in classroom experiences (Bergin & Bergin, 2009).

Positive peer relationships can be promoted in several ways. Peer tutoring or cross-aged tutoring can promote feelings of responsibility and compassion, as well as mastery and a sense of belonging for both the helper and the helped (Topping, 2005). Social and emotional curricula aim to encourage team work and provide competencies across listening, empathy, conflict management and group problem solving. Teachers can model empathy, respect and team work in their interactions with colleagues, students and families. Teachers might also provide activities in class which require team work so they can practice various social skills, including conflict resolution and delegation. Teachers might also offer activity groups in classrooms based on common interests to further increase a sense of belonging and give students opportunities to be accepted by their peers. Likewise, interest and support groups in schools may also promote school belonging. These might include special interests such as choirs, gymnastics or support groups for students with specific needs. For example, lesbian, gay, bisexual and transgender (LGBT) students rarely receive school support (Lee, 2002) but in support groups may obtain shared, uncompetitive and positive bonding relationships (Lee, 2002).

Teacher–student relationships

Teachers play a key role in what happens for children, both academically and psychologically. The quality of their relationships with students will influence what and how students learn, how engaged students are and how much they feel they belong. Mashburn et al. (2008) found that after adjusting for prior skill levels, child and family characteristics and program characteristics, teachers' emotional and instructional interactions predicted children's social skills in their first year of school. Thus, policies, program development and professional development efforts that improve teacher–child interactions can facilitate children's school readiness and later success.

Teacher–student relationships are important, not only for academic outcomes (Hattie, 2009) but also for a sense of belonging to a school community (Allen et al. 2016). Teven (2001; 2007) found that when teachers are empathic, understanding and responsive, students are more engaged and see teachers as more competent. Likewise, surveys from Year 8, 10 and 12 students in the USA found that academic progress was high for students who felt that their teachers actively listened, demonstrated interest in them and encouraged their success (Muller, 2001). In this way, when students consider their teachers to be caring and accepting, they are more likely to adopt the academic and social values of their teachers and, in turn, how they feel about school work and how much (or how little) they value it (Ulmanen et al. 2016). Teachers influence students, but students influence teachers are well. Teachers describe closer relationships with students who are able to work independently and exhibit high levels of self-regulation (Birch & Ladd, 1998) in a mutually reinforcing process, as these students then will receive more support from them (Hughes, Cavell & Willson, 2001).

Teachers can foster relationships with students by showing an interest in them, acknowledging success in and out of the classroom, offering emotional support to students and asking for and trying to understand students' points of view. When students want to discuss problems in their lives, active listening by teachers can promote students' sense of belonging (Gordon & Burch, 2003). The time teachers provide to students can convey that they have confidence in them, are willing to consider their feelings without judgement and that they care (Gordon & Burch, 2003).

In a study by Reupert and Maybery (2007), young people identified as at risk for mental illness nominated teachers who they considered provided exemplary support. One of the key ways that teachers showed they cared was in the manner in which they established and maintained relationships with students. The teachers in that study made it clear that they did not provide a counselling service or "talk in depth" (p. 200) with students about their circumstances, but instead "chatted" to students and "made extra time" (Reupert & Maybery, 2007, p. 200). They described encouraging children to fully engage in school life, for example by participating in school events such as sports and the school council. Though some teachers referred children to the school counsellor, they considered their relationship with the child as ongoing, regardless of any additional counselling support the student might be accessing. It is important that these relationships focus not only on students' wellbeing but also on their learning. Jennings and Greenberg (2009) argued that caring for students is not sufficient to promote mastery in learning; instead, they suggest that care and concern for students' learning is also required. Likewise, Reupert and Maybery (2007) found that teachers show they care when they hold students to high academic standards and have high but reasonable expectations.

Positive relationships between students and teachers are often characterised as caring. There has always been a legal obligation and "duty of care" for teachers in terms of children's physical safety, custody and the protection. However, Fletcher-Campbell (1995) distinguished between "caring for", which involves a teacher's contractual obligations, and "caring about", which involves a teacher's personal beliefs and commitment. Caring for students typically involves "the establishment of meaningful relationships, the ability to sustain connections, and the commitment to respond to others with sensitivity and flexibility" (Goldstein & Lake, 2000, p. 862). In practice, this can be defined by being responsive and by actively listening (Murphy, Delli & Edwards, 2004).

Relationships with students are especially important for those at risk of academic failure. Hamre and Pianta (2005) found in their study of 910 at-risk first grade children that at the end of the year, children in classrooms in which teachers infused "everyday interactions" with emotional support had achievement scores commensurate with their low-risk peers. In contrast, at-risk students placed in less supportive classrooms had lower achievement scores and experienced more conflict with teachers. Others have found that when students feel comfortable with teachers, they are more willing to persist with learning and grapple with challenging material (Garbacz, Swanger-Gagné & Sheridan, 2015; Hurd & Deutsch, 2017). In sum, Rogers and Webb (1991) summarised, "good teachers care, and good teaching is inextricably linked to specific acts of caring" (p. 174).

Caring is a useful concept because it extends past a helping relationship or one that is affectively based. Velasquez, West, Graham and Osguthorpe (2013, p. 182) explicitly embed caring into pedagogy when they argue that the "caring pedagogy is the act that results from a symbiotic caring relation between student and teacher, in which learning happens through modelling, dialogue, practice and confirmation at the individual and community levels". Similarly, caring teachers might challenge students because they want them to learn and do better (Goldstein & Lake, 2000). In this way, caring has been described as "students and teachers working together" (Laletas & Reupert, 2015, p. 14).

Laletas and Reupert (2015) found that caring could also be established through the way in which teachers respond to and address behavioural challenges. Illuminating the complexity in managing students' behaviour, Weinstein (1998) found that US teachers dichotomised the notion of care as different from maintaining order in the classroom and that achieving "order" was aligned with "being mean" while "caring" was associated with "wanting to be nice" (p. 161). Indeed, it has been said that teachers find it difficult to navigate their dual roles as both caring and authority figures (Aultman, Williams-Johnson & Schutz, 2009).

There is, however, some controversy around teachers and their caring relationships with students and what this might look like. In their interviews with primary pre-service teachers, Kemp and Reupert (2012) found that some were not sure about whether they should or could "touch" students, though most participants considered hugging or putting an arm around the shoulders of a student an acceptable form of caring. Likewise, one of the female teachers interviewed by Reupert and Maybery (2007, p. 201) described providing support to a female student:

> I did give her a gentle embrace . . . this breaks the rules, I know. But on one hand I am parent in loci and at the same time I am her teacher . . . you can't just stand there.

Some teachers have their own "rules" around touch, for example, one of the pre-service teachers interviewed by Kemp and Reupert (2012, p. 120) indicated that "with the younger children they at times gravitate towards you and I have had children embrace me . . . I would never push a child away from an embrace but I would not instigate the embrace". The issue of touch is especially challenging for male teachers, some of whom need to find alternative ways of caring that are less culturally "suspect" for men (Hansen & Mulholland, 2005). One of the teachers interviewed by Reupert and Maybery (2007) suggested that there are "two extremes of being either detached or a sexual perpetuator . . . I think we need to find the middle ground" (p. 201).

Another related controversy is around caring too much. Aultman et al. (2009) suggested that there is "a line" between caring for students and not becoming too involved. They continue by pointing out that outside of policy guidelines around sexual relationships with students, the caring "line" is somewhat arbitrary, contextualised and highly individualised. Notwithstanding the uncertainty about the "line", boundaries in the student–teacher relationship are required in certain areas including institutional (for example, driving a student home), financial (e.g. lending money) and communication (for example, involving inappropriate high levels of self-disclosure) (Aultman et al. 2009). In more recent times, Morris (2015) suggested that though Facebook (and other related media) might be seen as one way of establishing teacher–student relationships, communications across these platforms are susceptible to misinterpretation and lack security and confidentiality. Aultman et al. (2009) found it was often younger, less experienced teachers who expressed a need to be liked or to be friends with students and sometimes overstepped the "line".

How teachers and schools manage and react to student behaviour, especially challenging behaviour, will do much to shape school culture and climate and will be explored, in depth, in the next chapter.

References

Adelman, H. S., & Taylor, L. (2003). *Mental health in schools. Engaging learners, preventing problems and improving schools*. Thousand Oaks, CA: Corwin:

Allen, K. A., Kern, M., Vella-Brodrick, D., Hattie, J., & Waters, L. (2016). What schools need to know about fostering school belonging: A meta-analysis. *Educational Psychology Review*, *30*(1), 1–34.

Astor, R. A., Meyer, H. A., & Pitner, R. O. (2001). Elementary and middle school students' perceptions of violence-prone school subcontexts. *The Elementary School Journal*, *101*, 511–528.

Aultman, L. P., Williams-Johnson, M. R., & Schutz, P. A. (2009). Boundary dilemmas in teacher-student relationships: Struggling with "the line". *Teaching and Teacher Education*, *25*, 636–646.

Australian Council for Educational Research (2018). *PISA Australia in focus number 1: Sense of belonging at school*. Retrieved January 18, 2019, from https://research.acer.edu.au/cgi/viewcontent.cgi?article=1031&context=ozpisa

Bergin, C., & Bergin, D. (2009). Attachment in the classroom. *Educational Psychology Review*, *21*(2), 141–170.

Birch, S. H., & Ladd, G. (1998). Children's interpersonal behaviors and the teacher-child relationship. *Developmental Psychology*, *34*(5), 934–946.

Bracy, N. L. (2011). Student perceptions of high-security school environments. *Youth & Society*, *43*(1), 365–395.

Bryk, A. S., & Schneider, B. (2002). *Trust in schools: A core resource for improvement*. New York: Russell Sage Foundation.

Centre for Education Statistics and Evaluation (2015a). *Student engagement and wellbeing in NSW*. Retrieved January 18, 2019, from www.cese.nsw.gov.au/images/stories/PDF/LearningCurve7_TTFM_May2015.pdf

Centre for Education Statistics and Evaluation (2015b). *Student wellbeing*. Retrieved January 18, 2019, from www.cese.nsw.gov.au/images/stories/PDF/student_wellbeing_LR_AA.pdf

Centers for Disease Control and Prevention. (2009). *School connectedness: Strategies for increasing protective factors among youth*. Atlanta: U.S.: Department of Health and Human Services. Retrieved January 19, 2019, from www.cdc.gov/healthyyouth/protective/pdf/connectedness.pdf

Day, C., Gu, Q., & Sammons, P. (2016). The impact of leadership on student outcomes: How successful school leaders use transformational and instructional strategies to make a difference. *Educational Administrative Quarterly*, *52*(2), 221–258.

Dowdy, E., Quirk, M. P., Chin, J. K. (2012). School-based mental health. In J. Hattie, & E. Anderman (Eds.), *International guide to Student achievement* (pp. 125–127). London: Routledge.

Dunn, A. (2018, October 14). *Don't skirt the issue*. The Age.

Felner, R. D., Jackson, A.W., Kasak, D., Mulhall, P., Brand, S., & Flowers, N. (1997). The impact of school reform for the middle years: Longitudinal study of a network engaged in Turning Points-based comprehensive school transformation. *Phi Delta Kappan*, *78*, 528–532.

Flath, B. (1989). The principal as instructional leader. *ATA Magazines*, *69*(3), 19–22.

Fletcher-Campbell, F. (1995). Caring about caring? *Pastoral Care in Education*, *13*, 26–28.

Freiberg, H. J., & Stein, T. A. (1999). *Introduction to school climate: Measuring, improving, and sustaining healthy learning environments*. Philadelphia, PA: Falmer Press.

Fuchs, D., & Fuchs, L. S. (2017). Critique of the national evaluation of response to intervention: A case for simpler frameworks. *Exceptional Children*, *83*(3), 255–268.

Gabriel, J. G., & Farmer, P. C. (2009). *How to help your school thrive without breaking the bank*. Alexandria, VA: ASCD.

Garbacz, S. A., Swanger-Gagné, M. S., & Sheridan, S. M. (2015). The role of school-family partnership programs for promoting student social and emotional learning. In J. Durlak, T. Gullotta, C. Domitrovich, P. Goren, & R. Weissberg (Eds.), *The handbook of social and emotional learning* (pp. 244–259). New York: Guildford Press.

Garrett, Z., Newman, M., Elbourne, D., Bradley, S., Noden, P., Taylor, J., & West, A. (2004). *Secondary school size: A systematic review*. Research Evidence in Education Library. London: EPPI-Centre, Social Science Research Unit, Institute of Education, University of London. Retrieved January 19, 2019, from http://eppi.ioe.ac.uk/cms/Portals/0/PDF%20reviews%20and%20summaries/s_s_rv1.pdf?ver=2006-03-02-125040-877

Gillen-O'Neel, C., & Fuligni, A. (2013). A longitudinal study of school belonging and academic motivation across high school. *Child Development*, *84*(2), 678–692.

Goldstein, L., & Lake, V. (2000). "Love, love, and more love for children": Exploring preservice teacher's understandings of caring. *Teaching and Teacher Education*, *16*, 861–872.

Goodenow, C., & Grady, K. E. (1993). The relationship of school belonging and friends' values to academic motivation among urban adolescent students. *The Journal of Experimental Education*, *62*(1), 60–71.

Gordon, T., & Burch, N. (2003). *Teacher effectiveness training: The program proven to help teachers bring out the best in students of all ages*. New York: Three Rivers Press.

Gray, J., Galton, M., McLaughlin, C., Clarke, B., & Symonds, J. (2011). *The supportive school: Wellbeing and the young adolescent*. Cambridge: Cambridge Scholars Press.

Hallinger, P. (2003). Leading educational change: Reflections on the practice of instructional and transformational leadership. *Cambridge Journal of Education*, *33*(3), 329–351.

Hamre, B. K., & Pianta, R. C. (2005). Can instructional and emotional support in the first grade classroom make a difference for children at risk of school failure? *Child Development*, *76*(5), 949–967.

Hansen, P., & Mulholland, J. A. (2005). Caring and elementary teaching: The concerns of male beginning teachers. *Journal of Teacher Education*, *56*, 119–131.

Hattie, J. (2005). The paradox of reducing class size and improving learning outcomes. *International Journal of Educational Research*, *43*(6), 387–425.

Hattie, J. (2009). *Visible learning: A synthesis of meta-analyses relating to achievement*. London: Routledge.

Hattie, J. (2015). High-impact leadership. *Educational Leadership*, *72*(5), 37–40.

Heffernan, A. (2018). The influence of school context on school improvement policy enactment: An Australian case study. *International Journal of Leadership in Education*, *21*(6), 621–623.

Hemmelgarn, A. L., Glisson, C. and James, L. R. (2006), Organizational culture and climate: Implications for services and interventions research. *Clinical Psychology: Science and Practice*, *13*, 73–89. doi:10.1111/j.1468-2850.2006.00008.x

Hughes, J. N., Cavell, T. A., & Willson, V. (2001). Further support for the developmental significance of the quality of the teacher – student relationship. *Journal of School Psychology*, *39*(4), 289–301.

Humphrey, N., & Wigelsworth, M. (2016). Making the case for universal school-based mental health screening. *Emotional and Behavioural Difficulties*, *21*(1), 22–42.

Hurd, N., & Deutsch, N. (2017). SEL-focused after-school programs. *Future of Children*, *27*(1), 95–115.

Ikeda, M. J., Neessen, E., & Witt, J. C. (2007). Best practices in universal screening. In A. Thomas, & J. Grimes (Eds.), *In best practices in school psychology* (pp. 103–114). Bethesda, MD: National Association of School Psychologists.

Jenkins, J. R., Hudson, R. F., & Johnson, E. S. (2007). Screening for at-risk readers in a response to intervention framework. *School Psychology Review*, *36*, 582–600.

Jennings, P. A., & Greenberg, M. T. (2009). The prosocial classroom: Teacher social and emotional competence in relation to student and classroom outcomes. *Review of Educational Research*, *79*(1), 491–525.

Juvonen, J. (2001). *School violence: Prevalence, fears, and prevention*. RAND Issue paper. Retrieved June 18, 2019, from https://www.rand.org/pubs/issue_papers.html

Kemp, H., & Reupert, A. (2012). "There's no big book on how to care": Primary pre-service teachers' experiences of caring. *The Australian Journal of Teacher Education*, *37*(9), 114–127.

King, M. A., Sims, A., & Osher, D. (1998). *How is cultural competence integrated into education?* Washington, DC: Center for Effective Collaboration and Practice, American Institutes for Research.

Laletas, S., & Reupert, A. (2015). Exploring pre-service teachers' understanding of care. *Teachers and Teaching: Theory and Practice*, *22*(4), 485–503.

Lee, C. (2002). The impact of belonging to a high school gay/straight alliance. *The High School Journal*, *85*(3), 13–26.

Leithwood, K., & Jantzi, D. (2008). Linking leadership to student learning: The contributions of leader efficacy. *Educational Administration Quarterly*, *44*(4), 496–528.

Mashburn, A. J., Pianta, R. C, Hamre, B. K., Downer, J. T., Barbarin, O. A., Bryant, D., . . . Howes, C. (2008). Measures of classroom quality in prekindergarten and children's development of academic, language, and social skills. *Child Development*, *79*(3), 732–749.

Mathis, W. J. (2017). The effectiveness of class size reduction. *Psychosociological Issues in Human Resource*, *1*, 176–183.

Mayer, M. J., & Leone, P. E. (1999). A structural analysis of school violence and disruption: Implications for creating safer schools. *Education and Treatment of Children*, *22*, 333–356.

McNeely, C. A., Nonnemaker, J. M. and Blum, R. W. (2002), Promoting school connectedness: Evidence from the national longitudinal study of adolescent health. *Journal of School Health*, *72*, 138–146. doi:10.1111/j.1746-1561.2002.tb06533.x

Merten, E. C., Cwik, J. C., Margraf, J., & Schneider, S. (2017). Over-diagnosis of mental disorders in children and adolescents (in developed countries). *Child and Adolescent Psychiatry and Mental Health*, *e11*(5).

Messick, S. (1989). Validity. In R. L. Linn (Ed.), *Educational measurement* (3rd ed., pp. 13–103). New York: Macmillan.

Morris, Z. (2015). Contemporary professional boundaries and their relationship with teacher and student well-being. In C. M. Rubie-Davies, J. Stephens, & P. Watson (Eds.), *The Routledge international handbook of social psychology of the classroom* (pp. 372–382). Abingdon Oxon: Routledge.

Muller, C. (2001). The role of caring in the teacher – student relationship for at-risk students. *Sociological Inquiry*, *71*, 241–255.

Murphy, P. K., Delli, L., & Edwards, M. (2004). The good teacher and good teaching: Comparing beliefs of second-grade students, preservice teachers, and inservice teachers. *The Journal of Experimental Education*, *72*(2), 69–92.

Office of Career, Technical and Adult Education (2009). *School size*. Retrieved January 18, 2019, from https://www2.ed.gov/about/offices/list/ovae/pi/hs/schoolsize.html

Osher, D., & Berg, J. (2017). *School climate and social and emotional learning: The integration of two approaches*. Edna Bennett Pierce Prevention Research Center, Pennsylvania State University. Retrieved January 19, 2019, from http://prevention.psu.edu/uploads/files/rwjf443059.pdf

Osher, D., Sprague, J., Weissberg, R., Axelrod, J., Keenan, S., Kendziora, K., & Zin, J. (2008). A comprehensive approach to promoting social, emotional, and academic growth in contemporary schools. *Best Practices in School Psychology*, *4*, 1263–1278.

Perumean-Chaney, S. E., & Sutton, L. M. (2013). Students and perceived school safety: The impact of school security measures. *American Journal of Criminal Justice*, *38*(4), 570–588.

Pittman, L., & Richmond, A. (2007). Academic and psychological functioning in late adolescence: The importance of school belonging. *The Journal of Experimental Education*, *75*(4), 270–290.

Reupert, A. E., & Maybery, D. J. (2007). Strategies and issues in supporting children whose parents have a mental illness within the school system. *School Psychology International*, *28*(2), 195–205.

Rickwood, D., Deane, F. P., Wilson, C. J., & Ciarrochi, J. (2005). Young people's help-seeking for mental health problems. *Australian e-Journal for the Advancement of Mental Health, 4*(3), 1–34.

Rogers, D., & Webb, J. (1991). The ethic of caring in teacher education. *Journal of Teacher Education, 42*(3), 173–182.

Subotic-Kerry, M., King. C., O'Moore, K., Achilles, M., & O'Dea, B. (2018). General Practitioners attitudes towards an online school-based mental health service: Implications for the design and delivery of youth e-mental health. *JMIR Human Factors, 5*(1), e12.

Teven, J. J. (2001). The relationships among teacher characteristics and perceived caring. *Communication Education, 50*, 159–169.

Teven, J. J. (2007). Teacher caring and classroom behavior: Relationships with student affect and perceptions of teacher competence and trustworthiness. *Communication Quarterly, 55*, 433–450.

Theriot, M. T., & Orme, J. G. (2016). School resource officers and students' feelings of safety at school. *Youth Violence and Juvenile Justice, 14*(2), 130–146.

Topping, K. J. (2005). Trends in peer learning. *Educational Psychology, 25*(6), 631–645.

Ulmanen, S., Soini, T., Pietarinen, J., & Pyhältö, K. (2016). Students' experiences of the development of emotional engagement. *International Journal of Educational Research, 79*, 86–96.

Velasquez, A., West, R., Graham, C., & Osguthorpe, R. (2013). Developing caring relationships in schools: A review of the research on caring and nurturing pedagogies. *Review of Education, 1*, 162–190.

Walcott, C. M., & Music, A. (2012). Promoting adolescent help-seeking for mental health problems: Strategies for school-based professionals. *Communique, 41*(1), 4–7.

Wang, M-T., & Eccles, J. S. (2011). Adolescent behavioral, emotional, and cognitive engagement trajectories in school and their differential relations to educational success. *Journal of Research on Adolescence, 22*(1), 31–39.

Weinstein, C. S. (1998). "I want to be nice, but I have to be mean": Exploring prospective teachers' conceptions of caring and order. *Teaching and Teacher Education, 14*, 153–163.

Willms, J. D. (2003). *Student engagement at school: A sense of belonging and participation: Results from PISA 2000*. Retrieved from the Organisation for Economic Co-operation and Development website: www.oecd.org/edu/school/programmeforinternationalstudentassessmentpisa/33689437.pdf

Wingspread Declaration on School Connections (2004). *Journal of School Health, 74*(7), 233–234.

Zyngier, D. (2014). Class size and academic results, with a focus on children from culturally, linguistically and economically disenfranchised communities. *Evidence Base, 1*, 1–24.

Chapter 6

Reconceptualising student behaviour

Teaching, at its essence, is a relational practice. It involves more than curricula (what is taught) and pedagogy (how to teach), as it also incorporates how teachers interact with students and the manner in which the learning environment is organised and managed. This chapter provides another way of considering behavioural issues in schools by examining students' behaviour within the context of their (dis)engagement with the learning environment. Viewing student behaviour from this perspective allows us to direct intervention efforts on teacher–student interactions and teaching practices, rather than blame or inadvertently pathologise students.

The relationship between learning, mental health and behaviour

The nexus among learning difficulties, mental health presentations and behavioural issues is well documented (Gest & Gest, 2005; Landrum, Tankersley & Kauffman, 2003; Martella & Marchand-Martella, 2015). The entwined relationship between these domains can perhaps be seen most obviously by the numbers of young men in juvenile detention centres, many of whom have a history of academic difficulties and behaviour issues. The school to prison trajectory can, however, be avoided. The former Chair of the UK Youth Justice Board, Rod Morgan (2007, p. xiii), argued that:

> It may be too much to say that if we reformed our schools, we would have no need of prisons. But if we better engaged our children and young people in education we would almost certainly have less need of prisons. Effective crime prevention has arguably more to do with education than sentencing policy.

Notwithstanding the promise of education as a transformative opportunity for disadvantaged young people, the present system of schooling does not appear to be working for a group of disengaged (usually male) students. Snow, Woodward, Mathis and Powell (2016) found that 87% of 85 incarcerated young offenders had experienced some form of school exclusion, with only 15% having undertaken any vocational training and only eight who had progressed in formal schooling beyond Year 10. Such data speaks to the need for schools to change the way they identify and address "bad boys" or students they perceive as exhibiting challenging or disruptive behaviour.

So, what should schools target – behaviour or learning difficulties? Consistent with other themes in this book, early intervention and preventive approaches are needed that target academic as well as children's social, emotional and behavioural domains. Typically, children who experience more failure than success at school end up feeling frustrated and angry (Scott, Nelson & Liaupsin, 2001). For these students, learning is seen as an activity to be avoided. And the more students find the classroom aversive, the more likely they are to exhibit behaviours that show their frustration and anger (Pierce, Wechsler-Zimring, Noam, Wolf & Tami Katzir, 2013). Payne, Marks and Bogan (2007) found that behaviour problems may cause a disruption in academic engagement, and hence, students may fail to obtain the necessary academic skills, such as literacy. Thus, it is important to improve students' engagement and academic skill levels to reduce the aversive impact of school and the likelihood of problem behaviours at school.

What is challenging behaviour?

Whether and how a child's behaviour is defined as challenging, disruptive or otherwise problematic is entirely reliant on the context and interpretation of that behaviour. For example, Attention-Deficit/Hyperactivity Disorder (ADHD) is a commonly diagnosed disorder among children and teenagers, with symptoms of attentional difficulties, emotional regulation and response inhibition. But not all the attributes associated with ADHD are necessarily maladaptive; it depends on what is expected and needed in any given environment. Fugate, Zentall and Gentry (2013) found that though gifted students with ADHD characteristics had significantly poorer working memory, they also demonstrated greater creativity than those gifted students without these characteristics. Thus, notwithstanding the difficulty for many students with ADHD to pay attention in class and organise their learning, their strengths in divergent thinking and creativity might be capitalised on and applied when developing educational programs. The same authors continued by arguing that "in the school setting, the challenge becomes how to create an environment in which creativity is emphasised as *a pathway* to learning as well as an outcome of learning" (p. 242, italics included).

If schools expect students with ADHD (or ADHD characteristics) to sit still, listen and learn, they are setting that child up for failure. Instead, if we work with the attributes these young people bring to school, that is, their energy, spontaneity and creativity, then their behaviour may no longer be is seen as "bad" but instead as an attribute to be extended and utilised as an academic skill. To this end, educational programs may need to incorporate problem-based learning activities and permit different products of learning (such as cartoons, videos, newspaper articles), rather than expecting these students to passively learn content.

Likewise, the behaviour that some children exhibit may be entirely appropriate given the child's previous experiences and the context in which it is placed. Such behaviour, however, may be interpreted as unacceptable by teachers or caregivers. How we interpret a child's behaviour will have direct implications for our response. For example, if we see a child misbehaving, punishments or consequences often follow. Alternatively, however, if we perceive a child's behaviour as an attempt at communicating basic needs or struggling with expectations, then we change our own behaviour accordingly.

Hence, students' behaviour and emotions need to be seen and understood within the context in which they occur, not necessarily as individual, pathological symptoms. This stance means that schools need to examine their own practices and procedures. For example, a student who fights with other students should not necessarily be seen as a student with anger problems that need to be "fixed". Instead, consideration needs to be given to why the child is getting angry and at what or who. School psychologists are often asked to facilitate "anger management" programs for young people who have been involved in fights or other acts of violence. These programs typically encourage participants to identify negative or unhelpful thoughts and learn behavioural strategies to physically calm down. Rather than focus attention on a young person's responses, consideration could be turned instead to the possible causes of their behaviour. Has the teacher provided work that the student cannot do? Is there potential for the student to be shamed in front of peers? Was the anger provoked by bullying? Seeking answers to these questions does not excuse the behaviour, but it does help to understand it. It is only from this position of understanding that an adequate response can be formulated. Taking these arguments further, Gillies (2011, p. 196) speaks to the broad societal context in which behaviour is interpreted when she writes, "distinctions between emotional disturbance and lack of social conformity can be complex and inevitably reflect and reinforce a range of gendered, racialised and classed assumptions".

Were (2006) defined discipline as "a system of guiding the individuals to make responsible decisions responsibly" (p. 710). This notion is reflected in the oft-cited quote from former National Association of State Directors of Special Education President Tom Herner (1998, p. 2) that reads:

> If a child doesn't know how to read, we teach.
> If a child doesn't know how to swim, we teach.
> If a child doesn't know how to multiply, we teach.
> If a child doesn't know how to drive, we teach.
> If a child doesn't know how to behave, we . . . . teach?
> . . . . punish?
> Why can't we finish the last sentence as automatically as we do the others?

Hence, schools need to promote, teach and foster positive behaviour with the same determination they teach academic subjects. In this way, attempts at discipline should be used to teach young people appropriate behaviour, not to punish or expel them. This also means that teachers and other school staff need to change their own behaviour (for example by teaching differently) before they can expect to change the behaviour of young people in their classes.

Models of classroom management: what's our end goal?

Is our aim, as educators, for children to sit still, behave and listen? Is it for children to engage in busy work so they are so preoccupied they do not have the opportunity to disrupt the the running of the classroom? Or is our goal to encourage young people to think critically, consider what is important to them now and in the future and engage in learning experiences that hold value and meaning for them?

It is my contention that we should not be asking how to get children to behave in ways that teachers think are appropriate, but should instead consider how schools and teachers might promote behaviour that is conducive to learning that has meaning for that particular child. While instruction and classroom management are often considered two different skill sets (as might be seen when we look at how pre-service teachers are trained; Woodcock & Reupert, 2013), we need to engage with students in the learning process in such a way that their behaviour is also acceptable. In other words, how teachers instruct and how they manage their classes are intimately intertwined (Reupert & Woodcock, 2018).

Moreover, how teachers instruct and manage their classrooms is informed by their personal philosophy and stance around control and collaboration. There are many models of classroom management, which may be placed on a continuum from student to teacher centred. These models range from the teacher-centred approach of Canter and Canter (1976), called Assertive Discipline, through to the more student-focused mode of classroom management of Glasser (1990). The principle difference across these approaches are around control: who takes (or aims to take) control of the classroom, the ways that decisions are made about what is taught and how behaviour is managed. Both curriculum and behaviour management approaches can be placed on a control continuum (see Figure 6.1).

Despite the fundamental differences in these approaches, one common feature is an acknowledgement of the need to consider the function or meaning of the child's behaviour and the need that particular behaviour might be addressing. In this way, all models consider behaviour as a form of communication or as means by which the child expresses what he or she does or does not like, or does or does not want to do – even if they are not able to articulate or acknowledge their preferences so clearly.

For example, positioned with Functional Behaviour Analysis, Sugai (2007) identified four functions of behaviour: to escape or avoid something, to get

84 Reconceptualising student behaviour

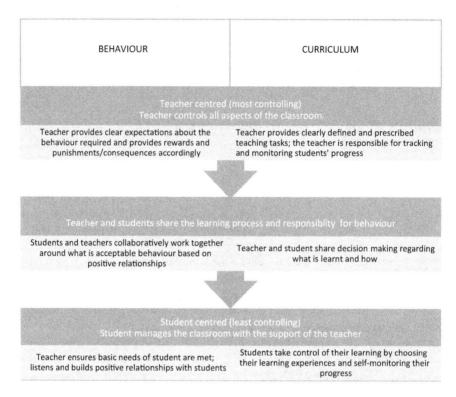

Figure 6.1 Continuum of control: behaviour and curriculum

attention from others, to obtain or get something and, finally, for sensory stimulation, because it feels good to them. On the other hand, Glasser (1998) argued that all behaviour is motivated by five basic needs, namely: (i) survival (need for food, shelter and safety), (ii) relationships, social connections, to give and receive affection and to feel part of a group, (iii) power (defined in terms of achieving and being recognised for our achievements and skill, to be listened to and have a sense of self-worth), (iv) to be free and independent and the ability to take control of the direction of one's life and (v) fun, to find pleasure, play and laugh. Notwithstanding the significant philosophical differences between the two positions, both attempt to understand a child's motivation for behaving as they do, and then use this information to inform an intervention or behavioural support program.

Regardless of which approach one assumes, effective teachers commonly do several things when it comes to classroom management. They have clear learning and behavioural expectations of students (that are either collaboratively decided on by the teacher and students, or by the teacher alone; see Figure 6.1); they generously acknowledge prosocial and on-task behaviour (privately and/or publicly); and finally, they discreetly but assertively correct (not punish) anti-social or disruptive behaviour (Lewis & Sugai, 1999; Richmond, 2007; Wong & Wong, 2005). Overall, the focus of effective teachers is on prevention and engaging students in the learning process. It is prevention focused, as students understand what is expected of them and are engaged in what they are doing.

"Teach more, manage less" (Richmond, 2007)

Similar to the relationship between teaching and classroom management (Figure 6.1), teachers might reflect on their respective foci of "managing" and "teaching". If teacher efforts are directed at maximising teaching time, they will need less time to manage behaviour; in other words, teachers can then "teach more, manage less" (Richmond, 2007). This notion needs to be reflected in the conversations teachers have with students; namely, teacher "talk" should be focused on engaging students in learning, not on behaviour. Conversely, when conversations are dominated by managing behaviour (for example, telling students how they should and should not behave), the learning experience is disrupted or at best minimised. See Table 6.1 for the two types of conversations, adapted from Richmond (2007). Table 6.1 highlights the respective time teachers give when holding dominant

Table 6.1 The relative time provided in dominant learning versus dominant managing behaviour conversations

Dominant learning conversations	Dominant managing conversations
Learning conversations (engaging students in learning)	Learning conversations (engaging students in learning)
	Managing conversations (conversations about behavioural expectations, correcting and directing students' behaviour)
Managing conversations (conversations about behavioural expectations, correcting and directing students' behaviour)	

Source: adapted from Richmond (2007).

conversations about learning (first column) or dominant conversations on managing behaviour (second column).

For example, when working with a student who is off task, a teacher might ask "would you please sit still?" Or, alternatively, the teacher might say "finish the next chapter, thanks". The first statement is focused on the student's behaviour (a "managing" conversation), while the second is focused on learning (a "learning" conversation). Holding regular learning conversations implies that teachers know how to engage students with the curriculum, that the curriculum is worth engaging in and the student can see its relevance. These sentiments are perhaps best summed up by Slavin (2009, p. 329), who argued:

> Students who are participating in well-structured activities that engage their interests, who are highly motivated to learn, and who are working on tasks that are challenging yet within their capabilities rarely pose any serious management problems.

By and large, however, teachers are not trained to think about classroom management and discipline in this way. Instead, repeated studies have shown that pre-service teachers from Australia, Canada and UK reply primarily on corrective strategies when they engage with students who are disengaged (Reupert & Woodcock, 2010, 2011; Woodcock & Reupert, 2017)

Promoting behaviour conducive to learning

The next chapter discusses pedagogy and curriculum in more detail, but at this point it is sufficient to say that teachers might promote behaviour that is conducive to learning by providing engaging lessons that tap into young peoples' interests, prior learning and goals and by ensuring that the work they do is meaningful. How this might be done varies depending on the context and government and community expectations. See, for example, a recent media piece about Finland's educational reforms:

> Finnish officials want to remove school subjects from the curriculum. There will no longer be any classes in physics, math, literature, history, or geography.
>
> The head of the Department of Education in Helsinki, Marjo Kyllonen, explained the changes, "There are schools that are teaching in the old-fashioned way which was of benefit in the beginning of the 1900s – but the needs are not the same, and we need something fit for the 21st century."
>
> Instead of individual subjects, students will study events and phenomena in an interdisciplinary format. For example, the Second World War will be examined from the perspective of history, geography, and math. And by taking the course "Working in a Cafe," students will absorb a whole body of knowledge about the English language, economics, and communication skills.

> This system will be introduced for senior students, beginning at the age of 16. The general idea is that the students ought to choose for themselves which topic or phenomenon they want to study, bearing in mind their ambitions for the future and their capabilities. In this way, no student will have to pass through an entire course on physics or chemistry while all the time thinking to themselves "What do I need to know this for?"
>
> The traditional format of teacher–pupil communication is also going to change. Students will no longer sit behind school desks and wait anxiously to be called upon to answer a question. Instead, they will work together in small groups to discuss problems.
>
> (*Daily Times Monitor*, 2017)

Another approach is being trialled in Australia:

> Lindfield Learning Village won't be the kind of school most adults recognise. Teaching will happen around "waterholes" or "campfires". Students will take responsibility for their own learning. And high schoolers will mentor kindy kids.
>
> Lindfield will take a "stage not age" approach, in which students advance based on their progress rather than their year level.
>
> Pupils will be divided into K–12 "home bases" of about 350 to encourage a sense of belonging in what could otherwise be an overwhelming campus. Older students will be encouraged to mentor and teach younger ones.
>
> Each student will have their own "learning pathway", monitored by a "learning mentor". And the school will teach through projects that engage several disciplines together, rather than focusing on one at a time.
>
> For example, a robot project might engage maths, computer technology, science and, if they create an imaginary story for their robot, English.
>
> The layout of the school will reflect this. Rather than traditional classrooms, there will be waterhole spaces, used for big groups. In the campfire space, a small group will work with a teacher. And students can work by themselves in the cave.
>
> (Baker, 2018)

Though different, both approaches reject traditional notions of learning with students sitting at desks neatly arranged in rows with a single teacher at the front of the room, as the primary source of knowledge, and instead position students as autonomous, self-directed learners. Learning environments and adult support are provided that best facilitate this form of learning; this also relates to how teachers manage student behaviour. Though effective classroom management techniques (such as the positioning of desks, or the proximity of the teacher to students) are important, they should not be used purely for the purpose of maintaining order or discipline. Instead, teachers need to be encouraged to reflect on what is being taught and how, in ways most engaging and meaningful to students. This also means that within a developmental framework, it is important that younger children are provided with a curriculum that is creative, flexible and enjoyable. For older students, flexibility, autonomy and enjoyment are critical.

"Consequences have consequences" (Lewis, 2015)

Many classroom management models rely on behavioural systems based on consequences (rewards or punishments), for example, gold stars and prizes for "good" behaviour and punishments such as suspensions and expulsions for "bad" behaviour. The use of rewards and punishments as a means to motivate students is however contentious.

On one hand, consequences can be detrimental to the child. Lewis (2015) argued that

> consequences have consequences. Contemporary psychological studies suggest that, far from resolving children's behavior problems, these standard disciplinary methods often exacerbate them. They sacrifice long-term goals (student behavior improving for good) for short-term gain – momentary peace in the classroom.

In his book, tellingly titled *Punished by Rewards: The Trouble with Gold Stars, Incentive Plans, A's, Praise and Other Bribes* (1993), Kohn argued that rewards are not effective at changing behaviour. He prefaces his arguments with a quote from Hackman and Oldham (1980, as cited in Kohn, 1993, p. 37):

> Many of the early (and highly successful) applications of the principles of behavior modification have involved animals (such as pigeons), children, or institutionalized adults such as prisoners or mental patients. Individuals in each of these groups are necessarily dependent on powerful others for many of the things they most want and need, and their behavior usually can be shaped with relative ease.

This statement highlights the power relationships that might be found between teachers and students. The end result of these teacher directed interactions often involves conforming to classroom norms where students do not have a voice or contribution. Wilson (2015) pointed out that school administrators may be more likely to select certain behaviours for rewarding/punishing, associated with their own Eurocentric culture which may or may not necessarily represent the culture of the student body. Further extending these arguments, Hanus and Fox (2018) found that rewards do not sustain behaviour in the longer term, nor do they promote deep, authentic learning; moreover, they may have a detrimental impact on motivation as students only engage in any given task when there is a reward on offer.

Arguably more troubling is the use of punishments (or negative consequences) and its impact on young people. One study of close to one million

Texas public secondary school students found that when students are suspended or expelled, the likelihood that they will repeat a grade, not graduate or become involved in the juvenile justice system increases significantly (Fabelo et al. 2011). They also found that the same students were being suspended over and over again; that is, they found that 15% of students were suspended more than ten times during the course of their middle and high school years. Nonetheless, suspension and expulsion rates among schools varied significantly, even among those schools with similar student compositions and resources. Some schools are obviously doing something different, though the researchers did not explore this. Even more worryingly, black students were 31% more likely than white or Latino kids to be suspended or expelled for similar rule violations, while three-quarters of young people with diagnosed behaviour problems, such as Oppositional Defiant Disorder (ODD) and Attention-Deficit/Hyperactivity Disorder (ADHD), were more likely to be suspended or expelled at least once. Such data speaks to a system that is not working and is decidedly ineffective at managing challenging behaviour.

Motivating students

In this field, it is important to distinguish between intrinsic and extrinsic motivation (Deci & Ryan, 2000; Ryan & Deci, 2000a, 2000b). Intrinsic motivation is when a student engages in an activity out of genuine interest or pleasure. Conversely, someone is said to be extrinsically motivated when they engage in an activity for a particular reward or due to the pressure of others (Ryan & Deci, 2000a). In comparison to extrinsic motivation, intrinsic motivation is associated with deep learning, better performance and wellbeing (Deci & Ryan, 2000; Ryan & Deci, 2000a, 2000b). It has been argued that rewards encourage children to think about how they might please their teacher, rather than learning because they are inherently interested (Deci & Ryan, 2000).

Deci and Ryan (2008) described the three core components of intrinsic motivation: autonomy, competence and connectedness. When students are given autonomy over their learning, their intrinsic motivation improves, they persist longer and they learn at a deeper level (Yeager et al. 2014). They do not have to be forced or coerced in any way to do this, because they want to do learn it. Teachers wanting to promote students' autonomy can invite students to set their own learning goals to ensure that what is taught and learnt is personally meaningful.

Competence is when students feel capable of learning a particular subject. Though teachers need to have high expectations and challenge students in their learning, students also need to feel that they have the capacity and skills to meet these challenges. If students feel that they are competent, they are more likely to be motivated to learn (Deci & Ryan, 2000); conversely, if students feel that the learning tasks are outside of their abilities, they are more likely to give up (Boggiano, 1998). Teachers can promote competence by ensuring tasks are challenging but achievable (Bergin & Bergin, 2009). Giving formative feedback that is specific to the task can also provide scaffolding and cultivate competence.

Finally, in relation to promoting intrinsic motivation, students need to feel a connectedness or a sense of belonging with their teachers and peers (Deci & Ryan, 2000; Ryan & Deci, 2000a). When students feel that they belong, are cared for and develop meaningful relationships in a school setting, they learn better. The importance of belonging is especially important for minority students (Walton & Cohen, 2011).

However, the use of rewards might, on some occasions, promote autonomy. Drawing on Ryan and Deci's (2000a) argument that intrinsic motivation is based on autonomy, relatedness and competence, students' responses to rewards will vary, depending on how they value these rewards. Ryan and Deci (2000b, 2009) developed a continuum of motivational levels, from being completely unmotivated, for example, where the offered rewards do little to influence behaviour, through to intrinsic motivation which occurs when an individual engages in a task for the pure pleasure of doing so. Within these extreme ends of the continuum they include four different types of extrinsic motivation – external regulation, which is where an individual is motivated to satisfy some external demand or to achieve an external reward; introjection, where motivation is driven by wanting to avoid guilt or anxiety or to satisfy pride; identification, where an individual accepts the external reward as a part of one's own values and goals; and finally integration, which is driven by a desire to achieve an outcome separate from the activity itself. Ryan and Deci (2000b, p. 73) suggested that though integrated motivation shares many qualities with intrinsic motivation, it is still extrinsic because it is being "done to attain separate outcomes rather than for their inherent enjoyment".

Hence, within the context of different types of extrinsic motivations, rewards can be effective if they do not undermine students' feelings of autonomy and competence. Lin, McKeachie and Kim (2001) found that as long as students perceived rewards as being related to competence and self-determination, intrinsic motivation was not negatively impacted. Similarly, Cameron, Pierce, Banko and Gear (2005) found that if rewards are aligned with individuals' valued skills, the rewards are not seen as controlling and do not undermine intrinsic motivation.

Moreover, an individual may be both intrinsically and extrinsically motivated (Lepper, Corpus & Iyengar, 2005). For example, a student may be inherently interested in a subject and at the same time wanting a good grade. Indeed, Lepper, Corpus and Iyengar (2005) argued that it is adaptive for students to seek out activities that they find pleasurable while simultaneously paying attention to the consequences of those activities, such as a teacher's praise and attention. They suggested that

> Seeking only immediate enjoyment with no attention to external contingencies and constraints may substantially reduce a student's future outcomes

and opportunities. Conversely, attending only to extrinsic constraints and incentives can substantially undermine intrinsic interest and the enjoyment that can come from learning itself

(Lepper, Corpus & Iyengar, 2005, p. 191)

In sum, it can be counterproductive to provide extrinsic motivators or rewards to students who do not value them. Additionally, rewards that seek to control behaviour and undermine self-determination are ineffective as are rewards that cannot be sustained over time. These studies have direct implications for how we interpret students' lack of motivation. Rather than see students as lazy, instead we might look more closely at the reasons why they are "unmotivated". For example, is it because the student feels so overwhelmed, he or she does not know where to start (competence)? Or perhaps the task is not meaningful to them (autonomy)? Or is it because the learning does not relate to them (relatedness)? Instead of attributing blame to the child, we need to look at what is being asked of the student and how.

An approach based on mutual respect

Rather than doing things "on a child", the approach I am advocating here is to work with the child and on what his or her goals are and what they want to do. Their goals may not be related to educational success (as might be gleaned from high scores on exams) but may nonetheless still be accommodated within the constraints of the schooling system. This notion is probably best aligned with the Collaborative Problem-Solving Approach developed by Greene and Albon (2006; Greene, 2008), whose central tenet is that "children do well if they can". The Collaborative Problem-Solving Approach is an individualised, relational model that seeks to engage children in the process of learning to solve their own problems. It does this through the development of trusting, collaborative relationships between the child and important adults in his/her life.

As indicated earlier, most classroom management models have one thing in common – they seek to establish what the child's behaviour means for him or her and then try to address that. However, rather than sit at the back of a classroom with behavioural charts, I am suggesting we talk "with", not "to" students, and engage with them in an authentic conversation about their needs, wants and desires. Often students do not know why they are behaving as they do, or they may not see their behaviour as a problem. However, being open to these conversations and genuinely listening to students, and then together coming up with a collaborative plan of action, will make a difference to the way teachers respond and consequently the way young people react. Punishing a student does not address why he or she misbehaved in the first place. Instead, we need to see students as capable and developing people who have the capacity to work out what is best for them.

Vieno, Perkins, Smith and Santinello (2005) make the case that democratic practices, whereby various student voices are heard and considered, are critical to fostering student, class and school level belonging. Democratic school practices include student participation in determining classroom rules, the freedom for staff and students to express themselves and the perceived fairness of the rules (Vieno et al. 2005). A diverse range of voices needs to be heard, not only those who do well at school or are nominated by teachers (DeFur & Korinek, 2010; Vieno et al. 2005). Underlying a democratic approach is respect and due regard, if not admiration, for the individual standing in front of them. Some teachers and administrators consider that respect comes from being polite, using titles (i.e. Mr, Mrs,) and wearing the correct uniform. However, a child can call a teacher Mrs but inject it with heavy sarcasm and spite that in no way signifies a mutually respectful relationship.

When children start school, most are excited and want to be there; they do not start hating school or somehow want to be "bad". And that is the critical point. It is what happens afterwards that changes the child, namely, the school environment, the expectations placed on him or her and the subsequent interpretation of a child's response that describe or judge certain behaviours as challenging or problematic. Rather than see a child's behaviour as manipulative, disorderly, rowdy or attention-seeking, we need to reflect on what is instead driving that behaviour and work with the child on coming up with mutually agreeable solutions. Such a stance recognises that only students can really control or change their own behaviour. The teacher's task, then, is to demonstrate to students why they might behave in a certain way.

References

Baker, J. (2018). Rush to enrol in Lindfield learning revolution. *The Sydney Morning Herald*, July 13, 2018. Retrieved January 19, 2019, from www.smh.com.au/national/nsw/rush-to-enrol-in-lindfield-learning-revolution-20180706-p4zq0f.html

Bergin, C., & Bergin, D. (2009). Attachment in the classroom. *Educational Psychology Review*, 21(2), 141–170.

Boggiano, A. K. (1998). Maladaptive achievement patterns: A test of a diathesis-stress analysis of helplessness. *Journal of Personality and Social Psychology*, 74, 1681–1695.

Cameron, J., Pierce, W. D., Banko, K. M., & Gear, A. (2005). Achievement-based rewards and intrinsic motivation: A test of cognitive mediators. *Journal of Educational Psychology*, 97(4), 641–655.

Canter, L., & Canter, M. (1976). *Assertive Discipline: A take charge approach for today's educator*. Santa Monica, CA: Lee Canter & Associates.

Daily Times Monitor (2017). February 12, 2019. Retrieved January 19, 2019, from https://dailytimes.com.pk/29539/finland-will-become-the-first-country-in-the-world-to-get-rid-of-all-school-subjects/

Deci, E. L., & Ryan, R. M. (2000). The "what" and "why" of goal pursuits: Human needs and the self-determination of behavior. *Psychological Inquiry*, 11(4), 227–268.

Deci, E. L., & Ryan, R. M. (2008). Facilitating optimal motivation and psychological well-being across life's domains. *Canadian Psychology*, 49(1), 14–23.

DeFur, S. H., & Korinek, L. (2010). Listening to student voices. *The Clearing House: A Journal of Educational Strategies, Issues and Ideas, 83*(1), 15–19.

Fabelo, T., Thompson, M. D., Plotkin, M., Carmichael, D., Marchbanks, M. P., & Booth, E. A. (2011). *Breaking schools' rules: A state-wide study of how school discipline relates to students' success and juvenile justice involvement.* New York: Council of State Governments Justice Centre. Retrieved October 11, 2018, from http://csgjusticecenter.org/wp-content/uploads/2012/08/Breaking_Schools_Rules_Report_Final.pdf

Fugate, C. M., Zentall, S. Z., & Gentry, M. (2013). Creativity and working memory in gifted students with and without characteristics of attention deficit hyperactive disorder: Lifting the mask. *Gifted Child Quarterly, 57*(4), 234–246.

Gest, S. D., & Gest, J. M. (2005). Reading tutoring for students at academic and behaviorial risk: Effects on time-on-tasks in the classroom. *Education & Treatment of Children, 28*, 25–47.

Gillies, V. (2011). Social and emotional pedagogies: Critiquing the new orthodoxy of emotion in classroom behaviour management. *British Journal of Sociology of Education, 32*(2), 185–202.

Glasser, W. (1990). *The quality school.* New York: Harper Collins.

Glasser, W. (1998). *Choice Theory.* New York: HarperCollins.

Greene, R. W. (2008). *Lost at school: Why our kids with behavioral challenges are falling through the cracks and how we can help them.* New York: Scribner.

Greene, R. W., & Albon, J. S. (2006). *Treating explosive kids: The collaborative problem-solving approach.* New York: The Guilford Press.

Hanus, M. D., & Fox, J. (2018). Assessing the effects of gamification in the classroom: A longitudinal study on intrinsic motivation, social comparison, satisfaction, effort, and academic performance. *Computers & Education, 80*, 152–161.

Herner, T. (1998). *NASDE Counterpoint*, 2.

Kohn, A. (1993). *The trouble with gold stars, incentive plans, A's, praise, and other bribes.* Boston: Houghton Mifflin.

Landrum, T. J., Tankersley, M., & Kauffman, J. M. (2003). What is special about special education for students with emotional or behaviorial disorders? *Journal of Special Education, 37*(3), 148–156.

Lepper, M. R., Corpus, J. H., & Iyengar, S. S. (2005). Intrinsic and extrinsic motivational orientations in the classroom: Age differences and academic correlates. *Journal of Educational Psychology, 97*(2), 184–196.

Lewis, K. R. (2015). *What if everything you knew about disciplining kids was wrong?* Mother Jones. Retrieved January 19, 2019, from www.motherjones.com/politics/2015/07/schools-behavior-discipline-collaborative-proactive-solutions-ross-greene/

Lewis, T., & Sugai, G. (1999). Effective behaviour support: A systems approach to proactive schoolwide management. *Focus on Exceptional Children, 31*(6), 1–24.

Lin, Y.-G., McKeachie, W. J., & Kim, Y. C. (2001). College student intrinsic and/or extrinsic motivation and learning. *Learning and Individual Differences, 13*(3), 251–258.

Martella, R. C., & Marchand-Martella, N. E. (2015). Improving classroom behavior through effective instruction: An illustrative program example using SRA FLEX Literacy. *Education and Treatment of Children, 38*(2), 241–272.

Morgan, R. (2007). Foreword. In M. Stephenson (Ed.), *Young people and offending. Education, youth justice and social inclusion* (pp. xiii–xiv). Cullumpton, Devon: Willan.

Payne, L., Marks, L. J., & Bogan, B. L. (2007). Using curriculum-based assessment to address the academic and behavioral deficits of students with emotional and behavioral disorders. *Beyond Behavior, 16*(3), 3–6.

Pierce, M. E., Wechsler-Zimring, A., Noam, G., Wolf, M., & Tami Katzir, T. (2013). Behavioral problems and reading difficulties among language minority and monolingual urban elementary school students. *Reading Psychology, 34*(2), 182–205.

Reupert, A., & Woodcock, S. (2010). Success and near misses: Pre-service teachers' use, confidence and success in various classroom management strategies. *Teaching and Teacher Education, 26,* 1261–1268.

Reupert, A., & Woodcock, S. (2011). Canadian and Australian pre-service teachers' use, confidence and success in various behaviour management strategies. *International Journal of Educational Research, 50,* 271–281.

Reupert, A., & Woodcock, S. (2018). Creating engaging and motivating learning environments. In J. Allen, & S. White (Eds.), *Learning to teach in a new era* (pp. 309–334). Port Melbourne: Cambridge University Press.

Richmond, C. (2007). *Teach more, manage less: A minimalist approach to behaviour management.* Australia: Scholastic Press.

Ryan, R. M., & Deci, E. L. (2000a). Intrinsic and extrinsic motivations: Classic definitions and new directions. *Contemporary Educational Psychology, 25,* 54–67.

Ryan, R. M., & Deci, E. L. (2000b). Self-determination theory and the facilitation of intrinsic motivation, social development, and well-being. *American Psychologist, 55*(1), 68–78.

Ryan, R. M., & Deci, E. L. (2009). Promoting self-determined school engagement: Motivation, learning, and well-being. In K. R. Wentzel & A. Wigfield (Eds.), *Handbook of motivation at school* (pp. 171–195). New York, NY: Routledge.

Scott, T. M., Nelson, C. M., & Liaupsin, C. J. (2001). Effective instruction: The forgotten component in preventing school violence. *Education and Treatment of Children, 24*(3), 309–322.

Slavin, R. E. (2009). *Educational psychology: Theory and practice* (9th ed.). Upper Saddle River, NJ: Pearson.

Snow, P. C., Woodward, M., Mathis, M., & Powell. M. B. (2016). Language functioning, mental health and alexithymia in incarcerated young offenders. *International Journal of Speech-Language Pathology, 18*(1), 20–31.

Sugai, G. (2007). Promoting behavioral competence in schools: A commentary on exemplary practices. *Psychology in the Schools, 44*(1), 113–118.

Vieno, A., Perkins, D. D., Smith, T. M., & Santinello, M. (2005). Democratic school climate and sense of community in school: A multilevel analysis. *American Journal of Community Psychology, 36*(3–4), 327–341.

Walton, G. M., & Cohen, G. L. (2011). A brief social-belonging intervention improves academic and health outcomes of minority students. *Science, 331*(6023), 1447–1451.

Were, N. (2006). *Discipline: Guidance and counselling in schools.* Nairobi: Nehema Publishers.

Wilson, A. N. (2015). A critique of sociocultural values in PBIS. *Behavior Analysis in Practice, 8*(1), 92–94.

Wong, H. K., & Wong, R. T. (2005). *How to be an effective teacher: The first days of school.* Mountain View, CA: Harry K. Wong Publications.

Woodcock, S., & Reupert, A. (2013). Does training matter? Comparing the behaviour management strategies of pre-service teachers in a four year program and those in a one year program. *Asia-Pacific Journal of Teacher Education, 41*(1), 87–101.

Woodcock, S., & Reupert, A. (2017). A tale from three countries: The classroom management practices of pre-service teachers from Australia, Canada and the United Kingdom. *Teacher Development, 21*(5), 655–667.

Yeager, D. S., Henderson, M. D., Paunesku, D., Walton, G. M., D'Mello, S., Spitzer, B. J., & Duckworth, A. L. (2014). Boring but important: A self-transcendent purpose for learning fosters academic self-regulation. *Journal of Personality and Social Psychology, 107*(4), 559.

Chapter 7

Teaching and learning

Pedagogical practices and curriculum decisions are required that promote student wellbeing as well as academic learning. There is a plethora of literature on how to be an effective teacher, and some of this will be reviewed here. There is comparatively less research on the effective, evidence based teaching and learning pedagogies that can be used to promote young people's mental health and wellbeing. This chapter will describe those teaching and learning strategies that simultaneously promote students' mental health, wellbeing and academic learning. How mental health promotion can and should be embedded in what and how we teach, for all teachers, regardless of their subject matter or year level, is also presented. Undoubtedly, the quality of teaching and learning has a significant impact on students' wellbeing. Even if unintentionally, teacher actions will inevitably influence how young people feel about themselves. Hence, a positive teaching and learning environment will promote academic learning, adaptive behaviour and student wellbeing, resulting in synergistic progress in all of these areas.

There are several ways that teachers might promote both academic learning and students' wellbeing in their teaching practices, and each of these will be covered here:

- Pedagogy – the instructional strategies employed by excellent teachers
- Feedback and assessment strategies
- Teaching specific mental health topics and issues
- Explicitly teaching social and emotional competencies
- Teachers as role models.

How excellent teachers teach

The notion of who is an excellent teacher and what he or she does is contentious and relies on whose definition of excellence is being applied. Nonetheless, most of the work in this area investigates the pedagogical actions undertaken by teachers whose students perform academically well at school. John Hattie's (2003) synthesis of 800 meta-analyses related to student achievement is influential in this area. Rather than focusing on social and emotional wellbeing, Hattie (2003) unapologetically identifies those school, student, teacher and home factors that promote academic success. By doing so, he does not imply that other outcomes, such as student wellbeing, are not important, nor does he diminish the interrelationship between academic progress and self-confidence. Instead, he focuses on academic success as one measure of schooling. Nonetheless, while pertaining to academic success, these pedagogies are still relevant when promoting young people's wellbeing.

Hattie (2003, 2009) established that although students' abilities and aptitudes make up approximately 50% of the variance in academic achievement, teacher factors account for 30% (with the remaining dependent on peer influence (5–10%), schools including the principal around 5–10% and home 5–10%). He summarises that

> it is what teachers know, do and care about which is very powerful in this learning equation ... the person who puts into place the end effects of so many policies, who interprets these policies and who is alone with students during their 15.000 hours of schooling.
>
> (Hattie, 2003, pp. 2–3)

As stated earlier, his work has primarily focused on identifying teacher actions that have the most powerful impact on academic achievement – but not student wellbeing.

Hattie (2012) identified five actions that an expert or excellent teacher does to promote academic achievement (see Table 7.1). At the same time however, and as can be seen in Table 7.1, these actions have direct and implicit implications for the development of students' social and emotional capacities and their confidence and self-efficacy as learners.

Thus, a positive school culture is one where mistakes are not regarded as failures but instead as opportunities for learning – for both students and teachers. Effective pedagogical practices ensure that all students are given opportunities to be successful, while also being held to high academic standards. In sum, an excellent teacher promotes both academic learning and the mental health and wellbeing of students by having clearly defined learning goals and teaching strategies that promote student success. By continually monitoring the impact of these strategies on students' learning, teachers are able to identify and subsequently support students who are finding the work difficult.

Thus, being an "expert" teacher means inadvertently, if not intentionally, attending to students' mental health and wellbeing. One common teaching strategy highlighted in Hattie's work is the use of group work. How group work might be employed demonstrates how supporting students' academic success and wellbeing can occur simultaneously. It is not uncommon for teachers to provide group projects or ask students to work with their peers during class time towards a common goal. However, the interpersonal skills

Table 7.1 Implications of expert teachers' actions on student wellbeing and social and emotional development

Expert teacher actions (Hattie, 2012)	Implications for teachers' practice	Impact on student wellbeing and social and emotional development
Identify essential representations about the subject they are teaching	• Makes connections between the students' prior learning and new content; this means teachers need to know who their students are and their cultural as well as learning background • Can sequence information in meaningful and appropriate ways and predict what needs to happen next for students to best learn • Can predict what types of errors students might make when problem solving and teach accordingly • Responsive to the needs and interests of students while also keeping the lesson on track • Uses data to understand individual student (as opposed to whole of class) needs	• Feel that they belong in the classroom/school • Mastery of subject matter, thereby promoting self-confidence and efficacy
Creates an optimal classroom climate for learning	• Embraces the learning process and works with and does not avoid mistakes and stuck points • Increases opportunity to provide feedback to students • Invites students to ask questions and holds genuine discussions • Embraces and does not avoid the learning process, including making mistakes and being stuck or bogged down • Flexible and responsive to the needs of the learning environment, especially around students' needs	• Learn that feedback is not punitive but part of the learning process • Has the opportunity to listen and respond to feedback • Learn that errors are part of the learning process and not to be avoided or feared

(Continued)

Table 7.1 (Continued)

Expert teacher actions (Hattie, 2012)	Implications for teachers' practice	Impact on student wellbeing and social and emotional development
Monitors student learning and provides feedback	• Anticipates and prevents disturbances that might occur when students lose interest or are not understanding • Provides timely, responsive feedback to students on their learning progress • Applies and then evaluates different strategies to ascertain the effectiveness of his or her teaching	• Student receives feedback on academic progress **and** social and emotional development and understands that both are valued and require practice and development • Students who are struggling are identified and provided with effective, timely support
Attends to students' and their own emotions	• Demonstrates care and commitment to all students • Passionate about teaching and learning • Manages and models self-care • Appreciates and pays attention to appropriate student–teacher boundaries	• Sense of belonging and being cared for
Actively strives to influence student outcomes	• As well as academic goals, aims to enhance students' self-efficacy about learning • Provides challenging goals and tasks • Promotes "deep and conceptual understandings … developing multiple learning strategies" (Hattie, 2012, p. 32)	• Self-efficacy as a learner when meeting challenging goals

involved in working with groups is not intuitive for many children. Each of the skills involved in being able to be a part of a successful team or group may need to be taught and rehearsed. According to Johnson and Johnson (1990, p. 29), "simply placing students in groups and telling them to work together does not produce cooperation". Working in a group requires various social skills, including turn taking, listening and giving and receiving feedback and resolving conflict. Yoder (2014) suggested that effective cooperative learning is characterised by:

- Individual accountability – where students have their own individual challenges
- Positive interdependence – where students have to rely on others to find information
- Promoting one another's successes – where students acknowledge and celebrate the successes of others rather than working competitively
- Group processing – where the group needs to meet and discuss how to progress towards a certain goal.

Given this extensive list of skills, before the opportunity to practice group work is provided, teachers may need to actively teach, model and reinforce the various social and emotional skills required for productive group work. Extrapolating further, teachers might, for example, discuss the need to take turns or not dominate group conversations and how they might build on each other's ideas (Webb, 2013). Additionally, students may need to be prompted and taught to be assertive, probe each other's thinking and respond constructively to disagreements (Webb, 2013).

Another important pedagogical concept for teachers is scaffolding, which involves educators making informed decisions that build on children's existing knowledge, capacities and skills and, perhaps more importantly, looking forward to what they need to develop and learn. Scaffolding is also an important consideration for the teaching of social and emotional competencies. For example, scaffolding may be used to model the language of social interactions using puppets to reflect on children's understandings of acceptable ways of responding to a range of everyday scenarios. Intentional teaching in this sense requires educators to be deliberate, informed and thoughtful in their decisions and actions about what skills they teach and how. They need to be responsive to children as agents for their own learning and consider when it is appropriate to follow the child's lead, to work collaboratively in partnership with the child and when to lead the child to discover new knowledge and understanding.

There are many other ways that teachers, at all levels and subject areas, can promote children's mental health and the development of numerous social and emotional skills when teaching academic topics, as detailed further below.

Feedback and assessment

Usually, students respond to a question raised by a teacher when they are reasonably confident that they can respond correctly. Unfortunately, responding in this manner only shows that they have already learnt the answer and have no need for further learning. In such an environment, "errors, and learning from them, are rarely welcomed" (Hattie & Timperley, 2007, p. 101). Nonetheless, it has often been said that learning is all about making mistakes, which inevitably means obtaining feedback that conveys that message. At the same time, constantly receiving negative feedback does little for either learning or self-confidence and can impact adversely on student–teacher relationships. Though delivering feedback is at the heart of good teaching, it is critical that teachers do this in ways that promote both academic learning and student wellbeing.

Assessment scores are one way of giving students feedback on their performance. The value of assessment in promoting academic success is questionable to say the least and may not be positive for mental health either. In their review of over 500 studies, Black and Wiliam (1998, p. 17) concluded that traditional assessment practices

> encourages superficial and rote learning, concentrating on recall of isolated details, usually items of knowledge which pupils soon forget . . . teachers do not generally review the assessment questions that they use and do not discuss them critically with peers, so there is little reflection on what is being assessed.
>
> (p. 17)

Rarely do test scores provide feedback to students on what they are doing, how they going or what skills they may need to improve or further develop. While assessments are a necessity in this accountability and high stakes era, a test score alone requires further scaffolding to be meaningful to students (and teachers). Giving students feedback on what they are doing and how they might improve is an essential step in the assessment process. Hence, giving and receiving feedback is a critical teaching and learning skill that impacts profoundly on students' academic learning as well as students' wellbeing and can influence the development of students' social and emotional skills.

Hattie and Timperley (2007) developed a three-phase model for student feedback which can be applied to academic learning as well as the development of other areas associated with social and emotional competence. These three steps include:

- Where am I going? (What are the goals?)
- How am I going? (What progress is being made toward the goal?)
- Where to next? (What do I need to do to make better progress?)

Their three-phase process serves to reduce potential discrepancies between students' current understanding, their performance and their learning goals, and allows them to learn new concepts and strategies for learning. This process also provides students with clear guidance as to what they have done and where they need to go, with suggestions for future learning. Rather than sending a test score that might present an implicit message that they are "wrong" or "right", this three-step process provides concrete guidance about what students need to do and hence can promote mastery and self-efficacy. Used in this way, feedback can be an effective instructional tool to promote learning and give students the confidence to continue.

The three-step feedback process also supports the development of self-awareness (by becoming aware of one's thinking process), which Veenman, Kok and Blote (2005) argue is critical to children's academic development. According to Hamre and Pianta (2005), prompting students to think about their thinking (meta-cognition) can extend students' language skills, which in turn is associated with achievement success (Hamre & Pianta, 2005). Moreover, encouraging students to think about their thinking is an evidence-based strategy that can be used to treat dysfunctional thought processes such as worrying and rumination (having the same thought over and over) or dysfunctional beliefs about oneself and the world e.g. I can't stand it when I don't do well on my spelling test (Kühne, Meister, Jansen, Härter, Moritz & Kriston, 2017). Thus, prompts to think about their thinking can be generalised to thinking about better ways of managing mental health and wellbeing. Accordingly, strategies that encourage meta-cognition in children such as those used in Hattie and Timperley's (2007) three-step feedback process may yield both academic and mental health benefits.

The three-step process has other potential social and emotional benefits. For example, in the "how am I going" phase, students might be invited to reflect on their use of particular social and emotional skill, such as the way they are solving problems or contributions to group work, and consider how these might be improved. In the "where to next" phase, students might consider what emotional and social skills they used successfully (e.g. persistence or asking for help) and what they may need to further develop if they were to do the activity again. Teacher feedback might be specifically directed to students' social and emotional competencies, for example how they emotionally approached certain challenging or stressful tasks. Though all teachers can provide this feedback, the specific manner will vary depending on the context, age and cultural background of child.

Teachers will also need to consider how to manage students who struggle with school work and score poorly on assessments. Reflecting on whether teaching practices need to change to better accommodate students will be necessary, along with appropriate intervention support as required. Overall, students do not need to be told repeatedly that they are wrong and the work they produce is not up to standard. Such feedback has minimal positive effect on learning and may instead adversely and irreparably impact students' confidence and self-esteem. In these cases, further (and usually different) instruction and information, and/or more intensive, individualised support, are more effective than negative feedback, especially for students with low confidence (Kulhavy, 1977).

The intertwined nature between academic success and wellbeing is clear, especially when observing the experiences of those who struggle academically. Previous academic success fosters high academic self-concept and, conversely, high academic self-concept fosters academic success. The reverse is also true, in that academic failure breeds self-doubt, and self-doubt impacts a child's motivation and ability. The negative spiral between self-concept and academic success means that young people who do not perform well academically are likely to develop a poor academic self-concept, which in turn impacts adversely on academic performance, motivation and attitude to school (Marsh & Martin, 2011).

Mental health topics

Teachers across all year levels are in a position to teach specific mental health and wellbeing topics. Primary school and early childhood teachers might use a social and emotional lens as part of what they are teaching, for example, when discussing books or teaching history. Topics such as problem solving, emotional identification and empathy may be raised in this way and further elaborated on. Kassem (2002) described how children's literature can be used as a means of teaching various social and emotional skills, including but not limited to those books and poetry that explicitly identify emotions. She described how the book, *When Sophie Gets Angry – Really, Really Angry*, a picture book written by Molly Bang (1999), might provide a means to encourage discussion in the classroom about anger and how to resolve it.

For secondary teachers, there are numerous topics that teachers can purposefully teach, such as depression, anxiety, bullying and so on. This is easier in some subjects than others. For example, health and physical education teachers might cover topics related to drug education and sexuality. In these discussions, they may discuss topics related to peer group pressure and respectful relationships. A senior literature teacher might use the fiction book, *Saving Francesca* by Melina Marchetta (2003) to raise and discuss issues regarding how young people might cope with a parent with depression. Given that one in five young people grow up with a parent with a mental illness (Maybery, Reupert, Patrick, Goodyear & Crase, 2009), it is possible that in a class of 25, five students will be living with a parent experiencing mental illness. The national COPMI initiative (children of parents with a mental illness) provides further ideas regarding activities for teachers to use with this book, that aim to increase students' understanding of mental illness, reduce stigma and increase help-seeking behaviour (see www.copmi.net.au/images/pdf/saving-francesca.pdf). In particular, instructions on how the text might be used to generate class discussions in a safe, protective way (e.g. ensuring class discussions do not focus on personal experiences), the type of language to use and how to encourage young people to support each other are included.

Teaching social and emotional skills

Social emotional learning, or SEL, is the process of acquiring the competencies to recognise and manage emotions, persevere, develop empathy, establish positive relationships with peers and adults, make responsible decisions and handle challenging situations effectively (Elias, 2006). There are many social and emotional skills or competencies that teachers can intentionally teach, and many of these are related not only to living a more fulfilling life (such as resolving conflict or the ability to make friends) but also to learning how to learn, such as time management and problem solving.

The Collaborative for Academic, Social, and Emotional Learning (CASEL; www.casel.org) is based at the University of Illinois at Chicago and is a world leader in this area. CASEL identified five core competencies associated with SEL: self-awareness, self-management, social awareness, relationship management and responsible decision making (Zins et al. 2004). The competencies related to these five dimensions are as follows:

- **Self-awareness**: accurately assessing one's feelings, strengths, values and behaviours, including a sense of well-grounded confidence and optimism
- **Social awareness**: taking the perspective of others, ability to empathise with others, appreciation and respect of diverse cultural backgrounds, understanding of community norms for behaviour
- **Responsible decision making**: identifying and analysing problems, making constructive and helpful decisions, appreciating the consequences of behaviour and consideration of wellbeing of oneself and others
- **Self-management**: emotional regulation, managing stress, controlling impulses, setting personal and academic goals
- **Relationship skills**: establishing and maintaining healthy functional relationships with peers and adults, communicating clearly and listening, cooperating and resisting pressure, managing conflict and seeking help.

It is these skills that need to be taught, practiced and celebrated, in an explicit, purposeful manner, but also integrated into daily interactions and teaching practices.

Activities to promote social and emotional competence can be infused in curriculum teaching. For example, whether it is a problem related to a peer group or a challenging maths problem, children of all ages will face problems and challenges that they need to overcome. How they interpret these problems, generate and consider alternative solutions, engage in planning and reflect on the consequences of potential solutions may provide a template for how they might then approach and resolve other problems they face. This means that instead of getting frustrated or giving up, young people with effective problem-solving skills will regulate their emotions, persist and think creatively. All of these skills can be applied to learning challenges as well as other issues that may arise as children but also as adults. Likewise, Waters (2017, p. 8) convincingly argued that teachers can promote social and emotional competence while also teaching academic content:

> consider the maths teacher who strategically uses a challenging maths problem to help students understand their emotions (e.g. fear, uncertainty, excitement, curiosity), to help them bounce back when they make a mistake (e.g. resilience) . . . determines whether they believe that they can work through the problem or give up . . . consider the drama teacher who helps students find moments of flow on stage, to experience the satisfaction of mastering a difficult line, to develop oration skills and self-confidence.

Purposefully teaching social and emotional skills

Students will learn social and emotional skills in a manner similar to the way they learn other skills, by observing others, including school staff, and practising and applying these skills in activities in and outside of the classroom. Again, similar to learning varoius academic skills, a developmental approach is required so that children can learn to address increasingly complex situations after first acquiring relatively more foundational skills. Thus, a developmental progression is necessary where certain social, emotional and cognitive skills need to be acquired before others, just like in reading and writing, where foundational skills are required before tackling more complex texts. Ideally, planned, ongoing and coordinated instruction in social and emotional skills should begin in early childhood settings and continue through to high school.

Teachers can actively and purposefully teach specific social and emotional skills. One teaching example taken from the Intervention Program for the Social Skills Improvement System (SSIS) (DiPerna, Lei, Bellinger & Cheng, 2015) is outlined below. The model below is presented as one model of a practice-based scenario, where the steps are supported by a context and the actions of the teacher and the practice steps are positioned within meaningful contexts.

Tell

- Introduce the specific social or emotional skill
- Define it
- Discuss why it is important
- Outline the steps involved in undertaking this particular behaviour.

Show

- Model this particular behaviour (both positive and negative)
- Model each of the components of the behaviour
- Direct a role play of a typical situation (with a helper)
- Discuss the role play and the behaviour.

Do

- Ask children to define the skill
- Ask children to explain the steps required to enact the behaviour
- Ask children why the behaviour is important
- Repeat the steps needed to enact the behaviour
- Ask children to model the behaviour in role plays
- Ask other children to provide feedback on the role plays.

Practice (in meaningful contexts)

- Review and apply the skill in role plays
- Have pairs or small groups of children practice the skill and provide feedback to each other
- Encourage use of the targeted behaviour in other contexts.

Monitor progress

- Ask children to consider how well they are going with this particular behaviour.

Another framework comes from Durlak et al. (2011) in their review of evidence-based programs in this area, who generated a framework for how SEL skills need to be taught, using the acronym of SAFE:

- **S**equenced activities to teach skills
- **A**ctive forms of learning, practice and engagement
- **F**ocused time and attention on skill development
- **E**xplicit targeting of social and emotional skills.

There are other, similar, purposeful teaching strategies that teachers may employ through the course of the day, such as explaining, identifying, instructing, listening, making connections, modelling, negotiating and providing choices, questioning and so on (Fox & Lentini, 2006). These are all similar approaches that make clear the approach teachers might employ when teaching social and emotional skills.

Social and emotional learning programs

In schools, formal social and emotional learning programs (as outlined in Chapter 3) are designed to promote social and emotional skills in a systematic and comprehensive manner. School-wide social and emotional policies and curricula are typically implemented with the broad aim of fostering various social and emotional skills (in students and staff) as well as the promotion of caring relationships between teachers and students, conflict reduction among students and a sense of school safety (Zins et al. 2004). Accordingly, the teaching of SEL should not soley driven by individual teachers, but offered and integrated as a whole school approach to creating positive, caring and safe schools. Ideally, social and emotional skills learnt should be reinforced in a variety of contexts, namely school, home and community. All children, regardless of their background, benefit from some exposure to SEL. As promoted by CASEL and others (Zins et al. 2004), SEL programs should have a universal prevention and promotion focus, so that children's behaviour and emotional problems are prevented through the active promotion and teaching of SEL.

Durlak et al. (2011), in a review of more than 200 school-based universal social and emotional learning programs, found that those students who participated in evidence-based social and emotional learning programs demonstrated significant improvements in social and emotional skills, behaviour and attitudes, as well as in academic performance. A follow-up study found that benefits were sustained for an average of 3.75 years after participation (Taylor et al. 2017). Such programs have been found to be effective for students, regardless of race, ethnic or socio-economic background (Taylor et al. 2017).

Guides to selecting programs

As outlined in Chapter 3, there are many programs that schools might employ when promoting children's social and emotional competencies. There are several guides that have been developed for schools to apply when selecting a SEL (or other wellbeing) program or intervention. These guides provide an overview of program targets (e.g. age of children) and its aims, delivery details and evidence base:

- Early Intervention Foundation guidebook: http://guidebook.eif.org.uk/
- Kidsmatter: Australian Primary Schools Mental Health Initiative: www.kidsmatter.edu.au/primary/resources-for-schools/other-resources/programs-guide/programs
- The CASEL Guide (2012): https://casel.org/guide/
- Blueprints for Healthy Youth Development website: www.blueprintsprograms.org/.

In addition, when considering a program, the following questions may assist in deciding what program to use, who should be involved and how and when it might be delivered.

The setting

- How well known are the needs and strengths of this particular setting? Is there a shared understanding of these needs and strengths among stakeholders?
- What is already in place? How is that program received by staff, students and the community? What remaining gaps are there?
- What is the commitment of staff to work in this area? What is their readiness to change or to learn something new? How much time and effort are they prepared to provide to any new initiative?
- Who (or what team) will drive the initiative and be responsible for its implementation? What support is there for these individuals (time and money)?

Features of the program/approach

- Is the program based on sound theory?
- What are the goals of the program? Do these goals match the needs and strengths of the setting? Target group? Scope?
- Does the program have a rigorous evidence-base?
    - Has the program been used in similar school environments and communities? What was the impact? With whom does it appear to be most/least effective?
    - What is the impact of the program on academic success? On wellbeing?
- How much will it cost? In money, time and commitment?
- Are there specialised training requirements? Has the professional development for staff been evaluated? Is there any long-term, ongoing professional development required/provided?
- Is the program easily integrated with existing school practices?
- Will school staff be able to implement it as recommended or will modifications in time and resourcing be an issue?
- Does the program involve family and community partnerships?
- What are the implications of the program on school policy?
- What are the implications of the program for discipline and classroom management procedures?
- How sustainable is the program in this particular setting with this particular community?
- How will the school monitor and evaluate the impact of the program? Does the program include evaluation tools and suggestions as part of the approach? What will the program be evaluated against? Is there a benchmark that can be compared to? When will the program be evaluated, why, by whom and how often?

Program content

- Does it explicitly include the teaching of various social and emotional skills? For all students? For at-risk students? Does the program fit the school profile? What efforts are made to generalise learnings outside of the classroom into the community, playgrounds and at home?
- Does the program consider school climate, including relationships between and within students, teachers, caregivers and others in the community?
- Are engaging and effective teaching and learning practices incorporated, for example cooperative group work and feedback processes?
- Is the program developmentally and culturally inclusive?

When selecting a program, it is important to be mindful that there is no one approach or model that will address all the needs of any given context. Nonetheless, chopping and joining different programs together may not bode well for how the program should run or its intended benefits. Zins and Elias (2006) reported that ensuring fidelity of SEL programs leads to better outcomes, while poor fidelity results in decreased effectiveness. Though any uptake of formal programs will inevitably led to adaptations, Zins and Elias (2006) suggest that staff need to anticipate and plan for modifications needed to improve outcomes in a particular context, and at the same time maintain core program elements, or what is known as "evidence based kernels" (Embry & Biglan, 2008, p. 75).

Criticisms of social and emotional learning programs

There are several detractors of the teaching of social and emotional skills, primarily because most (if not all) SEL programs are based on Western cultural norms. The questions here pertain to who decides what competencies are worth emulating and how these should be best taught. Complicit in these arguments is the questionable view of a single model of emotional and social competency that is valid across all cultures (Kristjansson, 2006) and the manner in which formalised SEL programs promulgate a centralist view of how we expect students to behave and express their emotions. As found repeatedly in cross-cultural studies, norms, beliefs and values regarding emotional expression and social skills, such as shyness, aggression and cooperation, are highly dependent on culture (Chao, 1995; Chen & French, 2008; Kristjansson, 2006; Raver, 2004), and what is considered to be important and competent behaviour in one culture may not be in others. This presents challenges when deciding what social and emotional skills to teach, and how, especially when it comes to generalising skills across school, home and the community.

Hoffman (2009) builds on these criticisms when she argued that many SEL programs focus on what some consider to be students' individual deficits and, moreover, draws attention away from what teachers might be doing differently in terms of relationship building. She continued by asking more broadly

> what the consequences are for human relationships when the focus is on behavioral and cognitive skills and when emotion is valued as a means to success rather than as a good in itself. Unless a parallel emphasis is placed on the qualities of relationship that arguably should contextualize skills and behaviors, the discourse risks promoting a shallow, decontextualized, and narrowly instrumentalist approach to emotion in classrooms that promotes measurability and efficiency at the expense of (non-quantifiable) qualities of relatedness.
>
> (Hoffman, 2009, p. 539)

Thus, SEL programs and curriculum should not be delivered in isolation (as some of the commercially available programs appear to do). Instead, when deciding on a SEL approach, full consideration of the child and his or her cultural background, interests, strengths and vulnerabilities is required, with due regard to the relationships children currently have, and require from their school. Moreover, in the early years of schooling in particular, a focus on intentional teaching should not preclude opportunities for play and incidental learning in regard to managing emotions. Similarly, all children, regardless of their age, need to be actively involved in the learning process and acquisition of social and emotional skills. Teachers need to consider how each child's agency and autonomy may be promoted, so that children are able to make choices and decisions that influence events around them. It is in this way that children's values, interests, strengths and capabilities should be considered the vehicle to building social and emotional competence. Ensuring that a range and balance of pedagogies are used over time maximises opportunities for children to learn in ways that motivate and engage them, are active and creative, promote decision making and enhance their perceptions of themselves as capable, competent learners.

Teachers as role models

Teachers cannot teach students to develop social and emotional skills that they do not possess themselves. Accordingly, they need to demonstrate and model to students how they appropriately manage stress, regulate their emotions and interact positively and respectfully with students, parents and colleagues. According to Jennings and Greenberg (2009), teachers' social and emotional competence establishes a cyclical process that, when positive, results in better outcomes for students and themselves but, when negative, results in burnout. They assert that teachers with strong social and emotional competence have better relationships with students, more effective classroom management strategies and more successfully promote social and emotional competence in their students.

Thus, in addition to having the skills to teach social and emotional skills, teachers need to "practice what they preach" or, perhaps more precisely, "practice what they teach" (Reupert, Hemmings & Connors, 2010). Modelling is embedded in interpersonal interactions and is shown in different ways for teachers and students. It can be explicit and planned, such as when problem solving and scaffolding learning, and by the teacher "thinking out loud" as they go through the skill they are modelling. Modelling can also be spontaneous, such as a student overhearing or observing an interaction between staff, between a teacher and caregiver or between a teacher and another student. Teachers need to be aware that they are role models to students, even if that is not their intention. Thorsborne (2013, p. 49) urged school staff to "take the lead and change their behaviour first". Worryingly, however, in one Candian primary school, Reimer (2018) found stark inconsistencies in how conflict resolution was taught to students compared to how conflict was enacted by and among staff members. Some staff spoke out against this hypocrisy and in the words of one of the teachers interviewed,

> The kids see it and they see, like, well, they do it. You know, [a teacher] is mean to [another teacher] and she's allowed to do it. And she doesn't get in trouble for it. So why do I have to be nice? And kids will say that.
> (Reimer, 2018, p. 66)

Conversely, when students saw teachers manage conflict appropriately, they would take this on board, as another teacher further explained: "If it becomes a part of us, it will become a part of the kids" (Reimer, 2018, p. 8). Though the focus on children's social and emotional competence is crucial, it must be seen within the wider relational context of the relationships between school staff and leaders.

References

Bang, M. (1999). *When Sophie gets angry – really, really angry*. Melbourne: Scholastic Press.

Black, P., & Wiliam, D. (1998). Assessment and classroom learning. *Assessment in Education*, 5(1), 7–75.

Chao, R. K. (1995). Chinese and European American cultural models of the self-reflected in mothers' childrearing beliefs. *Ethos*, 23(3), 328–354.

Chen, X., & French, D. C. (2008). Children's social competence in cultural context. *Annual Review of Psychology*, 59, 591–616.

DiPerna, J., Lei, P., Bellinger, J., & Cheng, W. (2015). *Efficacy of the social skills improvement system – classwide intervention program (SSIS-CIP) in the primary grades*. SREE Spring 2014 Conference. Retrieved January 20, 2019, from https://files.eric.ed.gov/fulltext/ED562704.pdf

Durlak, J. A., Weissberg, R. P., Dymnicki, A. B., Taylor, R. D., & Schellinger, K. (2011). The impact of enhancing students' social and emotional learning: A meta-analysis of school based universal interventions. *Child Development*, 82(1), 474–501.

Elias, M. J. (2006). The connection between academic and social-emotional learning. In M. J. Elias, & H. Arnold (Eds.), *The educator's guide to emotional intelligence and academic achievement* (pp. 4–14). Thousand Oaks, CA: Corwin Press.

Embry, D. D., & Biglan, A. (2008). Evidence-based kernels: Fundamental units of behavioral influence. *Clinical Child & Family Psychological Review, 11*, 75–113.

Fox, L., & Lentini, R. (2006). "You've got it!" Teaching social and emotional skills. *Young Children, 61*(6), 36–42.

Hamre, B. K., & Pianta, R. C. (2005). Can instructional and emotional support in the first grade classroom make a difference for children at risk of school failure? *Child Development, 76*(5), 949–967.

Hattie, J. (2003). *Teachers make a difference: What is the research evidence?* Paper presented at the Building Teacher Quality: What does the research tell us ACER Research Conference, Melbourne, Australia. Retrieved January 20, 2019, from http://research.acer.edu.au/research_conference_2003/4/

Hattie, J., & Timperley, H. (2007). The power of feedback. *Review of Educational Research, 77*(1), 81–112.

Hattie, J. (2009). *Visible learning: A synthesis of meta-analyses relating to achievement.* London: Routledge.

Hattie, J. (2012). *Visible learning for teachers: Maximizing impact on learning.* London: Routledge.

Hoffman, D. (2009). Reflecting on social emotional learning. A critique perspective on trends in the United States. *Review of Educational Research, 79*(2), 533–556.

Jennings, P. A., & Greenberg, M. T. (2009). The prosocial classroom: Teacher social and emotional competence in relation to student and classroom outcomes. *Review of Educational Research, 79*(1), 491–525.

Johnson, D., & Johnson, R. (1990). Social skills for successful group work. *Educational Leadership, 47*(4), 29–33.

Kassem, C. L. (2002). Developing the teaching professional: What teacher educators need to know about emotions. *Teacher Development, 6*(3), 363–372.

Kristjansson, K. (2006). "Emotional intelligence" in the classroom? An Aristotelian critique. *Educational Theory, 56*(1), 39–56.

Kühne, F., Meister, R, Jansen, A., Härter, M., Moritz, S., & Kriston, L. (2017). Effectiveness of metacognitive interventions for mental disorders in adults: A systematic review protocol (METACOG). *BMJ Open, 7*, e015428.

Kulhavy, R. W. (1977). Feedback in written instruction. *Review of Educational Research, 47*(1), 211–232.

Marchetta, M. (2003*). Saving Francesca.* Camberwell, Victoria: Penguin.

Marsh, H. W., & Martin, A. J. (2011). Academic self-concept and academic achievement: Relations and causal ordering. *British Journal of Educational Psychology, 81*(1), 59–77.

Maybery, D., Reupert, A., Patrick, K., Goodyear, M., & Crase, L. (2009). Prevalence of children whose parents have a mental illness. *Psychiatric Bulletin, 33*(1), 22–26.

Reimer, K. (2018). The kids do a better job of it than we do: A Canadian case study of teachers addressing the hypocritical application of restorative justice in their school. *The Australian Educational Researcher, 46*, 59–73.

Reupert, A., Hemmings, B., & Connors, J. (2010). Do we practice what we preach? The teaching practices of inclusive educators in tertiary settings. *International Journal of Teaching and Learning in Higher Education, 22*(2), 120–130.

Taylor, R. D., Oberle, E., Durlak, J. A., & Weissberg, R. P. (2017). Promoting positive youth development through school-based social and emotional learning interventions: A meta-analysis of follow up effects. *Child Development, 88*(4), 1156–1171.

Thorsborne, M. (2013). A story of the emergence of restorative practice in schools in Australia and New Zealand: Reflect, repair, reconnect. In K. S. van Wormer, & L. Walker (Eds.), *Restorative justice today: Practical applications* (pp. 43–51). Thousand Oaks, CA: Sage.

Raver, C. C. (2004). Placing emotional self-regulation in sociocultural and socioeconomic contexts. *Child Development, 75*(2), 346–353.

Veenman, M.V. J., Kok, R., & Blote, A.W. (2005). The relation between intellectual and metacognitive skills in early adolescence. *Instructional Science, 33*, 193–211.

Waters, L. (2017). Visible wellbeing in schools: The powerful role of instructional leadership. *The Australian Educational Leader, 39*(1), 6–10.

Webb, N. (2013). Collaboration in the classroom. In J. Hattie, & E. Anderman (Eds.), *International guide to student achievement* (pp. 207–210). London: Routledge.

Yoder, N. (2014). *Teaching the whole child. Instructional practices that support social-emotional learning in three teacher evaluation frameworks.* Center on Great Teachers & Leaders. American Institutes for Research. Retrieved January 21, 2019, from https://gtlcenter.org/sites/default/files/TeachingtheWholeChild.pdf

Zins, J. E., & Elias, M. J. (2006). Social and emotional learning. In G. G. Bear, & K. M. Minke (Eds.), *Children's needs III* (pp. 1–13). Bethesda, MD: NASP.

Zins, J. E., Weissberg, R. P., Wang, M. C., & Walberg, H. J. (Eds.). (2004). *Building academic success on social and emotional learning: What does the research say?* New York: Teachers College Press.

Chapter 8

Partnerships

In schools, an ntegration of students' academic learning and mental health and wellbeing necessitates the involvement of multiple stakeholders. Reliance on any one institution to support young people's mental health and learning is neither sustainable nor effective. Indeed, relying on schools alone to support children's learning and wellbeing competencies does not align with an ecological model of prevention and early intervention, which sees young people impacted by their family and the community in which they live. A partnership approach will ensure that young people's functioning across school, home and the community is improved. Moreover, working in partnership with agencies and others in the community can coordinate sparse resources and staff expertise and reduce costs, thereby strengthening the ability of schools to provide support to all young people and their families. Different strengths and skills can then be brought into the school to contribute in ways that existing staff might not have the expertise, time or resources to provide. Along with improved access to services and supports, effective school partnerships can help to navigate within and between systems to find innovative solutions for students and families.

This chapter will outline the ways in which schools might partner with others when promoting children's mental health, wellbeing and academic achievement. Potential partnerships may occur with any one or more combinations of families, children and youth, professional and community services and policy makers. Partnerships may vary in duration and intensity depending on the goals of the partnership and who is involved. There are several processes that can be employed to identify and manage partnerships that promote young people's wellbeing and academic success. Each of these partnerships is ultimately formed around the interests and needs of young people (see Figure 8.1), whose voice and agency needs to be identified throughout.

Much of the literature in this area focuses on partnerships with external agencies when promoting young people's mental health, or partnering with families when promoting young people's academic learning. This chapter will extend the reach of both external agencies and families and explore opportunities for all stakeholders to be involved in fostering young people's academic learning and their wellbeing.

Professional collaborations

Schools might partner with other schools and educational institutions, as well as community groups and agencies, when promoting young people's mental health, wellbeing and academic achievement.

First, schools might network and share resources and specialist staff across schools or settings. Similarly, teachers and school personnel might collaborate with others in different schools but in similar roles; for example, school nurses from different districts or regions might share resources or support each other. Other opportunities for collaboration might arise when students are transitioning between educational settings e.g. early childhood to primary and from primary to secondary, and from secondary to employment or other educational institutions in recognition that these transitional periods are peak times for student stress and maladjustment. These transition times are also key times for young people to learn new skills and competencies, in cognitive as well as social and emotional domains, and thus represent important opportunities for schools and other agencies and community groups to collaborate. Organising and delivering joint professional development opportunities are other examples of collaborative school activities.

Second, schools might partner with external agencies when developing and/or co-delivering a health promotion program or when developing and delivering a curriculum that integrates social and emotional competencies. For instance, schools might provide the space and facilities for external providers to deliver counselling to individuals or groups of students. Schools can serve as a conduit for families to access external service providers by letting them know what services are available and offering assistance with the referral process (Reupert, Deppeler & Sharma, 2015). Finally, during crisis times, outside agencies and professionals might be called in to coordinate services and provide expert intervention.

External entities and organisations might also support learning programs. For example, the program Read Like a Demon aims to inspire a love of reading and improve literacy among primary school students (Monash University, 2018). It involves football players, as reading role models, working with students in reading and writing. Other partnerships in high schools might involve vocational education and training, where interested students undertake vocational training and courses as part of their school curriculum. Around the world, different countries have adopted very different schooling structures around this, with some providing vocational education that develops specific job-related skills, while others deliver a relatively more general education that provides students with broad knowledge and basic skills in mathematics and communication (Hanushek, Schwerdt, Woessmann & Zhang, 2017).

Successful school partnerships, especially those pertaining to external agencies, are characterised by strong leadership, well-defined and clear decision making and communication processes, previous successful collaborations and

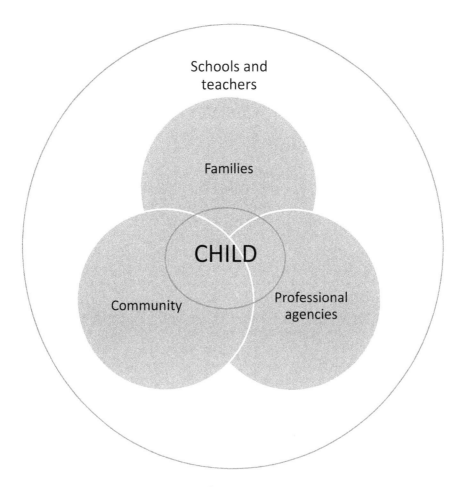

Figure 8.1 Children at the centre of school partnerships

sensitivity to context. Conversely, challenges to collaborative work include the additional workload that may arise from establishing and sustaining the collaboration, insufficient funding, power issues, different theoretical approaches and language discourse, conflict over interpersonal style and decision making and difficulties establishing common goals and objectives (Armstrong, 2015).

Though it is commonly assumed that school-based partnerships and relationships with others will be of benefit to young people, there is little research to confirm this belief (Suldo, Gormley, DuPaul & Anderson-Butcher, 2014). However, there is some evidence to suggest that external collaborations can help students in various ways. For instance, Owens and colleagues (2008) found that parents reported greater frequency and flexibility of appointments, and fewer transportation difficulties and experiences of stigma, when services were provided from the school rather than a clinic. Likewise, Puddy, Roberts, Vernberg and Hambrick (2012) reviewed case records of students with mental health problems and found that high quality, coordinated school-based mental health interventions predicted improvements in adaptive functioning and reduced disruptive behaviours.

Models of collaboration

Working effectively with others takes time. According to Mellin (2009), collaborative partners need to spend as much time attending to **how** they work together as much as they discuss what they do. A balance between process (decision making processes, attending to the relationship) and action is important. Working collaboratively requires knowledge of professional roles and in particular appreciating what others can and cannot do. Willingness to participate and share, confidence in others' abilities and expertise, and an acknowledgement that different professionals have different views are important attributes for working collaboratively (Barrett, Sellman & Thomas, 2005). In addition, structures for communicating, decision making, problem solving and resolving conflict are required. Support and commitment for collaboration at a senior level is necessary. Form needs to follow function; that is, the partners need to define how the partnership is going to work only once a rationale for why the partnership exists has been clarified.

Partnership models will vary depending on the purpose of the collaboration and the remit of different organisations involved. Sometimes all that is needed is an exchange of information and where agencies might share information or one might provide resources to the other. At other times and with different services, more is needed – for example, information exchange plus the sharing of staff or personnel for a specific issue. Synthesised from collaborative models in other fields (Hoskins & Angelica, 2005; Standards for Excellence Institute, 2014), partnerships might assume several forms (see Figure 8.2). Partnerships might change over time and become more or less collaborative depending on the needs of the particular community and government policy and funding.

Not all organisations will work together; indeed, some will be in competition with each other – for example, where two schools are actively trying to attract the same pool of students, or both are attempting to win limited funding from the same source. As outlined in the model (Figure 8.2), schools that simply communicate are engaging in a minimally intensive partnership with another organisation, which can be a one-way or two-way relationship. An example of one-way sharing is a school providing information on a family or a child to a mental health agency, but not receiving information back from the agency. Two-way sharing is where both the school and the agency exchange information on the family or child.

Figure 8.2 A continuum of collaboration between schools and external agencies and entities

Cooperative partnerships are usually formed between schools or between schools and other agencies for informal, one-time activities. For example, a school and a community group working together on an anti-bullying program for a particular year level. The most intensive collaboration is full integration, where two organisations are fully integrated and share the same goals and objectives, funding and staff; this might occur, for example, when two schools are merged.

The referral process

A key time for collaboration is when students are identified as having mental health issues, behavioural concerns and/or learning problems that require specialist intervention. Referral procedures are system- and country-specific, but some general guidelines can be made that ensure referrals to, as well as from, external providers are made sensitively. Rather than schools "dumping" students on external providers and hoping that they "fix" the problem, or conversely services "blaming" schools for putting undue pressure on students, a partnership approach is required that sees everyone working together to respond in the most effective way to meet the needs of the child and his or her family.

Working with young people who present with learning and/or mental health problems requires an ecological or multilevel perspective. The focus of intervention might be on the child, his or her peer group, the classroom, the school community and/or family. All components are determinants of a young person's mental health, wellbeing and learning and are valid, potential targets for intervention. If a teacher has a concern about a young person's mental health or learning, there need to be systems in place for that teacher, student and family to access more intensive support.

Issues that need to be addressed when managing the referral process are:

- Clarifying referral procedures, including confidentiality requirements and the involvement of the student and caregivers
- Clarifying the roles of the different stakeholders, including the teacher
- Identifying relevant formal and informal supports, including online supports
- Building sustained relationships with external providers
- Ensuring continuity of care
- Monitoring and evaluating progress from the perspective of the young person, family and other stakeholders.

The referral process and subsequent case management system is a collaborative process and core to the delivery of quality services designed to meet the needs of school students who have additional support requirements. Schools might provide or organise individual counselling, teaching and learning adjustments, flexible programming and/or different educational pathways that better meet the needs of that student. Mindful of including the views of students, the referral process should be student-focused and aim to develop, monitor and evaluate a plan of action to enable these students to function to the best of their ability and circumstances within and beyond the school system despite having additional support needs (de Jong, 2006).

Family partnerships

Children develop in the context of their environments, which include family, culture and community. The family plays the most critical role in a child's development and learning, and hence it is critical that schools respect the role of the child's family in the educational journey and actively encourage the involvement and input of caregivers and other family members.

Several large-scale meta-analyses have definitively concluded that caregiver involvement in children's education is positively associated with children's academic success (Jeynes, 2005) across age groups and population types (Hill & Tyson, 2009; Jeynes, 2005; Jeynes, 2007). Caregiver involvement not only impacts academic achievement but can also influence school engagement, intrinsic motivation, perceived competence and perceived control (Fan & Williams, 2010; Gonzalez-DeHass, Willems & Holbein, 2005). The most powerful way that caregivers impact positively on children's experience of school is through the values and attitudes that they convey to their children about the importance of learning (Hill & Tyson, 2009). There is abundant research that attests to the importance of caregiver involvement in children's education – the challenge for many schools is facilitating the involvement of all caregivers, those that are ready to engage as well as those who are more resistant, reluctant or unable to be part of the school community.

Valuing caregiver involvement seems to be the first step. Caregivers reported more ideas for home learning activities and an increased understanding of their child in classes where teachers strongly believed in caregiver involvement, compared to teachers who did not value their input (Epstein, 1986). Some teachers do not value caregiver input or interpret their reluctance to be involved in the classroom or school as lack of interest or concern. Other teachers may not have the time or feel adequately trained to work with families (Morris & Taylor, 1998). Chang, Early and Winton (2005) found that only 57% of teacher preparation programs for early childhood educators included education about collaborating with families. There is also a lack of clarity in national, state and local policy documents regarding the role of caregivers in schools (Haines et al. 2017).

Simultaneously, some caregivers are reluctant to be involved in school because of their own negative experiences of school, or lack of confidence to engage with school staff (Ceballo, Huerta & Epstein-Ngo, 2010). Other barriers for families include language differences and long working hours which make it difficult for caregivers to meet up with school staff (Ceballo et al. 2010). When they are consulted, caregivers may struggle to understand the educational jargon used by school staff. In a study about educational planning meetings for children with special needs, Martin et al. (2006) found that parents spoke for approximately 15% of recorded intervals during meetings, special educators spoke 51% of the time and the remaining time was used by other professionals. One parent participant in Zeitlin and Curcic's (2014) study described meeting with school professionals as being "overwhelmed by the power dominance of 10–12 professionals sitting on the opposite side of the table" (p. 379). There are often misunderstandings on both sides, where caregivers blame teachers for not providing individualising learning opportunities for their child, while teachers may blame caregivers for not following through. Though most schools typically do an adequate job engaging caregivers who are already actively involved in their children's education, they are less successful at engaging with disengaged caregivers.

There are different ways that caregivers and other family members might be involved in schools (see Figure 8.3); these range in intensity, duration and focus (Epstein, 1986; Hart, 1992; Hattie, 2009; Reschly & Christenson, 2009). Firstly, formal and informal procedures need to be established for families to communicate to the school and conversely for school staff to communicate to families. Communication needs to be welcoming and, frequent and to acknowledge the cultural and linguistic diversity across the school community. It may involve an exchange of information (from the school to the family or the family to the school) but should also provide an opportunity for learning and an exchange of ideas that consolidates both the school and caregivers as key players in a child's education journey. Regular and culturally appropriate communication needs to take place to ensure families are informed about and understand their child's progress academically, socially and emotionally. Opportunities for communication should be provided across different mediums such as email, face to face, telephone or Internet medium (e.g. zoom or skype). Caregivers may also be consulted and asked for feedback about a particular program or initiative. They may be invited to attend meetings or volunteer to help in learning activities, including reading groups. Weekend working bees on school groups may better suit some caregivers, for example, rather than activities during classtime. Caregivers may cooperate with school staff in developing programs or partner in the co-design and delivery of various initiatives. Finally, caregivers and other family members might take full responsibility for a program and share decision making governance decisions, including the hiring of staff.

Overall, caregivers need to be consulted and partner with the school on decisions impacting their child. The culture, traditions and values of the family need to be acknowledged, and schools should include learning activities that acknowledge and celebrate a child's background. Teachers should value and elicit the skills children bring from home. Schools might provide workshops or meetings for how caregivers can support young people's learning at home (for example, on literacy). There are key times when schools might partner with and

Figure 8.3 A continuum of collaboration between students/caregivers and school staff

engage families, such as when a child starts school or moves into a new setting, and these need to be capitalised on to ensure that school–home partnerships are initiated and then sustained.

Engaging with disengaged caregivers involves an accurate understanding of **why** they are reluctant to participate in collaboration with schools and then systematically and collaboratively addressing those barriers. Schools should try different ways of engaging with families that do not always rely on face to face meetings e.g. one-page handouts, flexible meeting times and a dedicated website, all of which may be especially useful for non-resident caregivers or those who are not able to attend functions during school times. Policies and procedures need to be established that enable effective family–school partnerships and reinforce the value of family involvement. A strength-based view of families is needed, where caregivers are acknowledged as the expert on their child and what is best for him and her. This means that school leaders need to promote family involvement by ensuring teachers and other school staff have the time to regularly communicate with family members. As well, evaluation procedures are required that investigate how effective the school is at engaging families, including who is engaged (and by implication not engaged), how satisfied families are in the partnership and how effective the school is in responding to and incorporating the voice of caregivers and other family members.

Children and youth

It goes without saying that developing strong partnerships with children and youth is at the core of good teaching. Rather than being passive recipients of learning, schools need to create the space and systems for students and teachers to work together as partners on teaching and learning. These collaborative learning partnerships have the potential to foster shared responsibility, respect and trust and to create conditions for teachers and students to learn from each other. Teacher–student partnerships allow both partners to contribute equally, though not necessarily in the same ways, to curriculum, pedagogy and classroom management. Placing students at the centre of our teaching and learning processes necessitates providing young people with the opportunities and resources to develop advocacy and communication skills, and these can be actively incorporated into a social and emotional curriculum and other curriculum areas. The level of intensity outlined in Figure 8.2 can be equally applied to different students at different times.

Fullan (2007, p. 170) noted that on those occasions when teachers do think about students, "they think of them as potential beneficiaries of change . . . they rarely think of students as participants in a process of school change and organizational life". He continued by advocating that schools need to engage with "all students, those doing okay but bored by the irrelevance of school, and those who are disadvantaged and find schools increasingly alienating as the move through the grades" (Fullan, 2007, p. 187). Likewise, Morse and Allensworth

(2015) argued that schools need to actively engage with all children, not only those who sit on student government or who are elected as school leaders. Children of all ages can be engaged; Serriere, Mitra and Reed (2011) described how children in primary or elementary school might be actively engaged in the issues that matter most to them.

There are several reasons for actively engaging young people in educational matters that affect them. According to Article 12 of the UNICEF Convention on the Rights of the Child (United Nations General Assembly, 1989), young people have the right to express an opinion and have that opinion taken into account, in accordance with their age and maturity. Additionally, the involvement of young people can promote student buy-in (Levin, 2000) and ensure that any given program is relevant and aligned with their needs and interests (Proctor et al. 2011). Adults, including their caregivers, often have views very different from young people (Maybery, Ling, Szakacs & Reupert, 2005), and so decisions that adults make may ignore or misconstrue their needs and perspectives.

As well, children can benefit from being involved in how their school is run in terms of enhanced feelings of competence, agency and belonging, and improved communication and problem solving abilities (Lansdown, Jimerson & Shahroozi, 2014). For example, peer mediation programs offer a dispute resolution process through which students are actively involved in resolving their own disputes. It is a process whereby students are trained to share the responsibility, with staff, for creating a safe and secure environment and provides a good example of partnering with students. Extensive evaluation research on peer mediation programs has confirmed that these programs are effective not only at teaching peer mediators conflict resolution knowledge and skills, but also at resolving conflict between students, reducing suspensions and discipline referrals and improving school climate (Harris, 2005).

Griebler, Rojatz, Simovska and Forster (2017) systematically summarised evidence for the impact of student participation in designing, planning, implementing and/or evaluating school health promotion measures. They found that students involved in these participatory practices were more satisfied and motivated and felt a greater sense of ownership than other students. Evidence for improving peer and student–adult relationships, as well as school climate, was also found.

Student input is also beneficial when elicited in traditional curriculum areas. Hagay and Baram-Tsabari (2015) described attempts by science teachers to incorporate relevance and personal context from the students' points of view by asking students to identify questions they wanted to know about science. The process ensured content was taught that students found meaningful, while allowing teachers the time to prepare and logically plan the unfolding of the topic. Likewise, in one primary school in Australia, every child in Year 6 assumes a leadership role, rather than assigning selected students to traditional positions of school captain, vice-captain and so on (Whitby, 2017). This enables all

Year 6 students to have a voice in the running of the school. The school also introduced flexible spaces throughout all their learning environments, allowing them to decide on the task they wanted to work on and how (in groups or individually). As the principal argued, this approach allowed students to be able to say, "this is where I'm heading, this is where I think I need to go" (Whitby, 2017).

Others described empowering students to deliver programs. Mellanby, Rees and Tripp (2000) compared school-based health education programs led by peers (that is, students delivering the program to their peers) versus those led by adults, all delivering the same material. They found that peer leaders were at least as effective than adults, if not more so. In another related study by some of the same authors, Mellanby, Newcombe, Rees and Tripp (2001) investigated the efficacy of peer-led and adult-led sex education for young people aged 13–14 years. They found that peer leaders were more effective in establishing conservative norms and attitudes related to sexual behaviour than the adults, though less effective than adults in imparting factual information and getting students involved in classroom activities. They conclude by suggesting that both adult-led and peer-led methods have their place, at least in effective sex education.

Collectively, such research attests to the value of partnering with students on a range of health, wellbeing and academic learning programs. Though referring to youth–community partnerships, the argument of Pittman, Martin and Williams (2007, p. 5) can be equally applied to student–school partnerships:

> Young people want to be engaged as change-makers in their lives, their families and their communities . . . they must be part of the solution . . . Change happens fastest when youth and community development are seen as two sides of the same coin and young people are afforded the tools, training and trust to apply their creativity and energy to affect meaningful change in their own lives and in the future of their neighbourhoods and communities.

Further extending this student-centred approach, Morse and Allensworth (2015, p. 793) developed three seemingly simple questions that underpin an open-dialogue approach with students about school policies, programs and services:

> What do students think about the planned policy, program or service?
> How will the policies, programs and services impact all students in the school?
> What would the students do differently if given the opportunity to do so?

It is these questions that challenge school leaders and staff to reflect on what they are doing, how and why. These issues will be further explored in the final chapter.

References

Armstrong, P. (2015). *Effective school partnerships and collaboration for school improvement: A review of the evidence.* Department of Education, UK Government. Retrieved February 25, 2019, from https://assets.publishing.service.gov.uk/government/uploads/system/uploads/attachment_data/file/467855/DFE-RR466_-_School_improvement_effective_school_partnerships.pdf

Barrett, G., Sellman, D., & Thomas, J. (Eds.). (2005). *Interpersonal working in health and social care.* Basingstoke: Palgrave Macmillan.

Ceballo, R., Huerta, M., & Epstein-Ngo, Q. (2010). Parental and school influences promoting academic success among Latino students. In J. L. Meece, & J. S. Eccles (Eds.), *Handbook of research on schools, schooling and human development* (pp. 293–307). New York: Routledge.

Chang, F., Early, D. M., & Winton, P. J. (2005). Early childhood teacher preparation in special education at 2-and 4-year institutions of higher education. *Journal of Early Intervention, 27*(2), 110–124.

de Jong, T. (2006). *A kit on effective school case management.* Australian Guidance and Counselling Association and MindMatters. Retrieved February 25, 2019, from http://citeseerx.ist.psu.edu/viewdoc/download?doi=10.1.1.489.6881&rep=rep1&type=pdf

Epstein, J. (1986). Parents' reactions to teacher practices of parent involvement. *The Elementary School Journal, 86*, 277–294.

Fan, W., & Williams, C. (2010). The effects of parental involvement on students' academic self-efficacy, engagement and intrinsic motivation. *Educational Psychology, 30*, 53–74.

Fullan, M. (2007). *The new meaning of educational change* (4th ed.). New York: Teachers College Press.

Gonzalez-DeHass, A., Willems, P., & Holbein, M. (2005). Examining the relationship between parental involvement and student motivation. *Educational Psychology Review, 17*(2), 99–123.

Griebler, U., Rojatz, D., Simovska, V., & Forster, R. (2017). Effects of student participation in school health promotion: A systematic review. *Health Promotion International, 32*, 195–206.

Hagay, G., & Baram-Tsabari, A. (2015). A strategy for incorporating students' interests into the high-school biology classroom. *Journal of Research in Science Teaching, 52*(7), 949–978.

Haines, S. J., Francis, G. L., Gershwin Mueller, T., Chiu, C., Burke, M. M., Kyzar, K., . . . Turnbull, A. P. (2017). Reconceptualizing family-professional partnership for inclusive schools: A call to action. *Inclusion, 5*(4), 234–247.

Hanushek, E. A., Schwerdt, G., Woessmann, L., & Zhang, L. (2017). General education, vocational education and labour market outcomes over the lifecycle. *Journal of Human Resources, 52*(1), 48–87.

Harris, R. D. (2005). Unlocking the learning potential in peer mediation: An evaluation of peer mediator modeling and disputant learning. *Conflict Resolution, 23*(2), 141–164.

Hart, R. A. (1992). *Children's participation: From tokenism to citizenship.* Florence: UNICEF Innocenti Research Centre. Retrieved January 20, 2019, from www.unicef-irc.org/publications/pdf/childrens_participation.pdf

Hattie, J. (2009). *Visible learning.* New York: Routledge.

Hill, N., & Tyson, D. (2009). Parental involvement in middle school: The meta-analytic assessment of the strategies that promote achievement. *Developmental Psychology, 45*(3), 740–763.

Hoskins, L., & Angelica, E. (2005). *Forming alliances: Working together to achieve mutual goals.* Saint Paul: Fieldstone Alliance.

Jeynes, W. (2005). A meta-analysis of the relation of parental involvement to urban elementary school student academic achievement. *Urban Education, 40*, 237–269.

Jeynes, W. (2007). The relationship between parental involvement and urban secondary school student academic achievement: A meta-analysis. *Urban Environment, 42*, 82–110.

Lansdown, G., Jimerson, S. R., & Shahroozi, R. (2014). Children's rights and school psychology: Children's right to participation. *Journal of School Psychology, 52* (1), 3–12.

Levin, B. (2000). Putting students at the centre in education reform. *Journal of Educational Change, 1*(2), 155–172.

Martin, J. E., Van Dycke, J., Christensen, W. R., Greene, B. A., Gardner, J. E., & Lovett, D. L. (2006). Increasing student participation in IEP meetings: Establishing the self-directed IEP as an evidence-based practice. *Exceptional Children, 72*(3), 299–316.

Maybery, D., Ling, L., Szakacs, E., & Reupert, A. (2005). Children of a parent with a mental illness: Perspectives on need. *Australian e-Journal for the Advancement of Mental Health, 4*(2), 1–11.

Mellanby, A., Rees, J., & Tripp, J. (2000). Peer-led and adult-led school health education: A critical review of available comparable research. *Health Education Research, 15*(5), 533–545.

Mellanby, A. R., Newcombe, R. G., Rees, J., & Tripp, J. H. (2001). A comparative study of peer-led and adult-led school sex education. *Health Education Research, 16*(4), 481–492.

Mellin, E. A. (2009). Unpacking interdisciplinary collaboration in expanded school mental health: A conceptual model for developing the evidence base. *Advances in School Mental Health Promotion, 2*, 4–14.

Monash University (2018). *2018 Read like a demon program guide*. Retrieved February 25, 2019, from http://deezone.com.au/wp-content/uploads/2013/04/Read-Like-a-Demon-Program-Guide-2018.pdf

Morris, V. G., & Taylor, S. I. (1998). Alleviating barriers to family involvement in education: The role of teacher education. *Teaching and Teacher Education, 14*(2), 219–231.

Morse, L., & Allensworth, D. (2015). Placing student at the centre: The whole school, whole community, whole child model. *School Health, 85*(11), 785–794.

Owens, J. S., Murphy, C. E., Richardson, L., Girio, E. L., & Himawan, L. K. (2008). Science to practice in underserved communities: The effectiveness of school mental health programming. *Journal of Clinical Child and Adolescent Psychology, 37*(2), 434–447.

Pittman, K., Martin, S., & Williams, A. (2007). *Core principles for engaging young people in community change*. Washington, DC: The Forum for Youth Investment, Impact Strategies, Inc. Retrieved January 20, 2019, from http://forumfyi.org/files/FINALYouth_Engagment_8.15pdf.pdf

Proctor, E., Hiie, S., Ramesh, R., Hovmand, P., Aarons, G., Bunger, A., ... Hensley, M. (2011). Outcomes for implementation research: Conceptual distinctions, measurement challenges, and research agenda. *Administration and Policy in Mental Health and Mental Health Services Research, 38*(2), 65–76.

Puddy, R. W., Roberts, M. C., Vernberg, E. M., & Hambrick, E. P. (2012). Service coordination and children's functioning in a school-based intensive mental health program. *Journal of Child and Family Studies, 21*, 948–962.

Reschly, A., & Christenson, S. (2009). Parents as essential partners for fostering students' learning outcomes. In R. Gilman, E. S. Huebner, & M. Furlong (Eds.), *Handbook of positive psychology in schools* (pp. 257–272). New York: Routledge.

Reupert, A., Deppeler, J., & Sharma, U. (2015). Enablers for inclusion: The perspective of parents with autism spectrum disorder. *Australasian Journal of Special Education, 39*(1), 85–96.

Serriere, S. C., Mitra, D., & Reed, K. (2011). Student voice in the elementary years: Fostering youth-adult partnerships in elementary service-learning. *Theory & Research in Social Education, 39*(4), 541–575.

Standards for Excellence Institute (2014). *Strategic partnerships*. Retrieved February 25, 2019, from www.thearc.org/file/documents_nce/Strategic-Partnerships.pdf

Suldo, S. M., Gormley, M. J., DuPaul, G. J., & Anderson-Butcher, D. (2014). The impact of school mental health on student and school-level academic outcomes: Current status of the research and future directions. *School Mental Health: A Multidisciplinary Research and Practice Journal*, *6*(2), 84–98.

UN General Assembly (1989). *Convention on the rights of the child*. Geneva: United Nations. Retrieved February 25, 2019, from www.un.org/documents/ga/res/44/a44r025.htm

Whitby, G. (2017). *Students as partners in learning*. Teacher. Evidence + Insight + Action. ACER. Retrieved February 25, 2019, from www.teachermagazine.com.au/articles/students-as-partners-in-learning

Zeitlin, V. M., & Curcic, S. (2014). Parental voices on individualized education programs: "Oh, IEP meeting tomorrow? Rum tonight!" *Disability & Society*, *29*(3), 373–387.

Chapter 9

Inclusivity
Celebrating diversity

To accommodate the academic and mental health needs of a diverse student body, provisions must be made so that all students, regardless of their gender, race, sexual identity, disability, learning characteristics or social background, can succeed in school. In educational settings, inclusive education means that all students, regardless of who they are, are eligible and welcome to attend age appropriate, regular classes and given appropriate and adequate support to learn and participate in all aspects of school life (Alquraini & Gut, 2012). Udvari-Solner and Kluth (1997) explicitly address the issue of exclusion when they describe an inclusive school as one which

> propels a critique of contemporary school culture and thus, encourages practitioners to reinvent what can be and should be to realize more humane, just and democratic learning communities. Inequities in treatment and educational opportunity are brought to the forefront, thereby fostering attention to human rights, respect for difference and value of diversity.
> (p. 142)

Why inclusive education is important and how inclusive practices can promote students' wellbeing and academic learning is explored in this chapter. Rather than merely accepting and tolerating diversity, the case is made for explicit structural and individual teacher strategies that actively include all students and ensure they receive equitable opportunities to succeed, academically and socially, at school.

Why is inclusion important?

First and foremost, inclusive education is concerned with students' rights to a full education in mainstream or regular settings. Endorsed by the Salamanca statement (UNESCO, 1994) and signed by 92 countries, inclusive education is based on the tenet that is the right of all children to be provided with the same educational and social opportunities, regardless of their gender, ability, culture, religion and sexuality (Lindsay, 2012). Based on social justice principles that advocate for equal access to all educational opportunities for all students, inclusion is regarded as a universal need and human right.

In schools today, there is a more heterogeneous group of students than ever before, in regard to race and ethnicity, social class, gender, sexual orientation and physical disability (Riehl, 2000). Many of these students will experience discrimination, alienation and rejection and, as a result, present with mental health or learning difficulties (Blanchett, Klingner & Harry, 2009). In a survey distributed to over 200 high school students in the USA, gender, race/ethnicity and placement in special education were all strong factors in influencing whether students perceived school as alienating and meaningless (Brown, Higgins, Pierce, Hong & Thoma, 2003). Likewise, students who identify as lesbian, gay or bisexual experience more victimisation, bullying and violence at school than other young people (O'Malley, Olsen, Kann, Vivolo-Kantor, Kinchen & McManus, 2014), with a subsequent higher risk of substance use and suicide risk (Johns et al. 2018). Students with disabilities, irrespective of type, are more likely to develop mental health problems than children without disabilities (Dix, Shearer, Slee & Butcher, 2010). Some estimate that students with an intellectual disability present with mental health concerns three to four times more often than their peers without disability, with between 4% and 18% receiving a mental illness diagnosis (Sturgeon, 2006).

One factor that influences the mental health and academic progress of students from diverse backgrounds is the attitudes of others, and the often disadvantageous ways that school systems have been constructed around them. Diaz and Kosciw (2009) found that 80% of the sampled lesbian, gay, and bisexual students in their study experience verbal abuse and hear homophobic remarks at school. Drawn from a sample of Latino, African American and Asian American youth, Benner and Graham (2013) reported discrimination from teachers associated with grades and school engagement, whereas discrimination (rejection, bullying) from peers was associated with psychological wellbeing. Some students with disabilities have difficulties establishing friendships (Dix et al. 2010; Schwab, 2015), possibly because they are not provided with opportunities to participate in everyday activities such as might occur during break times. It has been found that students with disabilities experience limited classmate interaction and recess participation compared to peers without disabilities (Eriksson, Welander & Granlund, 2007). This also means that students with disabilities have fewer friends to support them, another risk factor for mental health problems.

Whether the point of intervention should be the individual child or the context within which he or she is placed speaks also to how disability or difference might be construed. For example, some students with a disability, such as those with Autism Spectrum Disorders, find it difficult to express emotions and to read and process social cues, and so find it challenging to form and maintain friendship groups. Indeed, previous research has found that students with Autism Spectrum Disorders experience twice the loneliness of students with other types of disability (Bossaert, Colpin, Pijl & Petry,

2013). However, are these students lonely because of something inherently deficit in the individual or because those around him or her are not able to understand what that individual is trying to say? In other words, are the problems located within the individual, the environment or both? Such questions are important because they provide a focus as to where we need to be directing our efforts around intervention and change. The principles of inclusion point to the need for schools to address the stigma, bullying and victimisation associated with being "different" at individual, peer and school-wide levels. Overall, school failure and disengagement result from basic inequities that have not been addressed and where students have not been given equal opportunities to obtain a basic minimum standard of education. As students have different needs and come from different backgrounds, opportunities, accommodations and adaptations need to be targeted to make the education system fair.

Moreover, reflecting on how we perceive and act on "difference" also informs how we interact, and work with, young people. Pollak's (2002) interviews with 32 higher education students diagnosed with dyslexia found that how they had their dyslexic diagnosis explained to them shaped their beliefs about their ability. Those who understood dyslexia as a defect tended to have poorer self-esteem, while those who had their diagnosis explained to them as a cognitive difference were able to identify and apply their cognitive strengths and abilities. Such research highlights the importance of acknowledging the contextual factors that impact the wellbeing and functioning of individuals and the responsibility of schools to intervene. The need to assume a strength-based rather than deficit view of difference is paramount.

Gender diversity

An area that has increasingly been receiving much media and research attention has been the manner in which schools support gender diversity. Approximately 10% of young people below the age of 18 will experience feelings of same-sex attraction (Anagnostopoulos, Buchanan & Pereira, 2009). Moreover, 60% of same-sex attracted young people will experience verbal or physical abuse, with the greatest amount of abuse occurring in schools (Anagnostopoulos et al. 2009). Additionally, some 80% of young people will experience or witness gendered (often homophobic or transphobic) violence and harassment at school (Anagnostopoulos et al. 2009). Hence, promoting nuanced understandings of gender is crucial in an environment where LGBTIQ (lesbian, gay, bisexual, transgender/transsexual, intersex and queer/questioning) members of the community are between six and 15 times (depending on their identity) more likely to self-harm or attempt suicide than their heterosexual or cisgender peers (Rosenstreich, 2013).

There are several ways schools might acknowledge gender diversity. Relaxing the rules on school uniforms is a small but positive step in this direction, for example, where girls are allowed to wear trousers. The continued expectation that boys can only wear pants and girls can only wear dresses continues to reinforce traditional gender identities, which in the long run can be harmful to students. Mary Barry (2017), former CEO of Our Watch, a national organisation to prevent violence against women and their children, argued:

> Continuing to enforce limiting clothing regulations on girls is one of many ways they are reminded of their unequal status. It is seemingly "small" issues like this that, taken together, create a broader landscape of gender inequality across our society. But we can change this, a refreshing new approach to uniforms is just one example of how small changes can have a big impact, helping to break down restrictive stereotypes and enabling all children to be free to discover the world without unnecessary barriers. What better place to start than in schools? And what better time than now?

Other policy approaches allow students to use the toilets of the gender they identify with, rather than the toilets assigned to their biological sex, and allowing students to be called by their preferred name. There have been policy moves acknowledging gender diversity in Australia and the US, though not without a struggle and backlash from conservative groups.

Inclusive education benefits all students

The effectiveness of inclusive education is a question that teachers, parents, researches and policy makers have asked for many years. Questions of effectiveness and efficacy are complex, and answers vary depending on how effectiveness is defined (e.g. academic outcomes, social participation and integration, student wellbeing), the student body that is being assessed (particular disability groups for example), whose perspective is sought (student, parent, teacher, administrator), how much (or little) support is provided to teaching staff and, ultimately, what models of inclusion are being applied. Much of the research in this area has been conducted in reference to students with disabilities.

Notwithstanding these provisos, there is an emerging evidence base that when students are placed in inclusive classrooms, superior social and academic outcomes are reported, for all students (Alquraini & Gut, 2012; Hehir, Grindal, Freeman, Lamoreau, Borquaye & Burke, 2016). Hehir et al. (2016) conducted a systematic review of 280 studies from 25 countries, concluding that there is "clear and consistent evidence that inclusive educational settings can confer substantial short and long-term benefits for students with and without disabilities" (p. 1). They continued by pointing out that students with disabilities placed in inclusive settings develop stronger skills in reading and mathematics than those students who are segregated in specialist (or other) schools, are less likely to have behavioural problems and are more likely to attend class, complete secondary school and engage in post-secondary education (Hehir et al. 2016). At the same time, it should be noted that the Hehir et al. (2016) review did not include studies which employed control or comparison groups, nor did it consider possible differences between children with mild versus severe disabilities.

There is also research that participating in inclusive settings can result in substantial social and emotional benefits for students with disabilities. In Canada, Wiener and Tardif (2004) compared children with learning difficulties in four different educational settings on the attainment of several social and emotional skills. They found that children in the inclusive placements had more positive social and emotional functioning and were more accepted by peers, had more satisfying relationships with their best school friends, were less lonely and had fewer problem behaviours than similar children in less inclusive settings (Wiener & Tardif, 2004).

For students without disabilities, there are also potential benefits, both academic and otherwise. Hehir et al. (2016, p. 7) cited several studies to summarise that the impact of inclusive classrooms on students without disabilities can be "either neutral or positive". They found that the quality of instruction played a more substantial role in the achievement of students without abilities, rather than whether that student was in the same classroom as children with a disability. Interestingly, Salend and Duhaney (1999) found that students without disabilities received the same amount of attention as students in non-inclusive settings and obtained similar levels of academic achievement. Likewise, in Switzerland, Dessemontet and Bless (2013) found that including children with intellectual disabilities in general education classrooms did not have a negative impact on the academic progress of students without a disability.

Similar to their peers with disabilities, inclusion can also support the positive social and emotional development of students without disability. Staub and Peck's (1994) literature review found that inclusion can promote social and emotional competence in five positive ways. Learning in classrooms with students with disabilities resulted in other students being less fearful towards those who look or behave differently. These students may also experience a growth in social cognition (including tolerance and more effective communication). Another finding of the review was improvements in students' self-esteem, and a sense of belonging to the classroom when learning alongside students with disabilities. The review also found that inclusion resulted in less prejudice and higher responsiveness to the needs of others and, finally, warm and caring friendships with a variety of students. While dated, the review is supported by relatively more recent research. In Italy, Consiglio, Guarnera and Magnano (2015) compared the attitudes of children towards students with Down syndrome. Children with prior experience of students with Down syndrome held more positive and less prejudicial views about people with this syndrome when compared to students who had no prior contact.

Attainment grouping

Attainment grouping, sometimes called tracking or ability grouping, is the practice of grouping children together according to academic attainment. It may take various forms, including between-class ability grouping, where students in the same year are divided into low-, medium-, or high-level classes; within-class ability grouping, where students within a classroom are taught in groups based on their levels; cross-year subject grouping, where students in different year groups are combined into the same class depending on their prior achievement; and, finally, accelerated grouping, where students considered gifted are placed in classes with older peers. It is a contentious area, with some strongly advocating for the practice and others strongly arguing against it.

Proponents of attainment grouping argue that grouping students according to attainment allows teachers to adapt pedagogy and curriculum to the needs of both high and low achieving students. Detractors point out the negative impact of attainment grouping on low achieving students in terms of their confidence and school engagement. Others also highlight the concerns regarding the disproportionate number of number of boys, students from lower socio-economic groups and some minority ethnic groups allocated to low attainment groups (Dunne, Humphreys, Sebba, Dyson, Gallannaugh & Muijs, 2007). Conversely, mixed attainment classrooms avoid the negative labelling of students, the self-fulfilling prophesy of students who are expected to be low performing (from the point of view of teachers and students themselves) and the lack of movement once students have been sorted or allocated. The allocation of students impacts educational choices as well as employment and other opportunities (Smyth & Calvert, 2011). Others have suggested that students in the higher attainment groups are exposed to higher quality instruction, more content-laden and challenging curriculum and more teaching time than students assigned to lower attainment groups (Vogl & Preckel, 2014). Likewise, it has been argued that attainment grouping works for students in the higher groups but not for those placed in other groups. Parsons and Hallam (2014) investigated the relationship between attainment group and the academic progress made by children in England in Year 2 and found children in the "top" stream achieved more and made significantly more academic progress than children attending schools that did not stream, while children in the "middle" or "bottom" streams achieved less and made significantly less academic progress. Nonetheless, critics of mixed-attainment classes argue that mixed-attainment classrooms are demanding of teachers' time and resources and hold back high achieving students.

Students have their own opinions. Tereschchenko et al. (in press) analysed the attitudes of students of different attainment levels to mixed-attainment practice, drawn from group discussions and individual interviews with 89 Year 7 students from eight UK schools practicing mixed-attainment grouping in mathematics and English. High and mid-attaining students spoke positively about mixed attainment, as they believed the practice indicated that their school was committed to equity. They also found that mixed-attainment grouping was especially appreciated by students with low academic attainment, because of its inclusive and collaborative environment. Similarly, Hallam and Ireson (2006) found that disadvantaged students preferred mixed-attainment classes because of the cooperation, friendship and equality of learning opportunities. However, some students disliked mixed-attainment classes due to behavioural problems in class, and felt left out or behind (Hallam & Ireson, 2006), while some gifted students reported a preference for high attainment grouping (Adams-Byers, Squiller Whitsell & Moon, 2004).

Given the long-term potential adverse impact of streaming students into low attainment groups, it would appear that mixed-attainment classes are the most effective way of promoting all students' success. This recommendation is made, however, on the proviso that teachers have the time, resources and necessary abilities to teach challenging material in a mixed-attainment classroom.

Basic principles of an inclusive education

There are numerous policy and human rights documents that provide comprehensive coverage of the basic tenets involved in inclusive education. These documents share many similar features. The South Australian Department of Education (2018) guidelines (specific to disability) are demonstrative of one such document, outlined below, modified to apply to all forms of inclusion. Hence, regardless of ability, gender, race, religion, socio-economic status and sexuality, all children:

- Have the right to access and participate in all aspects of school life
- Have the right to be safe, physically, emotionally, socially and culturally, and to be treated respectfully
- Have the right to develop to the fullest potential
- Have the right to access an appropriate and adequate allocation of resources and support to encourage their full participation in school life
- Have the right to exercise choice and control in managing their educational experiences.

Such principles mean that respectful and inclusive language needs to be modelled by all school staff and a culture of acceptance should be fostered. A mutual understanding of expected behaviours in schools is explicit, where immediate responses to bullying and stigma are ensured. All school staff and students are responsible for being inclusive.

How to be inclusive

Inclusion is more than tolerating or accepting the diversity that exists in any given student body. It also means actively and consciously providing opportunities, at a structural as well as classroom level, for all students to succeed at school. Likewise, physically placing students with disabilities or other special needs into a regular school setting does not automatically result in inclusivity. There are many texts, books and papers that provide a comprehensive outline of research-based inclusive practices in schools. Nonetheless, here I will present some of the core dimensions of teaching and learning and administrative practice that emulate inclusivity.

Developed from Shulman's (2004) concept of three apprenticeships and Sharma's (2018) adaption of Shulman's concept, called the hearts, minds and hands approach, the following framework specifies targets for inclusive education (Figure 9.1). Though the individual teacher (knowledge, beliefs and practice) is the key to ensuring successful inclusion, specific policies and systems are required to support teachers' inclusive practices; it is not up to individual

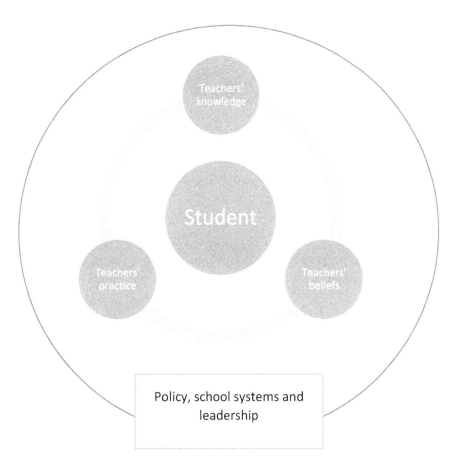

Figure 9.1 Framework of inclusive education

teachers to do this alone. Central to the model are students' needs and voices. Each component of this framework is unpacked further below.

Students at the centre

Students need to be at the centre of any approach to inclusive education, as subsequent actions, at either the teacher, policy or systems level, need to have their best interests at heart. This means understanding and responding to children as individuals rather than as representatives of any particular social or cultural group. It also means encouraging student agency and choice and providing multiple, culturally appropriate opportunities for students to have a voice in how classrooms and schools operate. Students' voices can be elicited in several ways, including but not limited to student council and class meetings. In addition, Dutro (2010) argued that a curriculum should "allow children to see themselves, access experiences that differ from their own, and foster talk about issues of equity and social justice" (p. 257). Thus, diverse perspectives need to be incorporated into the curriculum, e.g. by expanding reading lists beyond white male authors, ensuring information sheets, PowerPoint presentations and so on offer a variety of family types, social groups and individuals and avoiding generalising particular individuals or groups.

Teachers' beliefs

Regardless of funding, policy and resourcing, if teachers do not believe in the value of inclusion, it will be considerably difficult to implement. Thus, it can be argued that teachers' attitudes and beliefs towards inclusion are a central contributing factor to building inclusive environments (Carlson, Hemmings, Wurf & Reupert, 2012), especially given that their commitment and attitude to inclusion influences their intention to practice inclusively (Avramidis & Norwich, 2002). However, Sharma (2018) summarised previous research in this area by pointing out that a "large number of teachers (both in-service and pre-service) still continue to believe that inclusion is not good for *all* students . . . and they do not believe that inclusion is a good idea". Similarly, in a sample of primary and secondary US teachers, Quinn (2017) found that some held troubling racial attitudes, even if there are comparatively less teachers with these troubling views than others in the community. For example, approximately 30% of teachers attributed inequalities to a lack of motivation among African Americans, compared to 46% of people in the general community (30% is still an alarming number). Additionally, 44% of the sample did not consider insufficient educational opportunities to account for inequalities among different groups, suggesting they could not see their role as teachers in supporting social justice. In regard to gender diversity, Australian students who had disclosed their sexuality and/or gender diversity to one of their teachers were significantly more likely to report being rejected by teachers than same-sex attracted, cis-gender young people (Jones & Hillier, 2013).

Teacher attitudes can, however, be shifted. Burke and Sutherland (2004) found that prior experience, training and knowledge about students with disabilities was associated with teachers' positive attitudes towards inclusion. Targeted professional development can also positively shift teacher attitudes to race, culture and gender diversity (Hynds, Averill, Hindle & Meyer, 2017; Mason, Springer & Pugliese, 2017). However, teachers need not only to believe in inclusivity but also need to understand and know what it means to teach inclusively.

Teachers' knowledge

One way of ascertaining what teachers know about inclusive education is by examining what they learn as student or pre-service teachers. In a review of this area, Sharma, Forlin, Deppeler and Yang (2013) concluded that across the world, subjects on inclusion and special education were either offered in elective mode or not offered at all. Thus, it would appear that when they start teaching, knowledge about inclusivity is limited.

The question, as posed by Sharma (2018), is what should teachers know about inclusion. As he continued, the debate is typically framed around two opposing views: first, that teachers need knowledge about specific disabilities (and by inference, specific types of diversity) on the assumption that different groups have different teaching and learning needs; second, that teachers need to know about teaching and learning strategies for all learners, and how to address barriers to the participation of marginalised leaners. This second view is based on the premise that teaching approaches effective for students with a particular label (e.g. Down syndrome) are effective for **all** children. Davis and Florian's systematic review (2004, p. 6) confirmed this latter view; they found that effective teaching strategies for children with special needs were not sufficiently differentiated from effective strategies used to teach all children. They concluded that "the more important agenda is about how to develop a pedagogy that is inclusive of all learners". This, then, brings us to what teachers should be doing.

Teachers' practices

What teachers do in their classrooms will ultimately determine how included children are. There are several ways of identifying inclusive pedagogy, and most of these have been discussed in relation to students with disability, as can be seen in several text books and systematic reviews (e.g. Alquraini & Gut, 2012). Inclusive practices can also be identified by examining the practice of those who have been identified as exemplary inclusive educators (Carlson et al. 2012; Morningstar, Shogren, Lee & Born, 2015). It is outside of the scope of this chapter to provide a comprehensive coverage of these strategies, but there are some common features that tend to come up repeatedly when it comes to practicing inclusivity, and many of these align with the effective teaching strategies outlined previously by Hattie (2009).

One approach that encompasses inclusivity is called universal design for learning (UDL). UDL has been defined as those "methods and materials that are flexible and powerful enough to help all students, regardless of their ability, to maximize their progress" (Alquraini & Gut, 2012, p. 50). It is an approach to designing the curriculum, instruction, materials and content that aims to benefit all students by providing equal access to learning and not only to information. UDL involves offering multiple methods for learning the curriculum (e.g. videos, books or images), employs flexible ways of engaging in the learning process (e.g. independent work and group work) and provides different ways for the student to convey what they have learnt (Copeland & Cosbey, 2009). The UDL approach serves as a "blueprint for creating flexible goals, methods, materials, and assessments that accommodate learner differences" (Rose, 2001, p. 66). Moreover, students without disabilities or other special needs benefit from these same strategies (Spooner & Dymond, 2006). A significant component of UDL is curriculum accommodations involving quantity (how many items the learner is expected to do), time (provided for learning), level of support and alternate goals or expected outcomes. These accommodations do not change the curriculum but do reduce barriers to learning and participation so that all students can learn. Thus, the UDL approach implies that diversity is the norm and embedded into all aspects of teaching and learning.

Policy, school leadership and systems

Notwithstanding the importance of teacher attitude, knowledge and skill, the systems in which teachers work will impact their teaching and learning practises and beliefs. Forlin and Chambers (2011) found that teachers' confidence and knowledge of legislation were positively and significantly correlated with teachers' attitudes towards including students with disabilities and conversely negatively correlated with concerns about inclusion. However, they also found that increasing knowledge about legislation related to inclusion and improving confidence did not address their concerns or perceived stress associated with having students with disabilities in their classrooms. Indeed, while teachers are critical factors in fostering inclusive environments, they are influenced and supported by the systems in which they work and the leaders they report to.

School culture and policy must embrace the principles of inclusion and equity and work to eliminate school structures that marginalise students. Hehir et al. (2016) strongly advocated for national policies, publicly endorsed by national leaders, which affirm the right of students with disabilities to be included alongside their non-disabled peers. Similarly, policies that promote respect and safety for other marginalised learners need to be presented and endorsed by leaders in each country. Training and ongoing professional development opportunities need to be offered at both the university and in-service level that identify and confront negative and biased attitudes towards inclusion and diversity, actively teach evidence-based teaching and learning strategies for working inclusively and reduce the barriers of learning. In particular, the UDL framework, described earlier, can be used by teachers and schools in designing curricula to accommodate the diverse strengths and challenges of all learners. Likewise, Hehir et al. (2016) suggested that exemplary schools might serve as demonstration models for others to emulate and learn from.

The attitudes of principals and other school administrators are critical factors that shape how inclusion is implemented, though unfortunately they are not always supportive (Praisner, 2003). DeMatthews (2015) summarised social justice leadership as identifying oppressive and unjust practices and substituting these with equitable and culturally appropriate ones. Ryan (2006, pp. 17–18) suggested that being a leader meant being a role model for inclusivity and how decisions are made:

> inclusive leadership provides everyone with a fair chance to influence decisions, practices, and polices . . . Inclusive leadership relies on many different individuals who contribute in their own often humble ways . . . Inclusive leadership aims to achieve inclusion in all aspects of schooling and beyond the school.

Crockett (2002) summarised much of the sentiment in this area when she stated "what schools really require are responsive leaders – knowledgeable persons in positions of influence who are committed to ensuring context that supports learning for each and every student" (p. 157).

School structure also needs to be supportive of the principles and actions of inclusivity. The ten steps to equity in education written by the OECD in 2010, while dated, still hold relevance today. The first four relate to design and involve (i) limiting attainment grouping, especially in the early years, (ii) managing school choice so as to contain risks to equity, (iii) in upper secondary, providing meaningful alternatives, removing dead ends and preventing drop out, and (iv) offering second chances to gain education. A further three steps relate to practices, including (v) identifying and providing help to those who fall behind in their learning, while also reducing the practice of grade repetition, (vi) strengthening links between school and home so that parents can better help children learn, and (vii) respecting and responding to diversity to ensure the inclusion of minority groups in education. The final three steps involve resourcing: (viii) giving priority to early childhood education, (ix) directing resources to students and schools with the greatest needs and (x) setting targets for equity, especially those related to low school achievements and engagement.

References

Adams-Byers, J., Squiller Whitsell, S., & Moon, S. M. (2004). Gifted students' perceptions of the academic and social/emotional effects of homogeneous and heterogeneous grouping. *Gifted Child Quarterly, 48*(1), 7–20.

Alquraini, T., & Gut, D. (2012). Critical components of successful inclusion of students with severe disabilities: Literature review. *International Journal of Special Education, 27*(1), 42–59.

Anagnostopoulos, D., Buchanan, N. T., & Pereira, C. (2009). School staff responses to gender-based bullying as moral interpretation: An exploratory study. *Educational Policy, 23*(4), 519–553.

Avramidis, E., & Norwich, B. (2002). Teachers' attitudes integration/inclusion: A review of the literature. *European Journal of Special Needs Education, 17*(2), 129–147.

Barry, M. (2017). *School uniform changes would have a big impact.* The Sydney Morning Herald. Retrieved January 29, 2019, from www.smh.com.au/opinion/school-uniform-changes-would-have-a-big-impact-20170328-gv8132.html

Benner, A. D., & Graham, S. (2013). The antecedents and consequences of racial/ethnic discrimination during adolescence: Does the source of discrimination matter? *Developmental Psychology, 49*(8), 1602–1613.

Blanchett, W. J., Klingner, J. K., & Harry, B. (2009). The intersection of race, culture, language, and disability: Implications for urban education. *Urban Education, 44*(4), 389–409.

Bossaert, G., Colpin, H., Pijl, S. J., & Petry, K. (2013). Social participation of students with special educational needs in mainstream seventh grade. *Procedia – Social and Behavioral Sciences, 93*, 1952–1956.

Brown, M. R., Higgins, K., Pierce, T., Hong, E., & Thoma, C. (2003). Secondary students' perceptions of school life with regard to alienation: The effects of disability, gender and race. *Learning Disability Quarterly, 26*(4), 227–238.

Burke, K., & Sutherland, C. (2004). Attitudes towards inclusion: Knowledge vs experience. *Education, 125*(2), 163–172.

Carlson, L., Hemmings, B., Wurf, G., & Reupert, A. (2012). The instructional strategies and attitudes of effective inclusive teachers. *Special Education Perspectives, 21*(4), 7–20.

Consiglio, A., Guarnera, M., & Magnano, P. (2015). Representation of disability. Verification of the contact hypothesis in school. *Procedia – Social and Behavioral Sciences, 191*(2), 1964–1969.

Copeland, S. R., & Cosbey, J. (2009). Making progress in the general curriculum: Rethinking effective instructional practices. *Research and Practice for Persons with Severe Disabilities, 33*(4), 214–227.

Crockett, J. (2002). Special education's role in preparing responsive leaders for inclusive schools. *Remedial and Special Education, 23*, 157–168.

Davis, P., & Florian, L. (2004). Searching the literature on teaching strategies and approaches for pupils with special educational needs: Knowledge production and synthesis. *Journal of Research in Special Educational Needs, 4*(3), 142–147.

DeMatthews, D. (2015.) Making sense of social justice leadership: A case study of a principal's experiences to create a more inclusive school. *Leadership and Policy in Schools, 14*(2), 139–166.

Dessemontet, R., & Bless, G. (2013). The impact of including children with intellectual disability in general education classrooms on the academic achievement of their low-, average-, and high-achieving peers. *Journal of Intellectual and Developmental Disability, 38*(1), 23–30.

Diaz, E. M., & Kosciw, J. G. (2009). *Shared differences: The experiences of lesbian, gay, bisexual, and transgender students of color in our nation's schools.* New York: GLSEN.

Dix, K., Shearer, J., Slee, P., & Butcher, C. (2010). *KidsMatter for students with a disability: Evaluation report ministerial advisory committee: Students with disabilities.* South Australian Government. Australian Government. Retrieved January 29, 2019, from www.flinders.edu.au/ehl/fms/educationalfutures/kidsmatter/KidsMatter%20for%20Students%20with%20a%20Disability%20Evaluation%20Report.pdf

Dunne, M., Humphreys, S., Sebba, J., Dyson, A., Gallannaugh, F., & Muijs, D. (2007). *Effective teaching and learning for pupils in low attaining groups*. Research report DCSF-RR011. (DCSF). London: DCSF. Retrieved January 29, 2019, from https://dera.ioe.ac.uk/6622/1/DCSF-RR011.pdf

Dutro, E. (2010). What "hard times" means: Mandated curricula, class-privileged assumptions, and the lives of poor children. *Research in the Teaching of English, 44*, 255–291.

Eriksson, L., Welander, J., & Granlund, M. (2007). Participation in everyday school activities for children with and without disabilities. *Journal of Developmental and Physical Disabilities, 19*, 485–502.

Forlin, C., & Chambers, D. (2011). Teacher preparation for inclusive education: Increasing knowledge but raising concerns. *Asia Pacific Journal of Teacher Education, 39*(1) 17–32.

Hallam, S., & Ireson, J. (2006). Secondary school pupils' preferences for different types of structured grouping practices. *British Educational Research Journal, 32*(4), 583–599.

Hattie, J. (2009). *Visible learning: A synthesis of meta-analyses relating to achievement*. London: Routledge.

Hehir, T., Grindal, T., Freeman, B., Lamoreau, R., Borquaye, Y., & Burke, S. (2016). *A summary of the evidence on the inclusive education*. Instituto Alana. Retrieved January 29, 2019, from https://alana.org.br/wp-content/uploads/2016/12/A_Summary_of_the_evidence_on_inclusive_education.pdf

Hynds, A., Averill, R., Hindle, R., & Meyer, L. (2017). School expectations and student aspirations: The influence of schools and teachers on Indigenous secondary students. *Ethnicities, 17*(4), 546–573.

Jones, T., & Hillier, L. (2013). Comparing trans-spectrum and same-sex- attracted youth in Australia: Increased risks, increased Activisms. *Journal of LGBT Youth, 10*(4), 287–307.

Johns, M. M., Lowry, R., Rasberry, C. N., Dunville, R., Robin, L., Pampati, S., ... Mercer Kollar, L. M. (2018). Violence victimization, substance use, and suicide risk among sexual minority high school students – United States, 2015–2017. *MMWR Morbidity Mortal Weekly Report, 67*, 1211–1215. Retrieved January 29, 2019, from www.cdc.gov/mmwr/volumes/67/wr/mm6743a4.htm#suggestedcitation

Lindsay, G. (2012). Inclusive education. In J. Hattie, & E. Anderman (Eds.), *International guide to student achievement* (pp. 143–145). London: Routledge.

OECD (2010). *Overcoming school failure: Policies that work*. Retrieved January 29, 2019, from www.oecd.org/education/school/45171670.pdf

O'Malley Olsen, E., Kann, L., Vivolo-Kantor, A., Kinchen, S., & McManus, T. (2014). School violence and bullying among sexual minority high school students, 2009–2011. *Journal of Adolescent Health, 55*(3), 432–438.

Mason, E. C. M., Springer, S. I., & Pugliese, A. (2017). Staff development as a school climate intervention to support transgender and gender nonconforming students: An integrated research partnership model for school counselors and counselor educators. *Journal of LGBT Issues in Counseling, 11*(4), 301–318.

Morningstar, M. E., Shogren, K. A., Lee, H., & Born, K. (2015). Preliminary lessons about supporting participation and learning in inclusive classrooms. *Research and Practice for Persons with Severe Disabilities, 40*(3), 192–210.

Parsons, S., & Hallam, S. (2014). The impact of streaming on attainment at age seven: Evidence from the millennium cohort study. *Oxford Review of Education, 40*(5), 567–589.

Pollak, D. (2002). *Dyslexia, the self and higher education: Learning life histories of students identified as dyslexic*. Unpublished thesis. De Montfort University.

Praisner, C. L. (2003). Attitudes of elementary school principals toward the inclusion of students with disabilities. *Exceptional Children, 69*(2), 135–145.

Quinn, D. M. (2017). Racial attitudes of preK–12 and postsecondary educators: Descriptive evidence from nationally representative data. *Educational Researcher, 46*, 397–411.

Riehl, C. (2000). The principal's role in creating inclusive schools for diverse students: A review of normative, empirical, and critical literature on the practice of educational administration. *Review of Educational Research, 70*(1), 55–81.

Rosenstreich, G. (2013). *LGBTI people mental health and suicide* (2nd ed.). Sydney: National LGBTI Health Alliance. Retrieved January 29, 2019, from www.beyondblue.org.au/docs/default-source/default-document-library/bw0258-lgbti-mental-health-and-suicide-2013-2nd-edition.pdf?sfvrsn=2

Rose, D. (2001). Universal design for learning. *Journal of Special Education Technology, 16*, 66–67.

Ryan, J. (2006). *Inclusive leadership*. San Francisco, CA: Jossey-Bass.

Salend, S. J., & Duhaney, L. M. G. (1999). The impact of inclusion on students with and without disabilities and their educators. *Remedial and Special Education, 20*(2), 114–126.

Sharma, U. (2018). Preparing to teach in inclusive classrooms. In G. W. Noblit (Ed.), *Oxford research encyclopedia of education*. Oxford: Oxford University Press. Retrieved January 29, 2019, from http://oxfordre.com/education/view/10.1093/acrefore/9780190264093.001.0001/acrefore-9780190264093-e-113

Sharma, U., Forlin, C., Deppeler, J., & Yang, G. (2013). Reforming teacher education for inclusion in developing countries in the Asia Pacific region. *Asian Journal of Inclusive Education, 1*(1), 3–16.

Shulman, L. S. (2004). *The wisdom of practice: Essays on teaching, learning and learning to teach*. San Francisco, CA: Jossey-Bass.

Schwab, S. (2015). Social dimensions of inclusion in education of 4th and 7th grade pupils in inclusive and regular classes: Outcomes from Austria. *Research in Developmental Disabilities, 43–44*, 72–79.

Smyth, E., & Calvert, E. (2011). *Choices and challenges: Moving from junior cycle to senior cycle education*. Dublin: The Liffey Press.

South Australia Department of Education (2018). *Principles of inclusion for children and students with disability in education and care*. Retrieved January 29, 2019, from www.education.sa.gov.au/department/about-department/minister-education-and-child-development-decd/ministerial-advisory-committee-children-and-students-disability/principles-inclusion-children-students-disability

Spooner, F., & Dymond, S. K. (2006). Introduction to special issue on accessing the general curriculum what we know and need to know about accessing the general curriculum for students with significant cognitive disabilities. *Research and Practice for Persons with Severe Disabilities, 31*(4), 277–283.

Staub, D., & Peck, C. A. (1994). What are the outcomes for nondisabled students? *Educational Leadership, 52*(4), 36–40.

Sturgeon, S. (2006). Promoting mental health as an essential aspect of health promotion. *Health Promotion International, 21*, 36–41.

Tereschchenko, A., Francis, B., Archer, L., Hodgen, J., Mazenod, A., Taylor, B., ... Travers, M-C. (in press). Learners' attitudes to mixed-attainment grouping: Examining the views of students of high, middle and low attainment. *Research Papers in Education*.

Udvari-Solner, A., & Kluth, P. (1997). Inclusive education. In C. A. Grant, & G. Ladson-Billings (Eds.), *Dictionary of multicultural education* (pp. 141–144). Phoenix, AZ: Oryz Press.

UNESCO (1994). *The Salamanca statement and framework for action on special needs education.* Paris: UNESCO. Retrieved January 29, 2019, from www.unesco.org/education/pdf/SALAMA_E.PDF

Vogl, K., & Preckel, F. (2014). Full-time ability grouping of gifted Students: Impacts on social self-concept and school-related attitudes. *Gifted Child Quarterly, 58*(1), 51e68.

Wiener, J., & Tardif, C. Y. (2004). Social and emotional functioning of children with learning disabilities: Does special education placement make a difference? *Learning Disabilities Research & Practice, 19*(1), 20–32.

Chapter 10

Staff wellbeing

Teachers' mental health and wellbeing inevitably impacts students' mental health. It is impossible for teachers to promote mental health if they are not mentally well themselves. Equally, it is impossible for teachers to build students' social and emotional competencies if they have not acquired these skills themselves. Teachers' wellbeing will inevitably impact every aspect of what they do in the classroom, in particular, how they interact with students, their caregivers and colleagues and how they manage classroom behaviour and student engagement. Thus, teacher wellbeing impacts students, whose response in turn will impact teachers' wellbeing. It is within this iterative relationship that the following chapter is framed. Overall, it is noteworthy that what teachers need for their own wellbeing mirrors precisely what students need: a safe, welcoming environment that is intellectually stimulating and a place where people support and look out for each other.

Teacher social and emotional competence

Teachers bring more than their professional skills and knowledge to their role; they bring their personality, childhood experiences, biases, values and assumptions about what and how children learn, that is not always based on professional learning (Reupert, 2009). Thus, along with the necessary subject and pedagogical knowledge to teach their particular subject and year levels, effective teachers are those that have, and display, certain personal attributes and competencies to appropriately engage and interact with young people. Though it is acknowledged that teacher skill, confidence and competence develop over time, teaching effectiveness is also influenced by certain personal characteristics, including interpersonal skills and the ability to cope with a variety of stressors and demands. Indeed, Kunter, Kleickmann, Klusmann and Richter (2013) found that teachers' non-cognitive attributes make an incremental contribution to successful teaching **over and above** pedagogical content knowledge. Moreover, as outlined earlier, while several studies have demonstrated the efficacy of social and emotional learning programs for students, their successful implementation depends heavily on the capacity of the teacher to create an optimal learning environment in which various social and emotional skills may be practiced and modelled. It is his or her actions that will influence the ultimate success of these programs.

In the first instance, in order to competently teach various social and emotional skills, teachers should be able to model appropriate skills in the way they interact with students, their caregivers and colleagues and the way they manage their own stress levels and focus, plan and execute lessons (on any subject). In other words, we have to model what we preach and practice what we teach (Reupert et al. 2010). Given they are dealing with a large group of young people, with diverse interests and backgrounds, effective teachers will also need the ability to coach students through conflict situations and encourage cooperation among students during and outside of class time (Jennings & Greenberg, 2009).

However, staff rarely receive training and support in teaching students' social and emotional competencies (Lopes, Mestre, Guil, Kremenitzer & Salovey, 2012; Woodcock & Reupert, 2013). Accordingly, many teachers are not confident in delivering social and emotional programs, nor do they feel confident in responding to students' social, emotional and behavioural needs (Woodcock & Reupert, 2016). When they do receive training in evidence-based programs, they report being better able to implement positive classroom management strategies and to promote a positive classroom climate (Reupert & Woodcock, 2015). Training in this area needs to occur at the pre-service teacher level, during induction, and as ongoing professional development for in-service teachers.

Teachers' social and emotional competence can be defined in much the same way that it is defined for students – in terms of awareness of self and others, responsible decision making, emotional regulation and interpersonal effectiveness (Zins et al. 2004). Jennings and Greenberg (2009) further operationalised these competences when they suggested that, for teachers, self-awareness means being able to identify and use their emotions to motivate learning in themselves and others. Awareness of others involves understanding how their emotions might impact others and being empathic and culturally sensitive. Socially and emotionally competent teachers respect others, take the needs and perspectives of others into account when making decisions and know how to manage their own emotions, especially in challenging or stressful teaching situations (Jennings & Greenberg, 2009).

There is research to support the contention that teachers' social and emotional competence impacts their performance and student outcomes. Collie and Martin (2016) examined adaptability among teachers, defined as the capacity to adjust one's thoughts, behaviours and emotions in response to changing, novel or uncertain demands. They demonstrated that when teachers demonstrated higher adaptability, they experienced greater wellbeing, which in turn was associated with higher student attainment. Other research has shown that adaptive coping can assist teachers in managing their workloads and challenging interactions, which unsurprisingly can improve teacher wellbeing (Chang, 2009).

Teacher and principal stress and wellbeing

Teachers in many parts of the world experience high levels of stress and depression compared with the general population (Stansfeld, Rasul, Head & Singleton, 2011; Wieclaw, Agerbo, Mortensen & Bonde, 2005). For example, teachers in Great Britain report one of the highest levels of self-reported stress, anxiety and distress, caused or made worse by work, compared to other occupations (Health and Safety Executive, 2018). Likewise, Kidger et al. (2016) found that 19.4% of 555 teachers in England reported moderate to severe depressive symptoms. Stressors for teachers are numerous and can include long hours, workload (including administrative demands), disruptive student behaviour, overcrowded classrooms, isolation, managing change, an over-emphasis on testing, prescriptive curricula, teaching subjects that they do not have content knowledge in, a lack of input into decision making and the unavailability of support for students with additional needs (Bahr, Graham, Ferreira, Lloyd & Waters, 2018; Michie & Williams, 2003). In addition, Wilson, Douglas and Lyon (2011) found that from a sample of 731 teachers, the majority (80.0%) had experienced school-related violence at some point in their careers. Serious violence (actual, attempted or threatened physical violence) was less common but still concerning (28%). As well, school leaders need to manage relationships with and between staff, students, parents and the community and at times address threats and acts of physical violence (Lindle, 2004). They are however frequently inattentive to their own wellbeing (Dicke, Marsh, Riley, Parker, Guo & Horwood, 2018). Collectively, these factors can all lead to increased stress, low morale, adverse impacts on physical health and, ultimately, staff leaving the profession. There have been estimates that has many as 50% of new teachers leave the profession within the first five years of entering teaching, resulting in significant organisational and financial costs (Prilleltensky, Neff & Bessell, 2016).

A heuristic model synthesised from research conducted in organisational health (Hart & Cooper, 2001) and teacher social and emotional competence (Jennings & Greenberg, 2009) was developed to explain the relationship between individual and organisational factors, teacher wellbeing, stress and student outcomes (see Figure 10.1). As indicated by Figure 10.1, both individual and organisational factors contribute to teacher wellbeing and stress, which then impact their performance as teachers, which in turn impacts student outcomes. The influence of both individual and organisational factors are important, and as Rutter, Maughan, Mortimore, Ouston and Smith (1979, p. 39) concluded in their seminal study of the impact of schools on children, "teaching performance is a function of school environment as well as of personal qualities". The model also allows for reciprocal relationships in that organisational and individual factors will impact each other, and teacher wellbeing and teacher performance may impact each other. For example, how a teacher interacts with students and manages the class will impact on

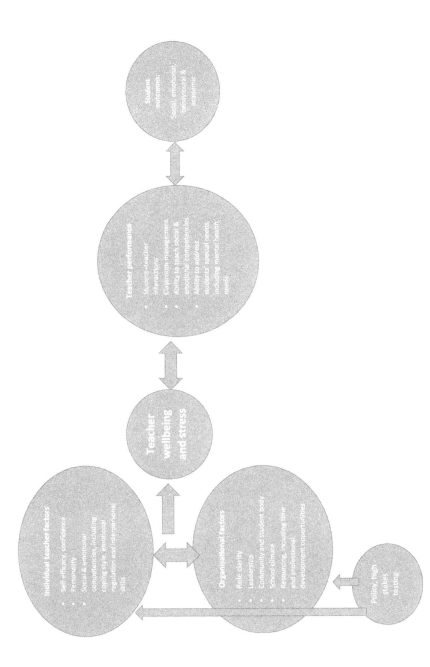

Figure 10.1 The relationships between individual and organisational factors, teacher wellbeing, stress and student outcomes

his or her mental health, and conversely, a teacher's mental health will impact on how he or he manages the class. Relatedly, students' outcomes (defined here in terms of social, behavioural, emotional and academic outcomes) are impacted by teachers' performance and then impact teachers' performance in a feedback loop. The context of the school and workload is informed by policy and, in particular, high stakes testing, which can exert pressure on teachers to teach to the test. How policy is interpreted and implemented by school leaders will influence teacher workload, stress and wellbeing. The model also provides a framework for intervention by highlighting both individual and organisational factors.

Given that approximately two-thirds of children will have experienced at least one adverse childhood experience (ACE) (Centers for Disease Control and Prevention, 2016), it is likely that teachers and other school staff will have lived experience of their own past (or current) adversity (Maybery & Reupert, 2018). School staff are also vulnerable to the vicarious or secondary trauma that may occur as a result of supporting and interacting with traumatised children (Wolpow, Johnson, Hertel & Kincaid, 2009), especially if the trauma experienced by a student triggers memories of their own trauma experiences (Felitti et al. 1998). Staff need to recognise the signs of trauma, in themselves as well as the students they work with, and model self-care.

Teachers' (potentially stressful) role in promoting young people's mental health and wellbeing

Schools play a critical role in the fostering of young people's mental health and wellbeing (as established in Chapter 2). Elias and Weissberg (2000) urged teachers to actively take part in the mental health promotion "revolution". The role of individual teachers in addressing student mental wellbeing usually involves the identification of children with special learning, behavioural and wellbeing needs; collaboration and consultation with psychologists, counsellors and other health and learning professionals; providing emotional and instrumental care and support to individual students; making adjustments and accommodations to the curriculum and pedagogy; and making efforts to be inclusive and conciliatory when dealing with student behaviour and conflict.

Teachers' efforts in supporting young people's mental health are especially critical given the shortage of appropriately qualified counselling personnel working in schools, in some countries at least. And teachers are filling in those gaps. In a national survey of mental health practices across English primary and secondary schools, Vostanis, Humphrey, Fitzgerald, Deighton and Wolpert (2013) found that many teachers, with no specialist mental health training, were delivering mental health and wellbeing programs, with less than 3% using external mental health specialists. Simultaneously, few schools considered training, support, supervision or counselling for their staff as a component of their approach to supporting students' mental health.

Notwithstanding the important contributions that individual teachers can make to the lives of students, there is ongoing tension about how, and the extent to which, teachers can and should work in this area. In a survey-based study examining 508 teachers' views regarding supporting children's mental health, one teacher recorded, "the expectations on teachers re social problems (bullying, abuse, neglect, parenting, safety, drugs) are ridiculous, unobtainable, unrealistic" (Graham, Phelps, Maddison & Fitzgerald, 2011, p. 492). Similarly, another argued:

> The problem I have is that most of us are so overwhelmed by work and stress that it is impossible to even start on student mental health. I am on five medications (for depression, sleep, ulcers, blood pressure). All of this and my staff of which there are six, four have high blood pressure, three have stress related illnesses, one has kidney stones and one has given up. Please don't use this to increase my workload. I'm doing the best I can. Please, please start by helping us because we are at our wits' end.
> (Graham et al. 2011, p. 492)

As evident from the survey responses, many teachers struggled to deal with the complexities of their roles and balance the many expectations placed on them. Though many were committed to supporting children and delivering mental health education programs, they emphatically stated that they needed "more time and resources" to do this (Graham et al. 2011, p. 492).

Many teachers responded to students' mental health issues by looking to "experts" from outside the school to assist, rather than considering what they might do themselves to support these students (Graham et al. 2011). They appeared to construct mental health as an issue that necessitated professional treatment or intervention outside of their expertise. For example, one teacher wrote: "Children need access to a caring individual on a daily basis who has qualifications and compassion to deal with their needs immediately" (Graham et al. 2011, p. 492). The strong theme that came out of this study was of teachers being isolated, ill-equipped, under-resourced and burdened by students' needs. Their responses also highlight training needs around what they might do to support students with mental health difficulties.

In comparison, Reupert and Maybery (2007) identified a myriad of creative ways that teachers used to support students' wellbeing. First, the researchers asked vulnerable young people, namely those whose home environment was marked by parental mental illness or substance misuse, to nominate school personnel who had provided them with exemplary support. The primary and high school teachers, leaders and school counsellors nominated in the study were then interviewed to ascertain the specific nature of this support. Interestingly, those nominated drew on their own personal (as opposed to professional) experience in this area, arising from their own mental health experiences or those of family members. In terms of support, they described addressing children's physical needs, such as offering breakfast. Though many described being torn in their curriculum obligations versus addressing children's needs, they reported creative and innovative ways in which children might be supported *through* and not instead of curriculum and pedagogy. For example, one primary teacher described how she was positive and encouraging via the child's school work and ensured the child was given opportunities to succeed (that is, ensuring there was something to be encouraging about). Another described being very clear about giving students boundaries and structure in terms of behavioural and academic expectations. For example, rather than giving open-ended extensions for homework, the teacher would negotiate different deadlines for different components of any given task.

The relationship that teachers have with students is another obvious way that children can be supported (as established previously). However, many teachers experience difficulty in setting boundaries around the student–teacher relationship. For example, many of the teachers interviewed by Kemp and Reupert (2012) used "the line" metaphor when describing their caring role, referring to boundaries that needed to be consciously and deliberately negotiated in some way. One participant referred to this boundary setting in the following manner:

> I want kids to know me... [but] there's still a line, and you've got to be careful not to cross that, because once you become more of a friend than a teacher then the boundaries are a little blurred.
> (Kemp & Reupert, 2012, p. 120)

Self-care featured largely in the narratives of some participants; for example, one participant reported that "at the end of the day they're [students] the parents' responsibility", while another stated, "I have to learn to switch off, I don't want to go home and think about 22 students all through the night" (Kemp & Reupert, 2012, p. 120). One teacher described the importance of self-care in terms of making her a better teacher: "if you're not caring for yourself and having time for yourself, then you can't have the energy to care for others and you get run down and stressed and physically stuffed" (p. 120). Role clarification as well as the appropriate time, resources, professional development opportunities and collegial and leader support are needed for teachers. Delineating the "line" around caring, and engaging in professional dialogue with other, experienced teachers around what caring for students means and how caring for students can be managed alongside teacher self-care, is strongly recommended. Targeted strategies for teachers to manage their own mental health and wellbeing are required at both an individual and systems level.

Promoting the wellbeing of school staff

Improving staff wellbeing and reducing staff stress, sickness and absence leads to improved teaching ability and performance (Greenberg & Jennings, 2009).

Moreover, when teachers' wellbeing is improved and stress lessened, attrition rates of teachers are reduced (Greenberg & Jennings, 2009). Teachers and school leaders will bring their own coping styles, resilience, perceptions of what a teacher is and should be and personality to their role, and these will inform how well they cope with the stressors associated with teaching. However, there is a limit to what individuals can and should do in the face of excessive work demands. Thus, efforts to promote teacher resilience or tolerance to stress will be unsuccessful if the work load is excessive and untenable and the work environment marked by conflict and violence. Notwithstanding the individual coping and personality factors that contribute to stress, the school management team also has an important role to play in promoting the wellbeing of school staff. Indeed, given that much of the stress experienced by teachers results from excessive demands of school life, it is also the responsibility of managers and policy makers to ensure that school environments are safe and foster and support teachers' wellbeing and mental health. The responsibility for promoting staff wellbeing is shared between individual staff members and school leaders.

There are various strategies directed to the individual that may be employed to foster wellbeing. Some programs invite staff to consider mindfulness, acceptance and a growth mindset, in order to respond adaptively to stress and learn how to manage negative feelings (Herman & Reinke, 2015). Likewise, Sutton (2005) provides some suggested activities to help teachers regulate their emotions, focus on being aware of one's emotions in the classroom, enhance awareness of positive emotions and build strategies for reducing negative emotions. Teachers will need to draw on informal and formal social and emotional supports and set aside time for family and interests outside of work. School leaders need to be role models for self-care in their own practice, and advocate for, and encourage collective wellbeing.

Other school efforts include mentoring and induction programs which can be used to counter the isolation and lack of support experienced by some teachers, especially beginning teachers (Prilleltensky et al. 2016). Other systematic strategies to support teachers and other school staff relate to school climate, in regard to an open and collaborative leadership style, ensuring teachers are provided with appropriate training opportunities and given the respect and autonomy required to promote job satisfaction. Additional protective factors against stress and burnout for teachers include feeling connected to students, support from colleagues and receiving recognition for their contributions (Flook, Goldberg, Pinger, Bonus & Davidson, 2013). Consultation around decision making processes in schools and policy for team work, delegation and feedback are all factors that can promote teacher wellbeing.

Leaders play a critical role in nurturing staff wellbeing. If leaders want staff to be warm, caring and responsive to students, then they need to model those same behaviours with staff. Similarly, all school staff will prosper in workplaces where they are treated with respect and engage in a consultative process on things that matter to them. Most staff will respect the outcome of a decision if they have been walked through the rationale for why a certain decision was made and the constraints facing administrators. Likewise, training and coaching approaches should acknowledge and draw on prior knowledge and experience rather than ignore or dismiss the learnings that staff bring with them. Given the stress associated with school management positions, leaders themselves need emotional and practical support for their own wellbeing; they will also need guidance in the ways they might support their staff on an individual and systemic basis.

It has been said that happy teachers make for happy students. This affective relationship applies not only to students' wellbeing but also equally to their academic engagement. Frenzel, Goetz, Lüdtke, Pekrun and Sutton (2009) investigated the relationship between teachers' students' enjoyment in mathematics. On the basis that "emotional transmission is based on socially perceivable hints about the emotional state of other persons" (p. 711), they found that in mathematics classes, teachers' enthusiasm and enjoyment and students' enjoyment were positively related and that the effect of teacher enjoyment on student enjoyment was mediated by teacher enthusiasm. A positive school culture, where teachers and others support each other and diversity among both the student body and staff are valued, will do much to promote staff wellbeing. In sum, ensuring teachers, school leaders and other school staff are mentally well not only improves their quality of life but will ultimately benefit the students that they teach, through supportive teacher–student relationships and improved teacher performance.

References

Bahr, N., Graham, A., Ferreira, J., Lloyd, M., & Waters, R. (2018). *Promotion of the teaching profession in Queensland*. Bilinga: Southern Cross University. Prepared for Queensland College of Teachers. Retrieved January 29, 2019, from www.qct.edu.au/pdf/Promotion_TPQ.pdf

Centers for Disease Control and Prevention (2016). *Adverse childhood experiences (ACEs)*. Retrieved January 29, 2019, from www.cdc.gov/violenceprevention/acestudy/index.html

Chang, M. (2009). An appraisal perspective of teacher burnout: Examining the emotional work of teachers. *Educational Psychology Review*, *21*, 193–218.

Collie, R. J., & Martin, A. J. (2016). Adaptability: An important capacity for effective teachers. *Educational Practice and Theory*, *38*, 27–39.

Dicke, T., Marsh, H. W., Riley, P., Parker, P. D., Guo, J., & Horwood, M. (2018). Validating the Copenhagen Psychosocial Questionnaire (COPSOQ-II) using Set-ESEM. Identifying psychosocial risk factors in a sample of school principals. *Frontiers in Psychology*, *9*, S. 800. Retrieved January 29, 2019, from www.ncbi.nlm.nih.gov/pmc/articles/PMC5936966/pdf/fpsyg-09-00584.pdf

Elias, M. J., & Weissberg, R. P. (2000). Primary prevention: Educational approaches to enhance social and emotional learning. *The Journal of School Health*, *70*(5), 186–191.

Felitti, V., Anda, R. F., Nordenberg, D., Williamson, D. F., Spitz, A. M., Edwards, V., . . . Marks, J. S. (1998). Relationship of childhood abuse and household dysfunction to many of the leading causes of death in adults. The adverse childhood experiences (ACE) study. *American Journal of Preventative Medicine*, *14*(4), 245–258.

Flook, L., Goldberg, S. B., Pinger, L., Bonus, K., & Davidson, R. (2013). Mindfulness for teachers: A pilot study to assess effects on stress, burnout and teaching efficacy. *Mind Brain Education*, *7*(3), 1–22. Retrieved December 4, 2018, from www.ncbi.nlm.nih.gov/pmc/articles/PMC3855679/pdf/nihms-532896.pdf

Frenzel, A. C., Goetz, T., Lüdtke, O., Pekrun, R., & Sutton, R. E. (2009). Emotional transmission in the classroom: Exploring the relationship between teacher and student enjoyment. *Journal of Educational Psychology*, *101*(3), 705–716.

Graham, A., Phelps, R., Maddison, C., & Fitzgerald, R. (2011). Supporting children's mental health in schools: Teacher views. *Teachers and Teaching: Theory and Practice*, *17*(4), 479–496.

Greenberg, M., & Jennings, T. (2009). The prosocial classroom: Teacher social and emotional competence in relation to student and classroom outcomes. *Review of Educational Research*, *79*(1), 491–525,

Hart, P., & Cooper, C. L. (2001). Occupational stress: Towards a more integrated framework. In N. Anderson, D. S. Ones, H. K. Sinangil, & C. Viswesvaran (Eds.), *Handbook of industrial, work & organizational psychology – Volume 2: Organizational psychology* (pp. 93–114). London: Sage.

Health and Safety Executive (2018). Work related stress depression or anxiety statistics in Great Britain, 2018. Retrieved June 23, 2019, from http://www.hse.gov.uk/statistics/causdis/stress.pdf Herman, K., & Reinke, W. (2015). *Stress management for teachers: A proactive guide*. New York: Guilford.

Jennings, P. A., & Greenberg, M. T. (2009). The prosocial classroom: Teacher social and emotional competence in relation to student and classroom outcomes. *Review of Educational Research*, *79*(1), 491–525.

Kemp, H., & Reupert, A. (2012). "There's no big book on how to care": Primary pre-service teachers' experiences of caring. *Australian Journal of Teacher Education*, *37*(9), 114–127.

Kidger, J., Brockman, R., Tilling, K. M., Campbell, R., Ford, T. J., Araya, R., . . . Gunnell, D. (2016). Teachers' wellbeing and depressive symptoms, and associated risk factors: A large cross sectional study in English secondary schools. *Journal of Affective Disorders*, *192*, 76–82.

Kunter, M., Kleickmann, T., Klusmann, U., & Richter, D. (2013). The development of teachers' professional competence. In M. Kunter, J. Baumert, W. Blum, U. Klusmann, S. Krauss, & M. Neubrand (Eds.), *Cognitive activation in the mathematics classroom and professional competence of teachers: Results from the COACTIV project* (pp. 63–77). (Mathematics Teacher Education; Vol. 8). New York: Springer VS. doi: 10.1007/978-1-4614-5149-5_4.

Lindle, J. C. (2004). Trauma and stress in the principal's office: Systematic inquiry as coping. *Journal of School Leadership*, *14*(4), 378–410.

Lopes, P. N., Mestre, J., Guil, R., Kremenitzer, J. P., & Salovey, P. (2012). The role of knowledge and skills for managing emotions in adaptation to school: Social behavior and misconduct in the classroom. *American Educational Research Journal*, *49*(4), 710–742.

Maybery, D., & Reupert, A. (2018). The number of parents who are patients attending psychiatric services. *Current Opinion in Psychiatry*, *31*(4), 358–362.

Michie, S., & Williams, S. (2003). Reducing work related psychological ill health and sickness absence: A systematic literature review. *Occupational Environmental Medicine*, *60*(1), 3–9.

Prilleltensky, I., Neff, M., & Bessell, A. (2016). Teacher stress: What it is, why it's important, how it can be alleviated. *Theory into Practice*, *55*, 104–111.

Reupert, A. (2009). Students' use of self: Teaching implications. *Social Work Education*, *28*(7), 765-777.

Reupert, A. E., & Maybery, D. J. (2007). Strategies and issues in supporting children whose parents have a mental illness within the school system. *School Psychology International*, *28*(2), 195–205.

Reupert, A., Hemmings, B., & Connors, J. (2010). Do we practice what we preach? The teaching practices of inclusive educators in tertiary settings. *International Journal of Teaching and Learning in Higher Education, 22*(2), 120–130.

Reupert, A., & Woodcock, S. (2015). Does a year make a difference? The classroom management practices of student teachers before and after a one year teacher education program. *Emotional and Behavioural Difficulties, 20*(3), 265–276.

Rutter, M., Maughan, B., Mortimore, P., Ouston, J., & Smith, A. (1979). *Fifteen thousand hours: Secondary schools and their effects on children.* Cambridge, MA: Harvard University.

Stansfeld, S. A., Rasul, F. R., Head, J., & Singleton, N. (2011). Occupation and mental health in a national UK survey. *Social Psychiatry and Psychiatric Epidemiology, 46*(2), 101–110.

Sutton, R. (2005). Teachers' emotions and classroom effectiveness. Implications from recent research. *The Clearinghouse, 78*(5), 229–234.

Vostanis, P., Humphrey, N., Fitzgerald, N., Deighton, J., & Wolpert, M. (2013). How do schools promote emotional well-being among their pupils? Findings from a national scoping survey of mental health provision in English schools. *Child and Adolescent Mental Health, 18*(3), 151–157.

Wieclaw, J., Agerbo, E., Mortensen, P. B., & Bonde, J. P. (2005). Occupational risk of affective and stress-related disorders in the Danish workforce. *Scandinavian Journal of Work, Environment & Health, 31*(5), 343–351.

Wilson, C. M., Douglas, K. S., & Lyon, D. R. (2011). Violence against teachers: Prevalence and consequences. *Journal of Interpersonal Violence, 26*(12), 2353–2371.

Wolpow, R., Johnson, M. M., Hertel, R., & Kincaid, S. (2009). *The heart of learning and teaching. Compassion, resiliency and academic success.* Olympia, WA: Office of Superintendent of Public Instruction (OSPI) Compassionate Schools. Retrieved January 29, 2019, from www.k12.wa.us/compassionateschools/pubdocs/TheHeartofLearningandTeaching.pdf

Woodcock, S., & Reupert, A. (2013). Does training matter? Comparing the behaviour management strategies of pre-service teachers in a four year program and those in a one year program. *Asia-Pacific Journal of Teacher Education, 41*(1), 87–101.

Woodcock, S., & Reupert, A. (2016). Inclusion, classroom management and teacher self-efficacy in an Australian context. In S. Garvis, & D. Pendergast (Eds.), *Asia-Pacific perspectives on teacher self-efficacy* (pp. 87–102). Sense Publishers: Netherlands.

Zins, J. E., Weissberg, R. P., Wang, M. C., & Walberg, H. J. (Eds.). (2004). *Building academic success on social and emotional learning: What does the research say?* New York: Teachers College.

Chapter 11

Trauma-informed schools

It is well established that the stress resulting from different types of trauma can adversely impact young people's developing brain, with often profound and deleterious educational and mental health implications. This chapter will provide an overview of the different types of trauma that might impact young people, and the ways in which schools might respond to the needs of young people who have been exposed to various traumas. How school and teacher responses align to efforts to promote academic learning and mental health will also presented.

Trauma and its impact on young people

Traumatic events may include direct violence in the home, including physical or sexual abuse, and indirect exposure, such as when children witness violent acts committed against a caregiver. Similarly, children may be traumatised through exposure to direct or indirect violence at school and in the community. Trauma events may involve natural disasters such as fire or flood and involvement in or witnessing of motor accidents (Nadeem, Jaycox, Kataoka, Langley, Stein & Wong, 2014). Such events may occur as singular traumatic experiences (e.g. school shootings, natural disasters) as well as ongoing trauma (e.g. living in dangerous neighbourhoods, ongoing sexual and/or physical abuse). The many and varied adverse childhood experiences (ACEs) – including physical abuse, substance abuse in the household and criminal behaviour of a household member, as discussed in Chapter 2 as a cause of mental illness – fit here as a source of trauma. It has been estimated that by the age of 16, approximately two-thirds of children are exposed to at least one traumatic event, such as violence, crime and abuse, including family and community violence (Le Brocque et al. 2017; Finkelhor, Turner, Ormrod, Hamby & Kracke, 2009).

Trauma can impact on young people in different ways. Compared to adults, children are particularly susceptible to trauma because of their developing brains; they have fewer coping strategies and depend on caregivers for protection. If a caregiver is the source of trauma (e.g. abuse), instead of providing a nurturing presence they may instead be a source of terror. Because of the importance of this early relationship for survival, the attachment patterns infants and young children have with their caregivers are projected onto others. This means that if a parent–child relationship is inconsistent, unhealthy or interrupted, it can be difficult for children to know that they can trust any adult. Instead, or as well, the caregiver may be similarly be traumatised (e.g. exposure to flood) or be victims themselves of abuse and unable to provide protection, comfort and reassurance. Children living in disadvantaged communities, and those with existing learning, behavioural and emotional difficulties, are often especially negatively impacted (Berger, Carroll, Maybery & Harrison, 2018).

Exposure to ongoing, severe and unpredictable stress can significantly impact a child's developing brain. Though the impact differs depending on the age of the child, exposure to trauma may cause a child to operate in the lower orders of the brain more frequently (Plumb, Bush & Kersevich, 2016). This means that children may experience hyper-arousal or hypo-arousal, which presents as fight, flight or freeze, resulting in children's attention focusing on survival and self-preservation, with other higher order brain functions reduced (Plumb et al. 2016). Not surprisingly, learning is not a focus when students are operating in the fight, flight or freeze mode. The longer the child experiences these hyper or hypo-states, the more normal and fixed they become and the less likely they are to be able to regulate their emotions and focus their attention on learning. Plumb et al. (2016, p. 40) concluded that

> it is important to understand that this is not a maladaptive behavior. The child's brain has learned that, in order to survive, it needs to remain in survival model at all times. Unfortunately children have no control over the development of their brain. A brain that is developed to survive, left without intervention will be a brain that has difficulty learning in school.

Every traumatic experience is different, and each child's response will vary depending on the frequency, severity and duration of the trauma event/s, and the child's age, resources, personality, intelligence and coping style as well as the level and quality of support they receive (Cole et al. 2009). Repeated traumatic experiences, especially those committed intentionally by a caregiver, are likely to result in different symptoms than a single traumatic event (Terr, 1991). Nonetheless, trauma has the potential to negatively impact children behaviourally, cognitively and socially.

Cole et al. (p. 21) asserted that "many of the obstacles traumatized children face in the classroom result from their inability to process information, meaningfully distinguish between threatening and nonthreatening situations, form trusting relationships with adults, and modulate their emotions". Thus, children who have experienced trauma may have their decision making abilities, abstract reasoning, memory and ability to concentrate compromised, and they may find it difficult to form close and trusting relationships with others; alternatively, they may form unhealthy relationships or isolate themselves (Beers & DeBellis,

2002; Plumb et al. 2016). Children exposed to trauma are more likely than other children to have decreased reading ability (Delaney-Black et al. 2002) and lower grade point averages (Hurt, Malmud, Brodsky & Giannetta, 2001), to receive special educational services (Shonk & Cicchetti, 2001), to report higher absenteeism (Beers & DeBellis, 2002) and, ultimately, to drop out of school (Grogger, 1997). Poor physical and mental health, homelessness, poverty and unemployment have all been positively associated with trauma exposure.

Schools and trauma

As schools are part of the community, they may either bear the brunt of the traumatic event (e.g. a school shooting) or may be called on to identify and support children and their caregivers impacted by trauma, such as might occur when the community is affected by fire or flood. The school may also need to identify and support any individual child exposed to trauma from their family and/or community. In response to community events, schools might be tasked with providing places of shelter or as points of distribution for food and other resources. They may provide counselling to members of the school community; for example, after the September 11, 2001 attacks on the World Trade Center and the Pentagon, most students who received counselling obtained this from school (Stuber, Fairbrother, Galea, Pfefferbaum, Wilson-Genderson & Vlahov, 2002). Importantly, schools can provide a welcome return to routine, normalcy and a pathway for the community to re-establish itself after a traumatic event. Other potential roles for schools in supporting children affected by trauma are outlined below.

School-based formal programs

There are various trauma-informed formal programs developed for schools, with some that focus on specific types of trauma such as fires, hurricanes and suicide (Le Brocque et al. 2017; Jaycox, Morse, Tanielian & Stein, 2006; Wasserman et al. 2015). Other programs are nonspecific, in that they are designed for schools to address the mental health needs of students exposed to "everyday" traumas that they might see at home or in their community. These include the Trauma Informed Positive Education (TIPE) model (Brunzell, Stokes & Waters, 2017) and the Attachment, Self-regulation and Competency (ARC) framework (Cole, O'Brien, Geron Gadd, Ristuccia, Wallace & Gregory, 2005). Depending on the trauma and exposure, some programs target the whole school while others are designed for selective or at-risk groups of students.

This section will consider generic trauma-informed teaching and learning strategies as well as the evidence-based ways in which schools might best prepare and respond to critical incidents. Rather than being an additional curriculum requirement or demand on schools, a synthesised approach will be presented, detailing how school-based, trauma-informed responses might be incorporated into general effective teaching and learning principles where opportunities to promote mental health and wellbeing are maximised for all students.

Trauma-sensitive school environments

School systems

A whole school approach ensures that the school culture is sensitive to the needs of all students, incorporating teaching and learning policies, classroom management guidelines and effective anti-bullying programs and approaches. Zero tolerance policies and harsh classroom discipline models can backfire as they have the potential to trigger children's reactions that amplify feelings of trauma. Instead, flexible but timely responses to behavioural problems are needed to de-escalate a situation rather than administering a prescribed and automatic punishment or consequence such as suspension. Policies and procedures for the identification and support for young people who require additional support is needed alongside strong partnerships with mental health and other external community providers. Appropriate training and induction for staff needs to be organised so that staff appreciate the needs of children and can behave appropriately.

The role of the teacher

Many teachers, at both the pre- and in-service level, are not trained in trauma-informed practices and subsequently feel diffident, overwhelmed and ill prepared to work with students who have been traumatised. Some may feel that working with children on trauma issues is beyond their role and expertise, while others see trauma as a home problem rather than a school problem and so might "blame" the child and/or the caregivers for problems the child is experiencing in school. They may also struggle to deal with the needs of one child while also working with the rest of the class.

Thus, it is perhaps not surprising that students report being dissatisfied with the manner in which teachers deal with traumatic events, such as the death of a classmate (Dyregrov, Wikander & Vigerust, 1999). However, given the prevalence of adverse experiences known to impact children, it is expected that many teachers will have at least some children in their class who have been traumatised, to at least some extent. Likewise, teachers may well have been brought up exposed to one or more adverse childhood event themselves, such as the mental illness or substance misuse of a family member (Maybery & Reupert, 2018). In the case of critical incident events that might impact a school, teachers often live in the same community as their students and may be similarly negatively affected by the same event. O'Toole and Friesen (2016) found that school staff reported high levels of emotional distress and post-traumatic stress disorder (PTSD) following a disaster. Thus, on these occasions, teachers may find it difficult to support children if they are not coping adaptively themselves. This finding also highlights the need for teachers to prevent "compassion fatigue", also referred to as "secondary traumatic stress", that may arise as a result of working with students exposed to trauma.

The difficulties for teachers when working with children negatively impacted by trauma arise because children may not express the distress they are feeling in ways that are easily recognisable; instead, they tend to present with behaviour that is aggressive or indicative of attention or learning problems (Downey, 2007). Additionally, family violence and abuse are taboo topics and are subsequently often kept secret from school staff, making it even more difficult for teachers to understand why a child is behaving as they are (Reupert & Maybery, 2007). Children's reactions to stress may thus mimic symptoms of Attention-Deficit/Hyperactivity Disorder (ADHD), or a conduct or learning disorder.

Cole et al. (2009) suggested that professional development programs for school staff should ideally promote an understanding of trauma and its impact on learning behaviours and interpersonal skills. It is important for teachers to appreciate children's behaviour as an adaptive response to stress, rather than attributable to low ability or behavioural problems (Goodman, Miller & West-Olatunji, 2012). Recognising that a child is reacting to trauma rather than being inherently bad or naughty will do much to change the manner in which staff respond to children. Additionally, school staff need to be familiar with court orders (e.g. restraining orders) and laws (for example, laws around managing disclosure) (Cole et al. 2009). School staff may need to learn how to work with caregivers who have been traumatised and help them feel comfortable and trusting of the school; Cole et al. (2009) argued that this trust will then transfer to their children. Finally, Cole et al. (2009) suggested that professional development needs to clearly outline to teachers their role in supporting children, not as mental health professionals, but instead focusing on what they can do to develop stable, supportive classrooms.

To this end, there are several things a teacher can do to support children who have experienced trauma. Given these children operate at a high level of arousal, teachers are ideally placed to model and teach children strategies for managing their anxiety and modulating their behaviour (Cole et al. 2009). Teaching these students to label and articulate their emotions and understand the connection between emotions and behaviour will need to be emphasised. The aim here is for students to learn how to de-escalate potentially triggering situations themselves and regulate their own emotions. The promotion of these skills needs to be part of a comprehensive social and emotional learning curriculum for the whole school. Additionally, accommodations such as a safe space in the classroom where students can go to when feeling overwhelmed and warning children about any loud noises before they occur (e.g. fire alarms) are other ways that can assist children to regulate their emotions (Cole et al. 2009).

Traumatised children may need strategies to improve executive functioning; again, those pedagogies that "excellent' teachers employ, as outlined in a previous chapter, will support this. For instance, teachers might break down tasks and assignments into manageable parts and use multiple ways of presenting information (e.g. written and oral instructions). Having explicit and behavioural goals will also help children regulate their emotions and think through what needs to be done and when.

Stability and predictability are especially important for children exposed to trauma. Older children may be prompted to use a day planner and provided with support at the end of the day to ensure homework requirements are understood. A daily schedule, for children of all ages, can provide some structure to the day, so teachers can post this for students to take note of during the day. Changes to the daily schedule should be made ahead of time. Transitions between activities are often a trigger for children who have been exposed to trauma, so teachers need to manage these in a calm and consistent manner so that children can predict what is going to happen and when. Likewise, teachers need to be clear about expected behaviours in the classroom and on school grounds, and teach rules and expected behaviours explicitly.

Teachers can work at repairing disrupted attachments so students know that their teacher can be trusted to keep them safe, both physically and emotionally, while at school. In this way, a caring teacher provides a role model and an alternative attachment template for healthy relationships. In particular, early childhood educators play an important role in this regard, because children's early classroom experiences influence their perception of school for years to come. It is in this way that teachers show children that there are adults who can support and guide them, even if their primary caregiver is not able to. Getting to know students, being genuinely interested in their progress, acknowledging their strengths outside of the classroom and being clear about expectations will provide a strong basis for student–teacher relationships. Ultimately, teacher actions to create a safe, welcoming space allow children to think that they belong and that they are worthy of someone's care.

Likewise, teachers need to employ classroom management practices that foster relational attachments and positive emotions, rather than run the risk of re-traumatising children. Focusing on the emotion behind the behaviour and not the behaviour itself may help teachers reframe how they understand the child and his or her actions. Understanding specific triggers that might set off a child's behaviour is an important component of understanding the child. Similarly, teachers need to model respectful, non-violent behaviour and relationships while at the same time setting clear and consistent limits for inappropriate behaviour. The importance of the student–teacher relationship cannot be emphasised enough for children who have been exposed to trauma; as Cole et al. (2009) argued, it is this relationship that creates the space needed for young people to learn.

Children whose behaviour is the most challenging are typically those who need the most social and academic support. Suspending or removing them from the classroom only serves to reinforce children's beliefs about their own unworthiness. Indeed, those children who are removed from the classroom are often the ones who need the most social, emotional and academic support. Though it is acknowledged that their behaviour may be challenging, removing these children will do little to "fix" the problem in the long term.

Instead, students need to be provided with opportunities for agency and control. Giving students genuine choices and finding opportunities throughout the day to set and achieve goals will provide students with a sense of self-control over their environment and promote self-confidence. Within a positive psychology paradigm, Brunzell et al. (2017) argued that, as well as rectifying student deficiencies, schools should develop young people's positive self-image, unrelated to academic achievement. This could involve assigning students particular jobs throughout the day, inviting them be a peer helper to someone else and encouraging their participation in extracurricular activities such as clubs, the arts and sports. Providing opportunities for success is critical in these examples.

Likewise, teachers need to maintain academic standards while also not pushing them too far. Cole et al. (2009) pointed out that children may interpret lowered standards as validation that they are worthless, a self-image perpetuated by the trauma experience. Instead, they suggest teachers encourage students to meet the high standards set for all students, with the help and support of the school.

Finally, as with any student, teachers can ask them directly what they can do to help – building genuine conversations throughout the day shows that they care and are willing to work with the student on making school a safe, calm space. Teachers do not necessarily need to know the source of the trauma but instead appreciate that the child is more than the behaviour he or she is presenting with. Wanting to reach out and understand the student will do much to support traumatised students.

Managing specific traumatic events

There are procedures that may be followed for various crises, such as suicides, traffic accidents, school shootings and natural disasters for example fire or flood (Robinson et al. 2013; Wasserman et al. 2015). Most programs in this area tend to follow a similar structure in regard to prevention and early intervention, as well as outlining strategies for how schools might respond both at the time of the crisis and afterwards. For example, Robinson et al. (2013) found four themes that underlie suicide prevention strategies in schools: universal approaches (involving the promotion of mental health and wellbeing to the whole school); selective approaches (for students not showing signs of suicidal behaviour but who are displaying risk factors that could place them at greater risk in the future); indicated interventions (for those who are already displaying suicidal behaviour, for example, who have expressed suicidal ideation or made a suicide attempt); and, finally, postvention (strategies and programs for the school community to apply after a suicide). In response to these four themes, training is typically offered to staff to better identify students who may be at risk for suicide and intervene appropriately so that a potentially suicidal student is identified, supported and, as required, referred for assessment and treatment (Wasserman et al. 2015). Other training initiatives might target students as peer leaders who, with adult mentoring, encourage their peers to identify trusted adults and disseminate messages about interpersonal and formal coping resources through social networking sites and presentations (Wyman et al. 2010). These four levels of support might inform procedures for responding to other critical incidents.

School shootings attract much media attention and can be especially traumatising for staff and students who witnessed the shooting as well as parents, teachers and students in communities within and outside of the area, and who may have ongoing feelings of danger about attending school. When it comes to prevention, a number of measures have been discussed, though on the whole efforts considered preventative tend to be of a punitive, reactive nature. For example, the Gun-Free Schools Act in the US called on states to enact laws that required schools to expel students who bring a firearm to school for a period of not less than one year (Borum, Cornell, Modzeleski & Jimerson, 2010). Other so-called prevention measures involve security measures such as searching lockers, requiring visitors to sign in and employing security guards (Borum et al. 2010). It is important to note that the majority of school attackers are male, and in more than three-quarters of incidents an adult had expressed concern about the attacker; nearly 75% had previously threatened or tried to commit suicide; more than half had a history of feeling extremely depressed; and in more than two-thirds of incidents, the attackers had felt persecuted or bullied by others (Borum et al. 2010). School shootings provide an example of the need for authentic prevention measures that can be applied equally to the whole student body, with follow up actions required for selective at-risk groups.

Crisis plans

Every school needs to have a crisis plan, which provides procedures to follow if or when a crisis such as a suicide or death occurs. It is equally important to develop and regularly review these plans, as when a crisis occurs, staff are typically caught up in the stress associated with the event and may not be thinking as clearly and rationally as they might otherwise. A comprehensive crisis plan should be forward-planning and outline strategies to employ during, immediately after a crisis and in the longer term (Department of Education and Science, 2007). Preparation covers training for staff about crises, the establishment of a critical incident management team and a checklist for policy and plans (Department of Education and Science, 2007). When an event occurs, schools will need to assess the impact of the event and mobilise their own resources and possibly other external supports to respond immediately and effectively. Counselling or psychological support may need to be provided to staff, students and others in the community, and screening conducted to identify those most at need of support, with clear procedures for referral as required. Usually it is best if students are supported by those they know best, and that is normally teachers rather than external "experts", who instead might advise and support school staff in helping students (Department of Education and Science, 2007). Consistent and reliable messages about the event need to be relayed to students, including the community and a strategy developed for dealing with the media. It is important to maintain routines and normalcy, though at the same time, provisions should be made to provide opportunities for students and staff to talk about what happened and what it means for them.

Synthesizing a trauma informed approach into school settings

A school with a tiered approach to identifying and responding to children's mental health and learning difficulties will already have many of the skills, frameworks and resources to help traumatised children. Hence, much of what has already been discussed in previous chapters of this book aligns with a trauma-informed school model. For example, discipline and behaviour policies in trauma-informed schools will advocate for children and focus on the causes of behaviour rather than merely attempting to manage the behaviour. Accordingly, accountability for behaviour needs to be addressed within an acknowledgement of the impact of trauma on children, with alternatives to punishment and suspension provided. Trauma-informed schools focus on respectful, positive and healing relationships between students, and between students and staff, and where school culture is sensitive to the needs of students and the community. Staff wellbeing is prioritised in recognition that staff are not able to attend to the needs of students if they are not mentally well themselves. The social and emotional curriculum needs to be modelled by staff and embedded within everyday lessons for all students, across all curriculum areas. Most, if not all, social and emotional learning programs incorporate emotional literacy and problem solving, two competencies that are recommended for intervening with children exposed to trauma (Payton et al. 2008).

A tiered approach to supporting young people's mental health, wellbeing and academic learning was outlined earlier (see Figure 4.1). The same approach applies here for students who have been exposed to trauma and, as shown in Figure 11.1, demonstrates how schools might identify and support these children. This might also be applied when schools are exposed to various adverse incidents. Erbacher, Singer and Poland (2014) developed a similar, three-tiered approach to managing suicide in schools which applies similar principles. For example, in their model and in tier two, students who may need specialist support after a class member commits suicide are supported in small groups where emotions and reactions are normalised or individually as required. Likewise, in tier two, some children exposed to trauma may benefit from small social-skills groups that teach children what behaviours are socially acceptable at school and discuss ways to make friends and ways to ask for help. Tier three usually involves

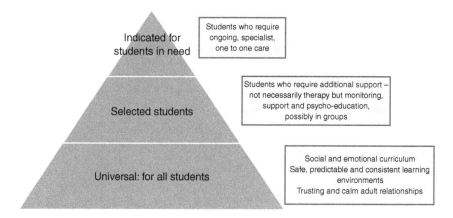

Figure 11.1 A school-based, tiered approach for supporting students exposed to trauma

a smaller number of students who require ongoing specialist care outside of the school, with links made back at the school to provide continued support and reinforcement.

For children exposed to trauma, school systems should be aligned with these three tiers and include classroom management and anti-bullying policies, pedagogy and curriculum offerings, strategies to promote staff wellbeing and procedures for identifying and screening at-risk students.

References

Beers, S., & DeBellis, M. (2002). Neuropsychological function in children with maltreatment-related posttraumatic stress disorder. *American Journal of Psychiatry*, *159*, 483–486.

Berger, E., Carroll, M., Maybery, D., & Harrison, D. (2018). The impact of a disaster on students and staff from a specialist, trauma-informed school in Australia. *Journal of Child & Adolescent Trauma*, *11*(4), 55521–55530.

Borum, W., Cornell, D. G., Modzeleski, W., & Jimerson, S. R. (2010). What can be done about school shootings? A review of the evidence. *Educational Researcher*, *39*(1) 27–37.

Brunzell, T., Stokes, H., & Waters, L. (2017). Trauma-informed positive education: Using positive psychology to strengthen vulnerable students. *Contemporary School Psychology*, *20*(1), 63–83.

Cole, S., O'Brien, J. G., Geron Gadd, M., Ristuccia, J., Wallace, D. L., & Gregory, M. (2005). *Helping traumatized children learn: Supportive school environments for children traumatized by family violence*. Boston, MA: Massachusetts Advocates for Children. Retrieved December 11, 2018, from https://traumasensitiveschools.org/wp-content/uploads/2013/06/Helping-Traumatized-Children-Learn.pdf

Cole, S., O'Brien, J. G., Geron Gadd, M., Ristuccia, J., Wallace, D. L., & Gregory, M. (2009). *Helping traumatized children learn. Supportive school environments for children traumatized by family violence*. Boston, MA: Massachusetts Advocates for Children. Retrieved January 29, 2019, from https://traumasensitiveschools.org/wp-content/uploads/2013/06/Helping-Traumatized-Children-Learn.pdf

Delaney-Black, V., Covington, C., Ondersma, S. J., Nordstrom-Klee, B., Templin, T., Ager, J., Janisse, J., & Sokol, R. J. (2002). Violence exposure, trauma, and IQ and/or reading deficits among urban children. *Archives of Pediatrics & Adolescent Medicine*, *156*(3), 280–285.

Department of Education and Science (2007). *Responding to critical incidents*. Guidelines for schools. Retrieved January 29, 2019, from www.sdpi.ie/other_des_publications/neps_critical_incidents_guidelines_schools.pdf

Downey, L. (2007). *Calmer classrooms: A guide to working with traumatised children*. Melbourne: Child Safety Commissioner.

Dyregrov, A., Wikander, A. M., & Vigerust, S. (1999). Sudden death of a classmate and friend: Adolescents' perception of support from their school. *School Psychology International*, *20*(20), 191–208. doi: 10.1177/0143034399202003.

Erbacher, T. A., Singer, J. B., & Poland, S. (2014). *Suicide in schools: A practitioner's guide to multi-level prevention, assessment, intervention, and postvention*. New York: Taylor & Francis.

Finkelhor, D., Turner, J., Ormrod, R., Hamby, S., & Kracke, K. (2009). *Children's exposure to violence: A comprehensive national survey*. Juvenile Justice Bulletin. Retrieved January 29, 2019, from www.unh.edu/ccrc/pdf/DOJ-NatSCEV-bulletin.pdf

Goodman, R. D., Miller, M. D., & West-Olatunji, C. A. (2012). Traumatic stress, socioeconomic status, and academic achievement among primary school students. *Psychological Trauma: Theory, Research, Practice, and Policy*, *4*(3), 252.

Grogger, J. (1997). Local violence and educational attainment. *Journal of Human Resources*, *32*, 659–682.

Hurt, H., Malmud, E., Brodsky, N. L., & Giannetta, J. (2001). Exposure to violence: Psychological and academic correlates in child witnesses. *Archives of Pediatrics and Adolescent Medicine*, *155*, 1351.

Jaycox, L. H., Morse, L. K., Tanielian, T., & Stein, B. D. (2006). *How schools can help students recover from traumatic experiences. A tool kit for supporting long-term recovery*. RAND. Gulf States Policy Institute. Retrieved January 29, 2019, from www.rand.org/content/dam/rand/pubs/technical_reports/2006/RAND_TR413.pdf

Le Brocque, R., DeYoung, A., Montague, G., Pocock, S., March, S., Triggell, N., ... Kenardy, J. (2017). Schools and natural disaster recovery: The unique and vital role that teachers and education professionals play in ensuring the mental health of students following natural disasters. *Journal of Psychologists and Counsellors in Schools*, *27*(1), 1–23.

Maybery, D., & Reupert, A. (2018). The number of parents who are patients attending psychiatric services. *Current Opinion in Psychiatry*, *31*(4), 358–362.

Nadeem, E., Jaycox, L., Kataoka, S., Langley, A., Stein, B. D., & Wong, M. (2014). Effects of trauma on students: Early intervention through the cognitive behavioral intervention for trauma in schools (CBITS). In M. Weist, N. Lever, C. Bradshaw, & J. Owens (Eds.), *Handbook of school mental health: Research, training, practice, and policy* (2nd ed.) (pp. 145–158). New York: Springer.

O'Toole, V. M., & Friesen, M. D. (2016). Teachers as first responders in tragedy: The role of emotion in teacher adjustment eighteen months post-earthquake. *Teaching and Teacher Education*, *59*, 57–67.

Payton, J., Weissberg, R., Durlak, J., Dymnicki, A., Taylor, R., Shellinger, K., & Pachan, M. (2008). *The positive impact of social and emotional learning for kindergarten to eighth grade students. Findings from three scientific reviews*. Chicago, IL: Collaborative for Academic, Social, and Emotional Learning. Retrieved December 11, 2018, from www.casel.org/wp-content/uploads/2016/08/PDF-4-the-positive-impact-of-social-and-emotional-learning-for-kindergarten-to-eighth-grade-students-executive-summary.pdf

Plumb, J., Bush, K. A., & Kersevich, S. E. (2016). Trauma-sensitive schools: An evidence-based approach. *School Social Work Journal, 40*(2), 37–60.

Reupert, A. E. & Maybery, D.J., (2007). Strategies and issues in supporting children whose parents have a mental illness within the school system. *School Psychology International, 28*(2), 195–205.

Robinson, J., Cox, G., Malone, A., Williamson, M., Baldwin, G., Fletcher, K., & O'Brien, M. (2013). A systematic review of school-based interventions aimed at preventing, treating, and responding to suicide-related behavior in young people. *Crisis: Journal of Crisis Intervention & Suicide, 34*(3), 164–182.

Shonk, S. M., & Cicchetti, D. (2001). Maltreatment, competency deficits, and risk for academic and behavioral maladjustment. *Developmental Psychology, 37*(1), 3–17.

Stuber, J., Fairbrother, G., Galea, S., Pfefferbaum, B., Wilson-Genderson, M., & Vlahov, D. (2002). Determinants of counseling for children in Manhattan after September 11 attacks. *Psychiatric Services, 53* (7), 815–822.

Terr, L. C. (1991). Childhood traumas: An outline and overview. *American Journal of Psychiatry, 148*(1), 10–20.

Wasserman, D., Hoven, C. W., Wasserman, C., Wall, M., Eisenberg, R., Hadlaczky, G., . . . Carli, V. (2015). School-based suicide prevention programmes: The SEYLE cluster-randomised, controlled trial. *The Lancet, 385*(9977), 1536–1544. http://dx.doi.org/10.1016/S0140-6736(14)61213-7

Wyman, P. A., Brown, C. H., LoMurray, M., Schmeelk-Cone, K., Petrova, M., Yu, Q., ... Wang, W. (2010). An outcome evaluation of the sources of strength suicide prevention program delivered by adolescent peer leaders in high schools. *American Journal of Public Health, 100*(9), 1653–1661.

Chapter 12

Making a difference
Are we there yet?

Much material has been covered in previous chapters. This chapter will provide a road map for a way forward, pull together various themes that have been raised and present a model that can be used to investigate whether and how school efforts make a difference to the young people they teach. The action research cycle is presented as a process to employ when deciding which changes may be necessary and documenting the impact they make (or do not make). The cycle provides a means of improving schools through learning and adaption and is iterative, dynamic and ongoing so schools can be responsive to the needs of children and the community over time. It is within this cyclic process that the chapter is subtitled "Are we there yet?", as it is positioned within the notion of never actually arriving but continually evolving and making refinements and improvements. Rather than "bolt on" programs or interventions, the position advocated in this chapter is about systems change for creating optimal conditions for supporting children's mental health and learning, driven by evidence-based practice in ways that are relevant and meaningful to end users, namely teachers, school staff and, most importantly, students.

What should schools be doing? Evidence-based programs and practice-based evidence

Schools are busy places, and it is easy for staff and school leaders to react as situations arise, rather than reflect on what they are doing, why and the impact their actions have on the students and families they work with. The importance of reflection and continually asking what difference our actions make to the young people we work with are at the core of good teaching practice. Effectively addressing children's mental health and academic needs means that the interests of children are at the centre of all school-based decision making processes. But how do schools decide what to do in this regard?

Evidence-based programs (EBPs) are those that have undergone a rigorous evaluation process and demonstrate effectiveness with specific population groups. They are commonly espoused as models of "gold practice" which teachers should be delivering. The term EBPs originally comes from medicine and is often reported in health and other medical trials. Chapter 3 provided an overview of many of the available EBPs for schools, which aim to foster a positive and engaging learning environment.

Notwithstanding the impetus to be evidence-based, Proctor et al. (2009) found that many health-related EBPs "languish" for 15–20 years before being implemented into clinical practice. Likewise, by and large teachers have failed to adopt the results of empirical research into practice (Hempenstall, 2006). There are many barriers to bridging the research–practice chasm in health as well as school settings, including inadequate management support, poor infrastructure, and a lack of time, resources and training opportunities (Reupert, 2018). With a particular reference to schools, Durlak and DuPre (2008) identified the factors that influence the implementation of EBPs, including leadership, staffing, resourcing, communication procedures, administrative support and community partnerships. There are also contextual issues that impede the effectiveness of EBPs and limit their transferability. Bartgis and Bigfoot (2010) argued that many programs which have been identified as evidence-based play little consideration to cultural issues which may be present. This makes their utility in real-world settings somewhat limiting.

The lack of uptake of EBPs in schools begs the question of what sources schools are drawing on when making decisions about wellbeing and learning approaches. How do they decide what to do if a child is struggling with reading, for example? How do they decide whether to move a child up a class or repeat the grade? How do they decide what to do if a child presents with distress or unhappiness? In a sample of over 700 English schools, Vostanis et al. (2013) found that only a third of schools reported providing evidence-based practices, with most reporting that interventions were developed locally. Thus, rather than turning to research to make decisions about supporting young people's mental health, it would appear that schools are doing "their own thing" and drawing on what they think is right, based on their own personal and professional experiences.

Moreover, when schools do turn to evidence-based programs they tend to adapt and change them according to their own needs and context. Program fidelity (the degree to which a program is delivered as intended) stipulates certain implementation guidelines around training, time and resources, but in schools, such stipulations are often not meet. Schools rarely implement a program as it was originally intended. The program may be changed in many ways; some elements might be removed because of time and resource limitations or other components added due to contextual demands or staff interest and expertise. Ringwalt et al. (2010) videotaped 23 teachers in their delivery of a drug prevention program to determine whether they omitted, added or changed prescribed content, or delivered it using different methods than what was required. Considerable variability in teacher performance was noted over time, with fewer steps covered and more material omitted than what was intended. The authors highlighted the need for ongoing support and training but also suggested that the prevention curricula may impose unrealistic expectations and burdens on teachers' abilities and classroom time.

As an alternative to EBP, practice-based evidence (PBE) provides a different way of thinking about evidence. Rather than driven by data collected by external experts, PBE is sourced from professional practice and built over time from experience and trial and error, in the "real world". For teachers, this means relying on what they have done in the past, reflecting on what worked and why and adjusting that learning to new contexts and students. Practice-based evidence has the potential to demonstrate what "works" with a variety of student groups, in a variety of settings. However, practice-based evidence is not an excuse to throw out the types of evidence and guidelines obtained from clinical trials and rigorous research. Shonkoff (2000) offers a means of bridging the research-practice gap by arguing that research is focused on what we do not know, and practice is focused on what should be done. Both are needed for applying knowledge that can make a difference to the lives of children and families. In practical terms, ongoing monitoring and evaluation activities are one way in which the research–practice chasm might be bridged.

The place of monitoring and evaluation

Given the global trend towards accountability, it is increasingly important for educators to use data to guide practice and keep stakeholders informed. As well as accountability, the collection and analysis of data provides opportunities for deep reflection and professional learning. Though governments in many parts of the world often focus on measures of academic achievement to gauge success, it is equally or perhaps more important to also collect ongoing reliable and valid measures of school climate and students' social and emotional competence, engagement in learning, connectedness to school, mental health and wellbeing.

The Educator Sector of UNESCO (2016, p. 7) defined monitoring as "the ongoing, systematic collection of information to assess progress towards the achievement of objectives, outcomes and impacts", while evaluation is defined as "the systematic and objective assessment of an ongoing or completed project, program or policy, its design, implementation and results, with the aim to determine the relevance and fulfilment of objectives, development efficiency, effectiveness, impact and sustainability". Monitoring activities tend to be immediate and ongoing and focus on processes or, in other words, ascertain whether plans were applied as originally intended. Evaluation efforts tend to present performance outcomes that provide a summative assessment of current school practice.

The objectives of monitoring and evaluation vary, depending on the end user, the activity being monitored and evaluated and the context in which it occurs. There are many reasons why individual teachers, groups of staff, school leaders or school communities might need to monitor and evaluate classroom and school practice, or be interested in doing so. Sometimes evaluation systems are required for accountability purposes; for example, high stakes assessment testing is one way of evaluating performance. Other stakeholders, such as caregivers or other professionals, may need to be informed about children's progress in particular areas. Screening data undertaken of children's learning or social and emotional wellbeing might be used to identify at-risk children and also used as baseline data against which subsequent progress is compared, especially if a new program or initiative has been introduced. Other reasons to monitor and evaluate might be to consider how effective a certain program is in terms of making a difference to young people's wellbeing, engagement, behaviour and/or learning. Similarly, a staff development program might be evaluated to ascertain how effective it was in changing staff attitude, confidence or behaviour. Evidence might be collected to identify children's strengths, skills and capabilities and how they best learn, at an individual, class or school level. Likewise, efforts might be made to track children's or a particular school's progress or learning gains from year to year (or less), and how much they improve. Other evaluation questions that might be investigated include determining the economic (and other) costs of any new program and how sustainable it might be in the future.

Overall, different types of data can be used for reflecting on whether what is being offered to students is appropriate and what subsequent changes might still need to be made. The key issue for all monitoring and evaluating activities in schools is ensuring that the data collected is used to inform planning and subsequent changes, which will ultimately serve to make schools a better place for all students and staff.

The action research cycle

There are various models of monitoring and evaluation that schools might employ. For example, many community and government bodies across Australia employ the Results Based Accountability (RBA) model (Fiscal Policy Studies Institute, n.d.). The model is framed around the following questions: "How much did we do?" "How well did we do it?" and "Is anyone better off?" The emphasis in the model is on collecting baseline data, considering other research or evidence and developing an action plan to improve current practice. Many school monitoring and evaluation models are linear; that is, they start at one data point, such as inputs (a new literacy program), and monitor learning processes (how teachers are implementing the literacy program) and then move to data outputs, in terms of grades, retention rates and test scores (see Matters, 2006).

In discussing the various evaluation and monitoring models that schools might employ, UNICEF (2009, p. 6) makes the point that monitoring and evaluation activities in schools tend to be

> done on schools rather than by schools or with schools... [schools] are not seen as research organizations, and teachers are not regarded as trained researchers. The prevailing view is that schools and teachers should not be involved with monitoring and evaluation beyond filling out questionnaires, answering interview questions and opening up their practice to observation.

Such models rely on the recommendations of outside "experts" to inform ongoing efforts of improvement. Conversely, when school communities assume responsibility of their evaluation and monitoring efforts, there is increased ownership, and importantly, results have the potential to be authentically grounded in the realities of school life and the communities in which they live. Additionally, school involvement in monitoring and evaluation ensures that a culture of continuous improvement is sustained.

One evaluation model that has been used extensively by and with schools is the action research cycle. Bassey (1998, p. 93) described action research as "an enquiry which is carried out in order to understand, to evaluate and then to change, in order to improve educational practice". See Figure 12.1 for the various steps involved in this cycle and the types of questions that might be framed at each step. These questions might necessitate the need for different data to be collected that can then be used to generate further questions.

Action research involves school staff in ongoing cycles of planning, acting, observing and reflecting. The primary objective of action research is to promote reflection and learning, which should then lead to positive change in

Figure 12.1 The action research cycle for schools

one's classroom or school. At the core of action research is reflection about what is being done, why, the impact of that work and, arguably most importantly, what needs to be done next. The problem solving process of action research might serve as a model for students in their own learning.

One critical component of the action research cycle is being prepared to make changes. The term action research includes the concept of disciplined inquiry (that is, "research") leading to concentrated efforts to improve the teaching and learning practices of the school and school environment (thus, "action"; Calhoun, 1994). Most schools engage in action research with the explicit goal of changing or improving the ways that thing are done, involving what Wadsworth (1998, p. 4) described as an imaginative leap from a world of "as it is" to a glimpse of a world "as it could be". Calhoun (1994) described three types of action research: that involving the individual teacher and his or her own practice; collaborative action research projects, where a team works together on a specific topic or initiative; and school-wide action research, for example where the aim might be to improve the social skills of students through implementing cooperative learning across the curriculum.

Collecting data is vital throughout each of these steps as the information collected can be used to guide, confirm or challenge thinking, give feedback on progress and evaluate outcomes. Matters (2006) argued that student learning can only be improved when data is used as basis of decision making. She cited Barry McGaw, who says that "without data, I'm just another person with an opinion" (Matters, 2006, p. 7). Schools routinely collect much of the data that might be used in an action research cycle, such as attendance records and discipline referrals. Depending on the issue under investigation, other forms of data might include classroom observations, student feedback, peer feedback, student work, test scores and so on. Data collection processes should be mindful and sensitive to the cultural and linguistic diversity of the group being sampled, and where the person or group collecting the data also reflects on their cultural assumptions, biases and values. In particular, culturally sensitive data collection incorporates knowledge of a cultural group, including their social norms.

Once collected, it is critical that data is used to inform decision making about change. It is in this vein that Matters (2006) made the distinction between assessment *of* learning and assessment *for* learning (where the latter leads to learning about what future actions are needed). How data are used to promote change will vary depending on the initial purposes of the data collection. Nonetheless, the various potential end users or recipients of the action research cycle are also collaborators in the process (Figure 12.1). Students are an obvious stakeholder in this process. On this note, Tognolini (2005, pp. 9–10) proposed that

> assessment is the collection of information for a purpose. I would not see a case, even in high stakes examinations where the assessment information that is collected should not be used to inform teaching and learning . . . I

believe that students, teachers and parents should be taught how to interpret data themselves ... teachers generally say to me "How am I expected to use the reports to give feedback to 40, 50 or 60 students in my class?" I am always perplexed by this question. Surely rather than go through each of the reports with the students it is more appropriate and efficient to teach the students themselves to analyse their own performance and tell you, the teacher, what they did wrong on those items they might have been expected to get right and how they might do in future to ensure that they get such items correct. In this way the learner is involved in the process.

Reflective practice

Within the action research cycle, reflective practice is core. Though pre-service education programs and ongoing professional development opportunities are important, neither is sufficient for teachers to successfully implement evidence-based approaches that promote young people's academic learning and mental health. In particular, one-off professional development workshops rarely led to long-term change in teaching practices (Guskey, 2000). Instead, learning opportunities that are embedded in the workplace, especially those that prompt self-reflection, will encourage the adaption of new practices.

Reflective practice is a vital way of extending professional understanding and learning about oneself. Schön (1983), in his influential book *The Reflective Practitioner*, developed the term "reflective practice", which included "reflection-in-action" (thinking on your feet) and "reflection-on-action" (thinking after the event). Schön (1983) argued that the most effective professionals use their previous experiences to better understand how and why things happen. Reflective teachers engage in an ongoing process of self-observation (looking at what they are doing) and self-evaluation (the impact of their actions). Critical reflection is a highly personal process that requires teachers to not only analyse their practice and the impact this has on children's learning and development but also turn inward and consider their personal values, biases and prior experiences before deciding how best to proceed.

The action research cycle involves repeated cycles of review and reflection, whereby teachers examine their practice, reflect on this and adjust their practice accordingly. Reflection provides an opportunity for educators to learn from their experiences and transform this knowledge to better understand what supports children's learning, development, health and wellbeing and the impacts educators are having on them. Teachers who regularly reflect on what and why they do what they do, will, over time, produce positive outcomes for children and families (MacNaughton, 2003).

There are various methods that might be employed to encourage or prompt reflection, and these can all be used within the action research cycle elaborated earlier. Diaries or logbooks, peer observations and student feedback are all methods that might be used as points of data to reflect on what is happening in practice. The following questions may be asked, using the data collected as a point of reference to guide understanding and self-reflection:

- What am I doing?
- Are students learning? Are students engaged?
- Which students are, and which students are not learning and engaging?
- Why or why not?
- What am I doing that facilitates learning and engagement?
- What am I doing that might be impeding learning and engagement?
- How can I better meet my students' needs?
- What options or other strategies are available? Who might I talk to about this?
- How can I encourage more student engagement and learning?

High quality mentoring is another process that through guidance, encouragement and feedback can prompt self-reflection. Chu (2012) encouraged mentors to adapt a co-learning stance that promotes curiosity, questioning and self-reflection.

Just do it

As a general rule, people and organisations are resistant to change, and teachers and schools are no exception. There is much comfort in the predictability of doing things the way things have always been done, and much cynicism in introducing change purely for the sake of change. Asking people to change their behaviour also implies that what they are currently doing is wrong or outdated and in need of correction. Finally, asking practitioners to add to their already demanding roles without something falling away is bound to fail, or lead to staff turnover or burnout. People will only change if they see the relevance, if they are convinced of the need for change or if they are "made to do it" (though staff have interesting ways of subverting mandatory requirements; see Tchernegovski, Maybery & Reupert, 2017).

Implementation science provides a plan for introducing change at a systems level. Implementation science is an area of study that stems from medicine, defined as "the scientific study of methods to promote the systematic uptake of research findings and other evidence-based practices into routine practice, and, hence, to improve the quality and effectiveness of health services" (Eccles & Mittman, 2006, p. 1). The same definition applies to schools when introducing any given evidence-based initiative, program or approach. Implementation science provides the template, map or guidelines for introducing change which ultimately aims to improve the teaching and learning environment for staff and students.

Short, Finn and Ferguson (2017) provided a list of organisational conditions they believed are foundational to effective school mental health promotion, and which can be generalised to introducing any school change. This included having a clear, focused vision and a commitment from stakeholders. In terms of implementation procedures, they suggested having a mental health leadership team, undertaking an assessment of need as well as capacity across the school community, delivering ongoing professional development opportunities for staff, working collaboratively with external stakeholders and ensuring that all activities are monitored and evaluated. CASEL (2006) also provided a comprehensive sequence of steps (readiness, planning and implementation) along with a set of sustainability factors that schools might use when implementing social and emotional learning programs, with many of the same features as already noted.

Figure 12.2 provides a synthesis of many of the above reported implementation strategies, along a continuum of phases. Incorporating the action research cycle, this implementation model provides one way to plan and introduce change for how schools might address students' mental health and learning

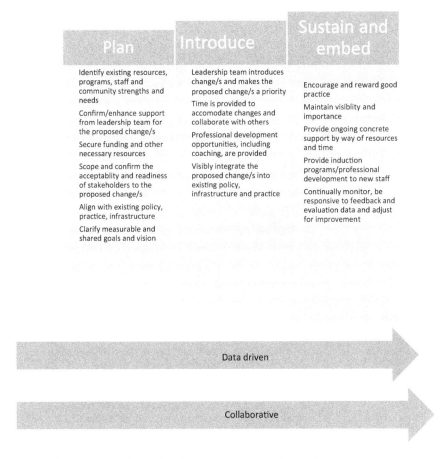

Figure 12.2 A three-phase plan for implementing change in schools

needs. Running throughout the three phases is the need to collaborate with others, including external partners, students, families and government officials. Another consistent feature is the collection and use of data to inform each phase as a means of monitoring progress and evaluating outcomes.

The planning phase is critical to identifying possible barriers and ascertaining the readiness of the school for change. If there are too many barriers, if the proposed change is not considered relevant, and/or if the school community is not ready for the proposed change/s, the likelihood of successfully introducing

Table 12.1 Common barriers for implementing change and possible responses

Perceived barrier	Possible responses
I don't have the time	• Negotiate for and provide adequate time • Condense materials/program (i.e. reduce time) • Deliver program/material in different format e.g. online (i.e. reduce time)
The timetable is already too busy/crowded	• Demonstrate how program/resources can be integrated into the existing curriculum • Provide suggestions of what might be dropped in the curriculum
It is too much and overwhelming	• Clarify role and set clear boundaries about what staff can/cannot do • Clarify and disseminate referral pathways to and from external providers • Clarify relationship and respective roles with external providers in the design/delivery/evaluation of program
It is not the role of the school	• Highlight the relationship between mental health, behaviour and learning • Ensure mental health/wellbeing/learning is visible e.g. in school policy, agenda items for meetings, part of leadership team responsibilities
It is not my job	• Highlight the relationship between mental health, behaviour and learning • Ensure mental health/wellbeing/learning responsibilities are clearly stated in position descriptions of staff • Include mental health/wellbeing responsibilities in induction programs for new staff • When advertising and recruiting for staff, be clear about expectations and roles
It is not a problem/It is not needed	• Present school-based, community and other data demonstrating that there is need to address student wellbeing/mental health/learning (including both qualitative and quantitative data)
It won't work	• Present data to demonstrate that the program has worked in other similar school environments • Present ongoing monitoring and evaluation data to highlight successes and areas for improvement • Be responsive to areas that need improvement
Lack of skills and confidence	• Provide professional development opportunities • Provide ongoing coaching, supervision opportunities

these change/s is low. Table 12.1 provides some suggestions for how perceived barriers might be addressed at an individual level with staff or community members. Many of these strategies are framed around ensuring that there are adequate resources and time devoted to addressing students' needs and simultaneously creating a culture that accepts the interrelationship between mental health and learning and the role of the school in addressing students' wellbeing. The support of leadership is vital as it provides an "authorising" environment which expects as well as supports a focus on students' mental health and learning (Reupert, Williamson & Maybery, 2017). A combination of quantitative data (e.g. prevalence, efficacy data) alongside qualitative data (e.g. interview excerpts from students or caregivers) can provide a compelling case for change. Finally, sustainability can only be achieved when proposed changes are aligned to current policy and system priorities.

As well as individual school efforts to introduce change, systems at a broader level should be put in place to coordinate programs and reduce duplication across regions and schools (Fixsen, Naoom, Blase, Friedman & Wallace, 2005).

It's about attitude

Banerjee, McLaughlin, Cotney, Roberts and Peereboom (2016) made the point that regardless of its evidence base, there is no guarantee that a program will have a positive impact on students, as other factors inherent to the population group and within the implementation process will invariably influence results. Success will depend on how well any given intervention or program is embedded through pedagogy, the school ethos, climate, daily routines and other school initiatives. Banerjee et al. (2016) argued that "any work in this area needs to be situated within an integrated school systems approach where it is connected with – rather than competing with – other school priorities" (p. 34). Efforts to promote student mental health and wellbeing are more than delivering "off the shelf" programs or a series of lessons; instead they are embedded in the attitudes, values and beliefs of school personnel and their practices and relationships. Strategies to promote young people's wellbeing and academic learning are successful when staff are committed and knowledgeable and when the school community values children's mental health and wellbeing.

Take home messages

As a way of conclusion, a number of take-home messages may be generated for schools when planning to simultaneously support young people's mental health and learning.

- Student mental health and academic learning are inseparable and interrelated; one will impact the other
- Schools have a vital role to play in fostering an environment that promotes students' wellbeing as well as their academic learning

- There are many things that schools can do that simultaneously enhance children's learning and mental health, including but not limited to
  - Promote a positive school climate that encourages a sense of belonging and a culture of care
  - Ensure staff model and actively teach a broad range of positive social and emotional skills in and out of the classroom
  - Sensitively identify students at risk of mental illness and/or learning difficulties, and prove more intensive support for those who need it
  - Sensitively identify those students experiencing serious distress and/or learning problems and facilitate referrals to and from appropriate agencies as required
- Responses to inappropriate and/or disruptive student behaviour need to address the cause/s of the misbehaviour from a systems point of view that does not pathologise or otherwise "blame" students
- Not only accept but work actively to include children from diverse backgrounds and with diverse learning and other needs into school life
- Ensure that staff wellbeing is monitored and actively supported through appropriate resourcing and support
- Appreciate the adverse impact a range of traumatising experiences might have on children's behaviour and learning
- Develop, employ and monitor systems to collaborate with others, including families and those in the community such as external providers
- Ensure children are at the centre of all decision making processes.
- Build systems that encourage and require teacher reflection as a means of professional development and evaluation
- Collect different types of data from various sources and stakeholders when making decisions and evaluating programs and initiatives.

Students are at the core of decision making when making changes in schools, and their "voice" is critical when determining what needs to change and how. If our goal is for students to become highly literate and numerate, have the ability to solve problems, communicate effectively and develop and maintain positive relationships within and beyond the family unit, then we need to build systems to ensure that their needs are at the forefront of all decisions made in regard to schooling. This means that schools have to consider the development and wellbeing of the whole child, including cognitive, social, emotional, physical and cultural domains. Such arguments align with UNESCO's definition of education for the twenty-first century, through learning to know, learning to do, learning to live together and learning to be (Delors, 2013).

Students' voices

This book started with Alice's story and will finish with children's perspectives about how schools might operate. In recognition that children have the ability and the right to articulate what they want and need (Awartani, Whitman & Gordon, 2008; Kangas, 2010), it is critical that children have an active role in the decision making process of improving learning environments. Efforts to elicit children's voices need to ensure there is an authentic and reciprocal relationship between those who are doing the asking (teachers, researchers) and children. It is also important to note that what children want can be very different from what parents or teachers believe they need. Maybery et al. (2005) asked young people facing multiple adversities what would help them. The young people overwhelming highlighted the importance of peer groups, while their parents and other health professionals suggested that external, professional support was the most important way to address their needs. Similarly, Piispanen (2008) asked children, parents and teachers to define their understanding of "good quality" learning environments. Students emphasised the physical dimension of the learning environment and indicated that they wanted schools to be as "home like" as possible, alongside opportunities to be physically active. Conversely, their parents stressed the social and psychological dimensions of school life, including being safe and learning how to socially interact with others, and the need to acknowledge children's individual learning needs. Teachers highlighted pedagogy in their discussion of good quality learning environments, including appropriate resources and teaching and learning strategies. Thus, children's views regarding what they need can be very different from what the adults in their life believe they need. Moreover, even when not formally asked, children will still communicate what their needs are, as might be ascertained through graffiti or nonattendance, both examples which tell us something about their experiences of school and school culture.

Children may also be asked to solve school and other societal problems. Problems with obesity have prompted schools to encourage physical activity. Hyndman (2016) conducted various focus groups with primary and secondary students to identify how they thought schools might promote physical activity. Children recommended adventure based activities such as rock-climbing walls, recreational physical activity facilities (e.g. jumping pillows), music during physical activity time and animal activity programs. Thus, it is incumbent on researchers and school staff to actively work with students when making decisions about how to promote student wellbeing and learning.

Children and youth: what is a happy school?

In 2017, three graduate students – Carolina Mueller, Elaine Chee-Ling Wong and Bay Cie (Betty) Lim – and I asked primary school-aged children in Australia and Malaysia to tell us what makes a happy school. In the Australian cohort of primary-aged students, one child was asked to explain why schools should promote student happiness. She reported, "Cause I want everyone to feel like they belong and know that they are part of the world". Another Australian primary student described the importance of having friends at school and explained that a happy school is a school where all children play together.

The important role teachers played in creating happy schools was also featured. In Malaysia, one secondary student described a good teacher as one who "lets us all speak our minds and we don't get judgment for it". She continued by suggesting that a happy school is one where a student can speak up in class with teacher acknowledgement, as opposed to an unhappy class where the teacher ignores disruptive or disengaged students. Interestingly, children in both countries noted that schools should balance what they considered to be "work" (learning) and play. One Malaysian secondary student described an unhappy school as "an environment where everything is very tense", while in comparison, a happy school was one where "they focus on their studies but ... they still ... encourage us to ... join [in] school activities".

The main business of school will always be academic learning but that does not take away the responsibility of school to actively promote children's mental health and wellbeing. Indeed, a focus on learning necessitates a focus on school belonging and positive peer and student–teacher relationships, as attested by children's representations of a happy school. Children appreciate the need for schools to integrate efforts to promote academic learning with efforts to enhance wellbeing. It is up to those of us who work and research in schools to ensure this occurs.

References

Awartani, M., Whitman, C.V., & Gordon, J. (2008). Developing instruments to capture young people's perceptions of how school as a learning environment affects their well-being. *European Journal of Education, 43*(1) 51–70.

Banerjee, R., McLaughlin, C., Cotney, J., Roberts, L., & Peereboom, C. (2016). *Promoting emotional health, well-being, and resilience in primary schools.* Working paper. Public Policy Institute for Wales, Public Policy Institute for Wales. Retrieved February 25, 2019, from http://sro.sussex.ac.uk/66449/

Bartgis, D., & Bigfoot, J. (2010). *Evidence based practice and practice based evidence: What are they? How do we know if we have one?* National Council for Urban Indian Health. Retrieved February 25, 2019, from www.ncuih.org/krc/D_bigfoot_EBP_PBE

Bassey, M. (1998). Action research for improving practice. In R. Halsall (Ed.), *Teacher research and school improvement: Opening doors from the inside* (pp. 93–106). Buckingham: Open University Press.

Calhoun, E. (1994). *How to use action research in the self-renewing school.* Alexandria, VA: Association for Supervision and Curriculum Development.

CASEL (2006). CASEL practice rubric for schoolwide SEL implementation. Retrieved February 25, 2019, from https://files.eric.ed.gov/fulltext/ED505360.pdf

Chu, M. (2012). Observe, reflect, and apply: Ways to successfully mentor early childhood educators. *Dimensions of Early Childhood, 40*(3), 20–29.

Delors, J. (2013). The treasure within: Learning to know, learning to do, learning to live together and learning to be. What is the value of that treasure 15 years after its publication? *International Review of Education, 59*(3), 319–330.

Durlak, J. A., & DuPre, E. P. (2008). Implementation matters: A review of research on the influence of implementation on program outcomes and the factors affecting implementation. *American Journal of Community Psychology, 41,* 327–350.

Eccles, M. P., & Mittman, B. S. (2006). Welcome to implementation science. *Implementation Science*, *1*, 1.

Fiscal Policy Studies Institute (n.d.). *What is results based accountability?* Retrieved February 25, 2019, from https://resultsaccountability.com/about/what-is-results-based-accountability/

Fixsen, D. L., Naoom, S. F., Blase, K. A., Friedman, R. M., & Wallace, F. (2005). *Implementation research: A synthesis of the literature*. Tampa, FL: University of South Florida, Louis de la Parte Florida Mental Health Institute, The National Implementation Research Network (FMHI Publication #231). Retrieved February 12, 2019, from https://fpg.unc.edu/node/4445

Guskey, T. (2000). *Evaluating professional development*. Thousand Oaks, CA: Corwin.

Hempenstall, K. (2006). What does evidence-based practice in education mean? *Australian Journal of Learning Disabilities*, *11*(2), 83–92.

Hyndman, B. (2016). A qualitative investigation of Australian youth perceptions to enhance school physical activity: The environmental perceptions investigation of children's physical activity (EPIC-PA) study. *Journal of Physical Activity and Health*, *13*(5), 543–550,

Kangas, M. (2010). Finnish children's views on the ideal school and learning environment. *Learning Environments Research*, *13*, 205–223.

MacNaughton, G. (2003). Reflecting on early childhood curriculum. In G. MacNaughton (Ed.), *Shaping early childhood* (pp. 113–120). England: Open University Press.

Matters, G. (2006). *Using data to support learning in schools. Students, teachers, systems*. Australian Council for Educational Research. Retrieved February 25, 2019, from https://research.acer.edu.au/cgi/viewcontent.cgi?article=1004&context=aer

Maybery, D., Ling, L., Szakacs, E., & Reupert, A. (2005). Children of a parent with a mental illness: Perspectives on need. *Australian e-Journal for the Advancement of Mental Health*, *4*(2), 78–88.

Piispanen, M. (2008). *Good learning environment. Perceptions of good quality in comprehensive school by pupils, parents and teachers*. Unpublished doctoral dissertation, University of Jyväskylä. Kokkola University Consortium Chydenius. Retrieved February 13, 2019, from https://jyx.jyu.fi/bitstream/handle/123456789/19018/1/978-951-39-3382-1.pdf

Proctor, E. K., Landsverk, J., Aarons, G., Chambers, D., Glisson, C., & Mittman, B. (2009). Implementation research in mental health services: An emerging science with conceptual, methodological and training challenges. *Administration and Policy in Mental Health and Mental Health Services Research*, *36*(1), 24–34.

Reupert, A. (2018). Research that makes a difference. *Advances in Mental Health*, *16*(2), 101–104.

Reupert, A., Williamson, C., & Maybery, D. (2017). How family orientated are primary care physicians? *Journal of Child & Family Studies*, *26*, 329–340.

Ringwalt, C., Jackson-Newsom, J., Gottfredson, N. C., Hansen, W. B., Giles, S. M., & Dusenbury, L. (2010). Three year trajectory of teachers' fidelity to a drug prevention curriculum. *Prevention Science*, *11*(1), 67–76.

Schön, D. A. (1983). *The structure of reflection-in-action. The reflective practitioner*. New York: Basic Books.

Shonkoff, J. (2000). Science, policy, and practice: Three cultures in search of a shared mission. *Child Development*, *71*(1), 181–187.

Short, K., Finn, C., & Ferguson, H. B. (2017). *System leadership in school mental health in Canada*. CASSA Discussion paper. Retrieved February 25, 2019, from https://opsoa.org/application/files/3415/1136/4074/CASSA_Discussion_Paper_on_System_Leadership_in_School_Ment.pdf

Tchernegovski, P., Maybery, D., & Reupert, A. (2017). Legislative policy to support children of parents with a mental illness: Revolution or evolution? *International Journal of Mental Health Promotion, 19*(1), 1–13.

Tognolini, J. (2005). *Using online assessment to inform teaching and learning in primary and secondary classrooms.* Australian Council for Educational Research. Conference archive. Retrieved February 25, 2019, from https://research.acer.edu.au/cgi/viewcontent.cgi?article=1005&context=research_conference_2005

UNESCO (2016). *Designing effective monitoring and evaluation of education systems for 2030: A global synthesis of policies and practices.* Retrieved February 25, 2019, from www.unesco.org/new/fileadmin/MULTIMEDIA/HQ/ED/pdf/me-report.pdf

UNICEF (2009). *Manual. Child friendly schools.* Chapter 8. Retrieved February 25, 2019, from www.unicef.org/publications/files/Child_Friendly_Schools_Manual_EN_040809.pdf

Vostanis, P., Humphrey, N., Fitzgerald, N., Deighton, J., & Wolpert, M. (2013). How do schools promote emotional well-being among their pupils? Findings from a national scoping survey of mental health provision in English schools. *Child and Adolescent Mental Health, 18*(3), 151–157.

Wadsworth, Y. (1998). *What is participatory action research?* Action Research International, paper 2. Retrieved March 4, 2019, from www.aral.com.au/ari/p-ywadsworth98.html

Index

Note: Page numbers **bold** indicate a table and page numbers in *italic* indicate a figure on the corresponding page.

2017 Annual PDK Poll 8–9

Aber, Lawrence 35
ability grouping 133–134
academic failure 15, 26–27; and inequity 130; interventions for at-risk children 38; and mental health 29; reasons for 27–28; school contribution to 15, 16; socio-economic factors 32, 33
academic incompetence model 29, 31
academic learning programs, Response to Intervention (RtI) 43
academic success 26; and children's social and emotional competence 33–35; and excellent teachers 95–96, 99; and mental health 19, 29; school impact on 35–36; and self-doubt 102; socio-economic factors 32, 33; three-step feedback process 101; *see also* attainment grouping
accountability 169
Acock, A. C. 34
action research cycle 167, 170–171, *171*, 172–173; data collection 172; implementation strategies 174–175, *176*, *177*; planning phase *176*, *177*; reflective practice 173–174
active listening 74
adaptive coping 145
Adelman, H. S. 68
adjustment erosion model 29, 29–30
adverse childhood experiences (ACEs) 14, 148; traumatic events 155
Albon, J. S. 91
Algozzine, B. 50
Allen, K. A. 69

Allensworth, D. 122
Allred, C. G. 51
Anderson-Butcher, D. 26
anger management programs 82
Angold, A. 12
anxiety 2, 5, 12, 13, 35; in teachers and principals 146
appropriate classroom behaviours 15
Assertive Discipline 83
assessment 26, 63, 100–102; high stakes 8, 148; Scholastic Assessment Test (SAT) 32
at-risk students 63, 64, 73, 129, 164; monitoring 169–170; and relationships 74; screening 62–63
attainment grouping 133–134
Attention-Deficit/Hyperactivity Disorder (ADHD) 12, 13, 15, 17, 34, 35, 63, 89; challenging behaviour 81–83; and memory 81
Australia: educational reforms in 86–87; Results Based Accountability (RBA) model 170; school policies 68
Autism Spectrum Disorders 129–130

Banerjee, R. 48, 177
Bang, Molly, *When Sophie Gets Angry – Really, Really Angry* 102
Banko, K. M. 90
Baram-Tsabari, A. 123
Barkham, G. E. 46
Barry, Mary 131
basic principles of inclusive education 134
behavioural problems in students 35; classroom management 83, 84–85; "managing" versus "teaching" 85, 86;

reasons for 27–28; relationship with mental health and learning 80–81; rewards and punishments 88–89
Belfield 20
benefits of inclusive education 131–132
Berg, J. 53
Bigfoot, J. 168
Biglan, A. 53
Bless, G. 132
Blote, A. W. 101
body mass index (BMI) 52
Bogan, B. L. 81
Bohon, C. 50
Bouffard, S. 53
Brackett, M. A. 19
Bradshaw, C. P. 53
Brown, J. L. 35
Brownlie, E. 16
bullying 15

Campbell, R. 18
Canter, L. 83
caregivers: barriers to seeking mental health treatment for their children 17–18; family partnerships 119–120, 122; as source of trauma in children 155–156; traumatized 159
caring 74, 75
"caring about" students 73–74
Caring School Community 20
cascade models 28–29, 34–35
case management, referral process 118–119
causes of mental illness 14–15, 16
challenging behaviour 81, 81–83; and trauma 159–161; triggers 160; *see also* disruptive behaviour
Chambers, D. 138
Chang, M. 119
Cheung, A. C. K. 45
Child Development Project, The 44
children: developmental needs of **36**; goals of 91; partnerships with 122–124; partnerships with children and youth 122–124; prevalence of mental illness in 11–13; and school partnerships *115*; traumatized 156–157, 158–159
children of parents with a mental illness (COPMI) national initiative 102–103
children's literature, as teaching tool 102
Cicchetti, D. 29
classroom, optimal size of 61–62

classroom management 83, 84–85, 102; Collaborative Problem-Solving Approach 91; democratic school practices 92; rewards and punishments 88–89
climate *see* school climate
collaboration 21, 148; group work 99; models of 116, 118; partnerships with children and youth 122–124; referral process 118–119; Responsive Classroom Approach 44
Collaborative for Academic, Social, and Emotional Learning (CASEL) 103–104, 106, 175
Collaborative Problem-Solving Approach 91–92
Collishaw, S. 13
competence 10–11, 89
competencies 34, 38
conduct disorder (CD) 12
connectedness 69–70; and physical safety 70–71; student-student relationships 72; teacher-student relationships 72–75
consequences, rewards and punishments 88–89
Cook, E. T. 52, 56
cooperative learning 99, 145
Copeland, W. 12
Coping Power program 50
Corpus, J. H. 90
Costello, E. J. 12
Cotney, J. 177
counselling 73, 162–163; one to one 44; professional collaborations 114
crisis plans 162–163
criticisms of social and emotional learning programs 108–109
cultural competence 70
culture 60; performance-driven 65; *see also* school culture
Curcic, S. 120
curriculum 8, 95, 122, 164; and academic failure 27–28; Australia's educational reforms 86–87; and behaviour management approaches 83, 84; Finland's educational reforms 86; and optimal size of classes 61–62; universal design for learning (UDL) 138–139
Cwik, J. C. 63
cyberbullying 14

data collection 172, 176
Dean, A. J. 12

Deci, E. L. 89, 90
decision-making skills 34, 103, 151; "policy enactment" 67–68
Deighton, J. 148
delinquency 35
democratic school practices 92
depression 2, 5, 10, 12, 13, 30, 35; prevention programmes 50; in teachers and principals 146–148
Dessemontet, R. 132
developmental cascade models 28–29, 34–35, 38; academic incompetence model 31; adjustment erosion model 29–30; shared risk model 31
developmental needs of children **36**
diaries 173–174
Diaz, E. M. 129
disabilities, students with 135, 137; benefits of inclusive education 131–132; exclusion 129
discipline: "managing" versus "teaching" 85, 86; and motivation 89–91; rewards and punishments 88–89; *see also* behavioural problems in students; disruptive behaviour
discrimination 129, 130; racial 136
disengaged students 80–81
disruptive behaviour 3, 5, 12, 15, 35, 81, 81–83; adjustment erosion model 30; triggers 160
diversity, gender 130–131
Domitrovich, C. E. 47, 56
Douglas, K. S. 146
dress code 68
Duhaney, L. M. G. 132
Dunn, A. 68
DuPaul, G. J. 26
DuPre, E. P. 46, 168
Durlak, J. A. 35, 46, 47, 56, 105, 168
dyslexia 1, 5, 130

Early, D. M. 119
economic arguments for children's mental health programs 19–20
education 1; inclusive 128–129, 130, 131–132, 134, 135, 136–139, 148; ten steps to equity in 139
Elias, M. J. 148
eliciting student voices 136, 179
Embry, D. 53
emotional competence 10–11
emotional regulation 33, 34
emotional self-efficacy 33

emotional transmission 152
equality: and inclusion 130; and mental health 20–21
ethos 54–55
evaluation 169–170; action research cycle 171, 172–173
evidence 169
evidence-based kernels 53, 54, 55
evidence-based programs (EBPs) 167–169, 177; implementation strategies 174–175, 176, 177; Promoting Alternative Thinking Strategies (PATHS) 42–43; recognizing, understanding, labelling, expressing and regulating emotions (RULER) 43; teacher training in 145
excellent teachers 95–96, 99
exclusion 80–81, 128; discrimination 129; homophobia 129; racial discrimination 136; *see also* inclusion
external regulation 90
externalising problems 10, 12–13, 16, 28–29; adjustment erosion model 29–30
extrinsic motivation 89, 90

Facebook 75
face-to-face intervention 63
false positives 63
family income, and SAT scores **32**
family partnerships 119–120, 122
Farkas, G. 31
feedback 100–102
Ferguson, H. B. 174
Ferron, J. 30
Finn, C. 174
Fitzgerald, N. 148
Flay, B. R. 51
Fleming, M. 17
Fletcher-Campbell, F. 73–74
follow-ups 63
Ford, T. J. 18
Forlin, C. 138
Forster, R. 123
Fox, J. 88
Frenzel, A. C. 152
Fullan, M. 122
functional behaviour analysis (FBA) 83–84

Gear, A. 90
gender: and behavioural issues 82; benefits of inclusive education 131–132; diversity 130–131; inclusion 128–129
Gentry, M. 81

Gillies, V. 82
Glasser, W. 83, 84
Goetz, T. 152
"gold practice" 167
"good quality" learning environments 179
Goodenow, C. 69
Goodman, R. D. 11–12, 18
Gormley, M. J. 26
Grady, K. E. 69
Graham, S. 129
Green, H. 18
Greenberg, M. T. 32, 73, 109, 145
Greene, B. A. 91
Griebler, U. 123
group work 99
guides to selecting SEL programs 106–108
Gun-Free Schools Act 162

Haertel, G. D. 19
Haggerty, R. J. 48
Hallam, S. 133, 134
Hambrick, E. P. 116
Hamre, B. K. 101
happy schools 179–180
Harpine, E. C. 31
Hattie, John 69, 95, 100
Hayatbaksh, R. 12
Health Promoting Schools Framework, The 51
healthy schools framework 51
hearts, minds and hands approach 135
Heffernan, A. 67
help-seeking schools 64–65
Herner, T. 82
high psychopathology 30
high stakes assessments 8, 148
homophobia 129
hot spot mapping 71
Humphrey, N. 148
hyper-arousal 156
hypo-arousal 156

identification 90
implementation strategies 174–175, 176, 177
inclusion 71, 128–129, 130, 135, 148; attainment grouping 133–134; basic principles of 134; benefits of 131–132; gender diversity 130–131; policy, school leadership and systems 138–139; students at the centre 136; teachers' beliefs 136–137; teachers' knowledge 137; ten steps to equity in education 139; universal design for learning (UDL) 138–139
indicated interventions 49, 161–162
initiatives 38
intrinsic motivation 89
instructional leadership 65–66, **66**
integrated mental health approach 47–48, 53, 54
integration 90
intellectual disabilities, benefits of inclusive education 131–132
intentional teaching 99
internalising problems 13, 16, 17, 30, 38
interpersonal skills 34, 96, 99, 110; of teachers 144
Intervention Program for Social Skills Improvement (SSIS) 104
interventions for at-risk children, referral process 118–119
intrinsic motivation 89, 90
introjection 90
Ireson, J. 134
Iyengar, S. S. 90

Jarosik, J. 17
Jennings, T. 73, 109, 145
Jones, S. M. 20, 35, 53
juvenile justice system 89

Kahn, J. 20
Kalogrides, D. 32
Kassem, C. L. 102
Kemp, H. 75, 150
Kern, M. 69
"kernels of influence" 54–56
Kim, Y. C. 45, 90
Kincaid, S. 50
Kleickmann, T. 144
Kluth, P. 128
Kohn, A. 88
Kok, R. 101
Kosciw, J. G. 129
Kunter, M. 144

lack of professional support for children's mental health 16–18
Laletas, S. 74
leadership 65–66, 67, 114, 123, 151; for implementing change 177; instructional 65–66, **66**; peer leaders 124; and policy 138–139

learning 95, 179; cooperative 99; feedback and assessment 100–102; pathways to 81; promoting behaviour conducive to 86–87; relationship with mental health and behaviour 80–81; scaffolding 99
learning programs, professional collaborations 114
learning-related skills 34
lesbian, gay, bisexual, transgender/transsexual, intersex and queer/questioning (LGBTIQ): benefits of inclusive education 131–132; gender diversity 130–131
literacy, Read Like a Demon 114
Lüdtke, O. 152
Lyon, D. R. 146

managing traumatic events 161–162
"managing" versus "teaching" 85, 86
Marchetta, Melina, *Saving Francesca* 102
Margraf, J. 63
Marks, L. J. 81
Marti, C. N. 50
Martin, A. J. 124, 145
Mashburn, A. J. 18
Mathis, W. J. 80–81
Maughan, B. 146
Maybery, D. J. 73–75, 149
McGaw, Barry 172
McGinnity, A. 18
McKeachie, W. J. 90
McLaughlin, C. 177
Mellin, E. A. 116
Mellor-Clark, J. 46
Meltzer, H. 18
memory, in ADHD students 81
mental health 26, 102–103, 129; academic incompetence model 31; and academic learning 9; and academic success 19, 29; adjustment erosion model 29–30; definition 10; and equality 20–21; relationship with behaviour and learning 80–81; role of teachers in promoting 148–150; school impact on 35–36; school-based support 18; screening 62–63; shared risk model 31; teachers' 144; *see also* developmental cascade models
mental health intervention 11, 37–38, 42; Child Development Project, The 44; economic arguments for 19–20; evidence base 45–47; evidence-based kernels 53; face-to-face 63; follow-ups 63; lack of professional support for 16–18; one to one counselling services 44; Positive Behavioural Interventions and Supports (PBIS) 43–44; "program drift" 46; program integration 50; Promoting Alternative Thinking Strategies (PATHS) 42–43, 45; randomised controlled trials (RTCs) 46; Reading, Writing, Respect and Resolution (4Rs Program) 35–36; recognizing, understanding, labelling, expressing and regulating emotions (RULER) 43, 45; Response to Intervention (RtI) 43; Responsive Classroom Approach 44; Schools for Health in Europe Network Foundation (SHE) 51–52; selected interventions 48; tiered approaches 48–49, 50, 52–55; universal approaches 48; whole school approaches 50–52; *see also* screening
mental health prevention 11
mental health promotion 11
mental illness 13–14; adverse childhood experiences (ACEs) 14; Attention-Deficit/Hyperactivity Disorder (ADHD) 15; causes 14–15, 16; definition 9–10; prevalence of in children 5, 11–13; psychopathology 30; at-risk students 63, 64, 73, 129; screening 62–63; socio-economic factors 32, 33
mentoring 174
Merikangas, K. R. 12, 16
meta-cognition 101
metal detectors 71
Metsäpelto, R-L. 31
mixed-attainment classrooms 133
modelling 110
models of classroom management 83, 84–85
models of collaboration 116, 118
money *see* socio-economic status
monitoring 169–170, 171; *see also* screening
Moore, M. 27
Morgan, P. 31
Morgan, R. 80
Moroney, D. 53
Morris, Z. 75
Morrison, F. J. 34
Morse, L. 122
Mortimore, P. 146
motivation 89–91
Mrazek, P. J. 48

Najman, J. 12
Node, P. 45

normal classroom behaviour 15
Nuthall, G. 27

one to one counselling services 44
one-way sharing 116
Oppositional Defiant Disorder (ODD) 89
optimal size for school classes 61
Organisation for Economic Cooperation and Development (OECD) 26–27; ten steps to equity in education 139
Orme, J. G. 71
Osher, D. 53
Our Watch 131
Ouston, J. 146
Owens, J. S. 115–116

parents, barriers to seeking mental health treatment for their children 17–18
partnerships 113; with children and youth 122–124; family 119–120, 122; models of collaboration 116, 118; professional collaborations 114, 115–116; referral process 118–119
pathways to learning 81
pedagogy 61–62, 74, 95, 122, 144, 148, 150, 164, 179; and excellent teachers 95–96, 99; fostering inclusiveness 137–138; practices associated with effective skill training 47–48; promoting behaviour conducive to learning 86–88
peer leaders 124
Peereboom, C. 177
Pekrun, R. 152
performance: academic failure 26–27; academic success 26; teacher 146, 148
performance-driven culture 65
Perkins, D. D. 91
Perumean-Chaney, S. E. 71
Pianta, R. C. 101
Pierce, W. D. 90
Piispanen, M. 179
Pittman, L. 124
policy 19, 72, 122, 136, 148; "enactment" 67–68; formal SEL programs 106; and school leadership 138–139; sentencing 80–81; and vision 67–69; zero-tolerance 158
Positive Action (PA) 50–51
Positive Behavioural Interventions and Supports (PBIS) 43–44, 50
positive psychology 161
post-traumatic stress disorder (PTSD) 158–159

postvention 161–162
practice-based evidence 169
prevalence of mental illness in children 11–13
principals: depression in 146–148; and stress 146–148, 149; see also leadership; teachers
problem solving 33, 34, 102, 116; Collaborative Problem-Solving Approach 91
professional collaborations 114, 115–116; referral process 118–119
program development 19
"program drift" 46
program integration 50, 53–54
Promoting Alternative Thinking Strategies (PATHS) 42–43, 48, 50; effectiveness of 45
promoting behaviour conducive to learning 86–88
psychopathology 30

Quinn, D. M. 136

racial discrimination 136
randomised controlled trials (RTCs) 46
Read Like a Demon 114
Reading, Writing, Respect and Resolution (4Rs Program) 35
recognizing, understanding, labelling, expressing and regulating emotions (RULER) 43, 48
Rees, J. 124
referral process 118–119
reflective practice 173–174
Reimer, K. 110
relationships 60, 71–72, 103, 109; caring 74; connectedness 69–70; interpersonal skills 96, 99; reciprocal 146; and at-risk students 74; student-student 72; student-teacher; teacher-student 72–75, 88, 151, 152
Response to Intervention (RtI) 43, 50
Responsive Classroom Approach 44
Results Based Accountability (RBA) model 170
Reupert, A. 73, 74, 75, 149, 150
rewards and punishments 88–89; motivation 89–91
Richter, D. 144
Roberts, L. 116, 177
Rohde, P. 50
Rojatz, D. 123
role models, teachers as 109–110

Rutter, M. 146
Ryan, R. M. 89, 90, 139

safe schools 70–71
safe spaces 159, 160, 161
Salamanca statement 128
Sandomierski, T. 50
Santinello, M. 92
scaffolding 99, 110
Schneider, B. 63
Scholastic Assessment Test (SAT) 32
Schön, D. A. 173
school climate 60; connectedness 69–70; inclusion 138–139; and leadership 65–66, 67; and school size 61–62; screening 62–63
school culture 54–55, 60, 96, 152; connectedness 69–70; cultural competence 70; inclusion 138–139; and leadership 65–66, 67; physical safety of students 70–71; and school size 61–62; screening 62–63
School Resource Officers (SROs) 71
school shootings 71, 162
school size, impact on school culture and climate 61–62
school uniforms 68
schools 8; academic failure 26–27; academic success 26; crisis plans 162–163; drop outs 19; economic arguments for children's mental health intervention 20; ethos 54–55; evidence-based kernels 55; evidence-based programs (EBPs) 167–169; "good" 53–54; happy 179–180; health-promoting framework 51–52; help-seeking 64–65; impact on children's mental health 15, 16, 18–19, 35–36; inclusion 128–129, 130; leadership 65–66, 67; mental health intervention 42, 42–44; mental health screening 62–63; models of collaboration 116, 118; one to one counselling services 44; partnerships 113; partnerships with children and youth 122–124; physical safety 70–71; policies 67–69; professional collaborations 114, 115–116; under-resourced 33; role of in promoting children's mental health 6–8; staff development program 170; staff wellbeing, promoting 150–152; student mental health support 18; suicide prevention strategies 161–162; synthesizing a trauma-informed approach into 163–164; trauma-informed formal programs 157–158; unhappy 180; vision 67–69; wellbeing programs 37–38
Schools for Health in Europe Network Foundation (SHE) 51–52
scores, assessment 100
screening 62–63, 169–170; false positives 63; at-risk students 63, 64; Smooth Sailing 63
selected interventions 48, 161–162
selecting SEL programs 106–108
self-awareness 101, 103
self-care 150, 151
self-management 34, 103
self-reflection 174
sense of belonging see connectedness
sentencing policy 80–81
Sequenced, Active, and Focused lessons with an Explicit teaching of skills (SAFE) 47–48, 105
sex education 124
Shanahan, L. 12
shared risk 29, 31
Sharma, U. 136
Sharp, A. 15
Shores, K. A. 32
Short, K. 174
Simovska, V. 123
Smith, A. 92, 146
Smooth Sailing 63
Snow, P. C. 80–81
social and emotional competence 100–101; and academic achievement 33–35; Sequenced, Active, and Focused lessons with an Explicit teaching of skills (SAFE) 105; Social Skills Improvement System (SSIS) 104–105; staff; student; teachers' 144–145; teaching 103–104, 104
social and emotional learning (SEL) interventions 20, 50, 103–104; children's literature as teaching tool 102; criticisms of 108–109; effectiveness of 45, 46–47; guides to selecting programs 106–108; Promoting Alternative Thinking Strategies (PATHS) 42–43; recognizing, understanding, labelling, expressing and regulating emotions (RULER) 43
social and emotional programs 145
social and emotional wellbeing 10–11; and equality 20–21; school impact on 18–19
social awareness 103
social competence 34
social inclusion 71

social justice 128–129
social media 14
Social Skills Improvement System (SSIS) 104–105
socio-economic status, association with academic performance and mental illness 32, 33
Sperling, R. A. 31
staff: development programs 170; evidence-based kernels 55
standardised testing 8, 8–9, 26
Stiles, W. 46
stress 10, 19, 150–151, 156, 159; principal; teacher; in teachers and principals 146–148, 149; *see also* traumatic events
student behaviour: disruptive 3, 5; normal 15
students: academic failure 26–27; academic success 26; "caring about" 73–74; connectedness 69–70; evidence-based kernels 55; feedback and assessment 100–102; goals of 91; and mental illness 13–14; motivating 89–91; physical safety of 70–71; voices, eliciting 136; *see also* teachers; teacher-student relationships
student-student relationships 72
substance abuse 35
Sugai, G. 84–85
suicidal ideation 12; screening 63
suicide prevention strategies 161–162
Suldo, S. 26, 30
Sutton, L. M. 71, 152

"talk in depth" 73
Tardif, C. Y. 132
Taylor, B. 68
teachers: "caring for" students 74–75; classroom management 83, 84–85; and connectedness 69–70; cultural competence 70; "duty of care" 73 74; EBP training 145; excellent 95–96, 99; "expert" 96, 99; feedback and assessment 100–102; fostering inclusiveness 137–138; "gold practice" 167; instructional leadership 65–66, **66**; interpersonal skills 144; knowledge of inclusive education 137; "line" metaphor 150; "managing" versus "teaching" 85, 86; mental health 144; physical safety of 70–71; promoting wellbeing of 150–152; reflective practice 173–174; role in promoting student mental health and wellbeing 148–150; as role models 109–110; social and emotional competence 144–145; stress 146–148, 149; trauma-informed practices 158–161
teacher-student relationships 72–75, 88, 150, 152
ten steps to equity in education 139
test scores 100
Thaljia, A. 30
"thinking out loud" 110
three apprenticeships 135
three-step feedback process 100–101
tiered approaches to mental health intervention 48–49, 50, 52–55, 163–164; evidence-based kernels 53–54; universal approaches 48–49, 50
Timperley, H. 100
tracking 133–134
traumatic events 155; counselling for 157; impact on children's mental health 155–156; managing 161–162; post-traumatic stress disorder (PTSD) 158–159; school shootings 162; synthesizing a trauma-informed approach into schools 163–164
Tripp, J. 124
truancy 2, 4
tutoring 72
two-way sharing 116

Uemura, R. 35
unhappy schools 180
UNICEF, 123, 170
United Kingdom: mixed-attainment classrooms 133–134; school policies 67–68
United Nations Convention on the Rights of the Child (2001) 7
United States, Gun-Free Schools Act 162
universal approaches 48, 49, 50, 161–162; to screening 62
universal design for learning (UDL) 138–139

Valentino, R. A. 32
VanGeest, J. 17
Vernberg, E. M. 116
vision and policy 67–69

Wingspread Declaration on School Connections 70
Wade, B. 27
Walberg, H. J. 19
Wang, M. C. 19
Waters, R. 69

Webb, J. 74
Weissberg, R. 148
wellbeing 10, 19, 26, 95, 96, 102, 113, 179; and academic success 37; and equality 20–21; role of teachers in promoting 148–150; in school staff, promoting 150–152; staff 163; student 1, 5, 8; of teachers 144
wellbeing programs 37–38
West, R. 45
whole school approach to mental health 42; examples of 50–52; Positive Action (PA) 50–51; Positive Behavioural Interventions and Supports (PBIS) 43–44; problems and future opportunities 56; rationale behind 47–48
Wigglesworth, M. 31, 33

Williams, C. 124
Wilson, C. J. 146
Winton, P. J, 119
Wolpert, M. 148
Woodward, M. 80–81
World Health Organisation (WHO) 12, 51; definition of mental health 10

Xie, C. 45

"year 9 dip" 69–70
Yoder, N. 53, 99

Zeitlin, V. M. 120
Zentall, S. Z. 81
zero-tolerance policies 158

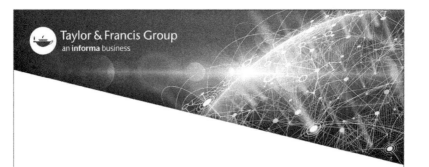

CPSIA information can be obtained
at www.ICGtesting.com
Printed in the USA
LVHW091931050919
630057LV00010B/277/P